Law and the Digital Economy

Daniela Copetti Cravo

Law and the Digital Economy

Unlocking Data through Regulation in Brazil and the European Union

Springer

Daniela Copetti Cravo
Attorney General's Office of the Municipality
of Porto Alegre
Porto Alegre, Brazil

ISBN 978-3-032-36671-9 ISBN 978-3-032-36672-6 (eBook)
https://doi.org/10.1007/978-3-032-36672-6

The original submitted manuscript has been translated into English. The translation was done using artificial intelligence. A subsequent revision was performed by the author(s) to further refine the work and to ensure that the translation is appropriate concerning content and scientific correctness. It may, however, read stylistically different from a conventional translation.

Translation from the Portuguese language edition: "Direito à Portabilidade de Dados" by Daniela Copetti Cravo, © The Author 2022. Published by Lumen Juris. All Rights Reserved.

This Springer imprint is published by the registered company Springer Nature Switzerland AG, part of Springer Nature.
The registered company address is: Gewerbestrasse 11, 6330 Cham, Switzerland

Competing Interests The author has no competing interests to declare that are relevant to the content of this manuscript.

Contents

Chapter 1
Introduction

Contemporary society is defined by a pervasive digital transformation driven by the rapid advancement of information and communication technologies (ICTs). In this landscape, the Internet acts as a powerful catalyst, reshaping how individuals live, work, and interact.

The unprecedented capacity to process, store, and disseminate information on a global scale, combined with the accelerated expansion of telecommunications networks, has fostered an environment of continuous and ubiquitous information flows. This reality has fueled the emergence of novel business models increasingly oriented around the use of data, which has consolidated its position as a strategic and highly valuable input in the digital economy.

In this context, information not only supports decision-making but also structures competitive dynamics, shapes innovation trajectories, and conditions participation in digital ecosystems. To secure access to this valuable resource, economic actors deploy a wide range of strategies, including the provision of seemingly "free" services dependent on user consent for data processing, alongside increasingly sophisticated mechanisms for large-scale information collection, storage, and analysis.

These practices, however, raise fundamental questions regarding the legitimacy of consent and the adequacy of safeguards ensuring the appropriate handling of personal data. Mass processing techniques such as profiling and large-scale analytics enable the extraction of strategic insights but simultaneously amplify individual vulnerability, creating risks of discrimination, exclusion, and violations of fundamental rights.

Against this backdrop, the protection of personal data has emerged as a regulatory priority—driven both by the immense economic value of data and by a limited public awareness of associated risks. In Brazil, this concern culminated in the enactment of the General Data Protection Law (Lei Geral de Proteção de Dados—LGPD) in 2018, aligning the country with a broader global movement toward comprehensive data governance frameworks. In Europe, the General Data Protection Regulation

D. Copetti Cravo, *Law and the Digital Economy*,
https://doi.org/10.1007/978-3-032-36672-6_1

(GDPR), which entered into force in 2018, represents the most influential and mature expression of this movement, establishing a robust, rights-based model that has shaped regulatory approaches worldwide and set a benchmark for accountability, transparency, and data subject empowerment.

Yet a data-driven economy demands more than the protection of personality and privacy rights. When data becomes a strategic input, it also becomes a locus of economic power. Competition increasingly hinges on access to data, and disputes over such access intensify under conditions shaped by powerful network effects and economies of scale in data processing.

These dynamics frequently generate "winner-takes-all" or "winner-takes-most" markets, in which the value of a service depends on the size of its user base—and its ability to attract new users depends on the value already accumulated. Once a dominant position is consolidated, the adhesion of additional users becomes almost automatic, while potential entrants face the classic "chicken-and-egg problem": without users, there is no value; without value, there are no users.

This environment incentivizes aggressive strategies of data accumulation and enclosure. Where a single firm controls a substantial share of market-relevant data, its incentive to innovate may diminish, and practices emerge that deepen lock-in, reduce user autonomy, and weaken competitive pressure. Barriers to switching become structural, translating into high transaction costs, technological dependence, and limited room for meaningful choice.

In light of these evolving challenges, regulatory and institutional mechanisms capable of preventing distortive market dynamics—while simultaneously safeguarding fundamental rights and preserving the integrity of digital ecosystems—become indispensable. Data is no longer merely an input for digital services; it has acquired the status of a geopolitical and economic asset, with access, localization, and control increasingly operating as instruments of strategic power in a context of technological competition and global interdependence. In this environment, governing data means more than protecting privacy: it requires treating data as a core strategic resource and investing in secure, high-quality, and interoperable datasets that can support innovation, resilience, and democratic oversight.

The rise of generative AI, large language models (LLMs), and agentic AI systems has intensified these pressures. Access to large-scale, diverse, high-quality, and domain-specific datasets has become a defining factor of technological leadership and industrial competitiveness. Empirical studies indicate exponential growth in dataset size, with estimates suggesting that, if current trends persist, the stock of publicly available training data may be exhausted within the next decade[1]—a structural constraint that disproportionately affects smaller firms, public institutions, and research actors. Against this backdrop, questions of who can access which data, under what conditions, and for what purposes acquire renewed regulatory significance.

[1] European Commission (2025).

Contemporary policy debates therefore increasingly move beyond a narrow focus on individual data rights and toward a broader architecture of access, sharing, and circulation of data. Within this architecture, multiple instruments coexist—portability rights, interoperability obligations, sector-specific data-sharing regimes, public-interest access mechanisms, and competition-driven remedies—often overlapping, interacting, and occasionally colliding. The central challenge is no longer limited to enabling individual control over personal data but to designing safe and legitimate pathways for data circulation across actors, sectors, and jurisdictions.

This broader perspective becomes even more salient as digital governance progressively encompasses not only personal data but also nonpersonal, industrial, and IoT-generated datasets, particularly in domains where access, reuse, and combination of data are essential to objectives such as innovation, safety, scientific research, mobility management, urban policy, and environmental monitoring. In these environments, the regulatory task involves mediating between individual rights, market dynamics, technological feasibility, and wider societal benefits.

Concepts such as interoperability by design, governance by design, and accountability by architecture emerge as key structuring principles. They signal a shift toward institutional arrangements in which data mobility is embedded within supervised, rights-compatible, and security-oriented frameworks, capable of reconciling economic dynamism with legal certainty, democratic legitimacy, and public trust.

The European Union's evolving regulatory framework—particularly the Digital Markets Act, the Data Governance Act, and the Data Act—exemplifies this systemic approach. Together, these instruments move beyond a model centered exclusively on privacy protection, advancing a vision in which the objective is not only to protect data but to unlock its economic and social value through structured access regimes, interoperability obligations, safeguards for confidentiality, and institutional coordination between regulators.

Recent policy developments in the European Union further reinforce the centrality of data governance in the digital economy. The Commission's *Data Union Strategy: Unlocking Data for AI* (COM(2025) 835) identifies three strategic challenges—data scarcity, regulatory complexity, and intensifying geopolitical competition—and highlights that many valuable datasets remain siloed or underused due to fragmented rules and uneven implementation across Member States. In this context, data is increasingly framed as a strategic resource, essential not only for innovation and competitiveness but also for Europe's technological autonomy and for the development of trustworthy artificial intelligence ecosystems.

At the same time, the Commission acknowledges that the interaction between the GDPR and sector-specific legislation has produced a complex and, at times, fragmented regulatory landscape, generating legal uncertainty and high compliance costs. The Digital Omnibus proposal (COM(2025) 837) seeks to streamline and consolidate elements of the EU's horizontal data acquis, combining simplification measures with targeted amendments designed to enhance legal clarity for data pooling, facilitate responsible reuse of data, and support innovation-oriented practices such as privacy-preserving AI training and interoperability across data ecosystems.

These developments expose the persistent challenges generated by what has often been described as a layered or "lasagna-style" regulatory landscape. The coexistence of general data protection rules, sector-specific regimes, competition-driven remedies, and emerging AI-related requirements frequently results in overlapping, fragmented, or inconsistently implemented obligations. This fragmentation increases regulatory complexity and compliance costs, particularly for SMEs, public bodies, and research institutions, and can inadvertently discourage responsible data sharing, hinder interoperability initiatives, and reinforce existing barriers to access.

In this context, harmonization and coordination become not merely technical aspirations but central conditions for a functioning and innovation-oriented data ecosystem. The challenge is to move from a model of cumulative regulatory layers toward coherent governance architectures capable of providing legal certainty, reducing unnecessary administrative burden, and supporting trustworthy data circulation, without diluting fundamental rights or weakening accountability.

Brazil, in turn, faces both the challenge and the opportunity of interpreting and adapting these paradigms within its own institutional and socioeconomic environment. The choice to place Brazil alongside the European Union in this analysis is not merely geographic or symbolic—it is analytical. Brazil represents one of the most dynamic and revealing environments for observing how the data-driven digital economy reshapes markets, social relations, and governance structures. Far from being a marginal or late-adopting jurisdiction, Brazil is today one of the world's most hyperconnected societies, with extremely high levels of platform use, social media engagement, and data-generating activity across everyday life. In this context, individuals act simultaneously as consumers, users, workers, economic agents, and continuous sources of data, making Brazil an especially rich empirical setting for examining the social and economic consequences of data circulation, concentration, and control.

Recent studies show that Brazil ranks second globally in average daily Internet usage, with users spending an average of 9 h and 13 min online every day—surpassing nearly every other country, except South Africa.[2] This staggering level of connectivity is not limited to adults. The TIC Kids Online Brasil 2023 report reveals that 93% of Brazilian children and adolescents aged 9–17 are Internet users—a population of over 24.5 million—with extremely high engagement on platforms like WhatsApp (70%), YouTube (66%), Instagram (60%), and TikTok (50%).[3]

The popularization of the Internet and social media has profoundly transformed social relations and spurred the emergence of new professions, such as that of the digital influencer—a term popularized in Brazil since 2015. Originally associated

[2] We Are Social and Meltwater (2024).

[3] CETIC.br. (2023).

with blogs, these professionals migrated to platforms such as YouTube, Instagram, and TikTok, creating diverse content and gaining influential power over behaviors, lifestyles, and consumer decisions.[4]

Brazil is also the global leader in the number of digital influencers on Instagram, with over 500,000 accounts boasting at least 10,000 followers. When other platforms like YouTube and TikTok are considered, Brazil ranks third worldwide in the influencer economy.[5] This growing ecosystem of content creators is not just a cultural phenomenon—it is a major economic force driving consumption, advertising, and platform monetization strategies.

The recognition of the commercial potential of influencers has led brands to invest heavily in advertising partnerships, generating revenues that in some cases reach significant amounts. In parallel, debates about the regulation of this activity have emerged in Brazil, reflected in legislative projects such as Bills 10,937/2018, 929/2020, 3130/2021, 1282/2022, 1335/2022, and 2347/2022, which aim to define the duties, competencies, and guarantees of influencers.[6]

The scale and intensity of digital participation in Brazil illuminate dynamics that are often less visible in European contexts. Brazil ranks among the global leaders in daily Internet usage, social media participation, and platform-based economic activities. Children and adolescents are embedded in digital ecosystems from an early age, while adults increasingly rely on platforms for communication, consumption, mobility, financial services, and work. The rapid expansion of the influencer and creator economy—of which Brazil is one of the largest markets in the world—illustrates how data-intensive business models restructure advertising, labor relations, identity construction, and consumer decision-making. These developments generate both opportunities for innovation and expression and heightened exposure to asymmetries of power, behavioral manipulation, and economic dependency, making the Brazilian experience especially instructive for global regulatory debates.

From a regulatory perspective, Brazil occupies a unique position: it is simultaneously a follower and an innovator. The LGPD draws conceptual inspiration from the GDPR, yet its implementation unfolds within a distinct institutional, socioeconomic, and enforcement landscape. At the same time, Brazil has pioneered ambitious initiatives in the field of digital governance—particularly through the *Estatuto Digital da Criança e do Adolescente (ECA Digital)*, which establishes a comprehensive framework for the protection of children and adolescents in online environments and requires digital platforms to adopt privacy-, safety-, and rights-protective measures whenever this vulnerable group interacts with technological services. Debates on platform governance, influencer regulation, and AI oversight further enrich this evolving ecosystem, revealing how emerging economies confront challenges similar to those faced in Europe but under conditions of greater inequality, heightened platform dependence, and persistent market concentration.

---

[4] de Faria and Marinho (2023).

[5] Valor Econômico (2024).

[6] de Faria and Marinho (2023).

For readers in the European Union, the Brazil–EU comparison thus offers more than a case study of external reception of European regulation. It provides a contrasting and complementary vantage point from which to examine how data governance operates in high-connectivity societies marked by strong platform penetration and intense social media engagement. The exchange is therefore bidirectional: Europe offers Brazil a reference framework and normative horizon, while Brazil offers Europe empirical insight, cautionary lessons, and alternative regulatory trajectories that enrich the understanding of how access, control, and circulation of data can be governed in diverse democratic and social contexts.

Furthermore, Brazil–EU regulatory dialogues, together with its growing participation in digital policy coalitions, positions it as a promising setting for testing cooperative mechanisms for international data transfers, model contractual clauses, public–private data-sharing arrangements, and trusted data environments that parallel—and potentially interoperate with—European initiatives such as data labs, common data spaces, and interoperability-oriented infrastructures.

Methodologically, this book adopts a problem-oriented and comparative regulatory approach, grounded primarily in doctrinal legal analysis and complemented by elements of institutional and policy-oriented analysis. The Brazil–EU comparison follows a functional–analytical perspective: rather than focusing on textual differences between statutes, it examines how distinct legal systems respond—in practice—to common challenges involving access to, circulation of, and control over data in increasingly data-driven digital ecosystems.

The core research material consists of the applicable legal frameworks, in particular, the GDPR, the LGPD, the EU Digital Markets Act, and the Data Act, together with sector-specific regimes and their Brazilian counterparts. Special attention is also given to the European Commission's 2025 Proposal for the Simplification of the Digital Legislative Framework (COM(2025) 837), which explicitly confronts the cumulative effects of regulatory layering, overlap and fragmentation—the so-called regulatory lasagna—and seeks to reduce compliance burdens, coordination frictions, and barriers to data access, interoperability, and reuse. These normative instruments are complemented by administrative decisions, judicial case law, and enforcement practices issued by authorities such as the European Commission, national data protection authorities, competition agencies, courts, and the Brazilian ANPD and CADE.

Rather than treating these regimes in isolation, the analysis investigates how data protection, competition law, consumer protection, and sectoral regulation intersect—and, at times, collide—in shaping the concrete conditions under which data portability, interoperability, and data sharing may operate. This cross-domain perspective is essential to understanding how regulatory fragmentation, institutional misalignment, and overlapping obligations can generate uncertainty, increase transaction and compliance costs, and ultimately obstruct socially valuable forms of data access and reuse.

This methodological design sustains the argumentative trajectory of the book. The analysis begins by establishing the conceptual and technological foundations of data as infrastructure, framing data not merely as an individual right or proprietary asset but as a strategic, socio-technical resource whose circulation, aggregation, and reuse condition innovation, competition, safety, resilience, and public interest objectives. It then advances through a cross-domain examination of portability as both an individual right and a structural governance mechanism, situated within a broader architecture of data access instruments—including interoperability mandates, sectoral data-sharing regimes, public interest access mechanisms, and competition-driven remedies.

Within this framework, the book addresses its central research problem in explicit terms: How can legal and institutional frameworks be designed to reduce fragmentation, lower regulatory frictions, and provide legal certainty for the safe and legitimate reuse of data?

Building on this core question, the analysis explores derivative issues such as (1) the limits and conflicts arising from the interaction between legal regimes; (2) the effects of regulatory fragmentation and cumulative compliance burdens on data access and interoperability; (3) the institutional and enforcement conditions under which portability contributes (or fails to contribute) to competition, innovation, and collective interests; and (4) how emerging initiatives may recalibrate the balance between rights protection, market dynamics, and technological feasibility.

The structure of the book follows the logic of the central research problem—namely, how legal and institutional frameworks can be designed to reduce fragmentation, lower regulatory frictions, and provide legal certainty for the safe and legitimate reuse of data—and progressively develops the argumentative thread from conceptual foundations to applied institutional analysis.

The opening chapters establish the conceptual, technological, and normative background necessary to frame this inquiry. They examine the transformation of data into a strategic infrastructure of the digital economy and the consolidation of data protection as a fundamental right in both the European Union and Brazil, thereby defining the baseline tensions between data use, control, and protection.

The intermediate chapters constitute the analytical core of the work and directly engage with the research problem. They explore how data concentration generates market power in digital environments and how different legal domains—particularly data protection law and competition law—shape, constrain, and enable access to and reuse of data. Within this framework, the book develops the concept of data portability as both an individual right grounded in informational self-determination and as a structural governance instrument capable of reducing lock-in effects, fostering competition, and facilitating controlled data flows.

Subsequent chapters advance the inquiry by examining the legal design and implementation of portability, focusing on interoperability, institutional coordination, and the management of conflicts between rights and regulatory objectives. Particular attention is given to the risks of fragmentation, overlapping mandates, and bureaucratic complexity, as well as to emerging mechanisms aimed at reducing these frictions and enhancing legal certainty in data-sharing environments.

The final analytical chapter situates these developments within the broader reconfiguration of digital markets, with emphasis on the evolving European regulatory framework—including the Digital Markets Act and the Data Act—as examples of attempts to operationalize more coherent and coordinated models of data governance, especially in relation to gatekeepers and structured data-sharing ecosystems.

The concluding chapter synthesizes the findings, explicitly answers the research question, and proposes normative and institutional pathways for designing more integrated, rights-compatible and innovation-oriented frameworks in Brazil and the European Union—capable of reducing fragmentation, lowering regulatory frictions, and ensuring legal certainty for the safe and legitimate reuse of data while preserving fundamental rights and systemic integrity.

References

CETIC.br (2023) TIC Kids Online Brasil 2023: survey on internet use by children and adolescents in Brazil. Comitê Gestor da Internet no Brasil, São Paulo. https://cetic.br/pt/pesquisa/kids-online/. Accessed 4 June 2026

Comissão Europeia (2025) Comunicação da Comissão ao Parlamento Europeu e ao Conselho Data Union Strategy: unlocking data for AI, COM(2025) 835 final. Comissão Europeia, Bruxelas. https://eur-lex.europa.eu/legal-content/ES/TXT/?uri=COM:2025:835:FIN. Accessed 4 June 2026

de Faria AC, Marinho MT (2023) Influenciadores digitais e a economia do compartilhamento: uma nova lógica de proteção dos trabalhadores. Revista de Direito do Trabalho 232:69–89

Valor Econômico (2024) Brasil lidera ranking mundial de influenciadores digitais. https://valor.globo.com/patrocinado/dino/noticia/2024/09/09/brasil-lidera-ranking-mundial-de-influenciadores-digitais.ghtml. Accessed 4 June 2026

We Are Social and Meltwater (2024) Digital 2024: 5 billion social media users. https://wearesocial.com/uk/blog/2024/01/digital-2024-5-billion-social-media-users/. Accessed 4 June 2026

Chapter 2
Data as Strategic Infrastructure in the Digital Economy

2.1 From the Information Society to Data-Driven Ecosystems

The transition from an industrial economy to a digital economy is not merely a sectoral shift but a structural reconfiguration of the sources of value creation, power, and governance. Whereas in the past the drivers of progress resided in physical infrastructure—such as railways, energy, and industries—in the twenty-first century they have shifted to data, algorithms, and digital platforms.

Data ceases to be merely informational records and becomes a strategic asset and essential infrastructure, whose possession, control, and processing capacity determine competitiveness, innovation, and economic sovereignty. This chapter reconstructs the historical and conceptual trajectory that led to the centrality of data, starting from the information society to the consolidation of data-driven ecosystems and platform power.

In this regard, it should first be noted that the present era is witnessing the consolidation of a profound postindustrial revolution, whose main characteristics are the increase in wealth independently of industrial production growth and the surpassing of industrial employment by employment in the services sector. This phenomenon, far from being a mere sectoral transition, represents a fundamental reconfiguration of the sources of value creation and economic power.

If the industrial era was powered by coal and steel, and structured by railways and electrical grids, the digital economy of the twenty-first century is driven by data and algorithms and structured by a complex and ubiquitous digital infrastructure. In this new paradigm, data transcends its status as mere records or isolated information to become a first-order capital asset, an essential infrastructure whose ownership and control determine competitiveness, innovation, and even sovereignty on the global stage.

Just as physical infrastructure was crucial to the functioning of the economy and modern society, data infrastructure has become the central nervous system of

D. Copetti Cravo, *Law and the Digital Economy*,
https://doi.org/10.1007/978-3-032-36672-6_2

commerce, governance, and social interaction. Understanding the rise of data to this strategic level is, therefore, the objective of this chapter.

The journey that has brought us to the current centrality of data has been evolutionary. Initially, the discourse focused on the emergence of an "information society," a concept that captured the growing importance of knowledge and communication in economic and social life. However, this notion, though pioneering, was still passive and abstract, treating information more as a good to be accessed and consumed than as a dynamic and productive resource.

The true turning point occurred with the transition to what is now defined as data-driven ecosystems. In this phase, information is transformed into data: a granular, processable, and, above all, actionable raw material.

These ecosystems are not limited to storing or transmitting information; they are designed to create continuous feedback loops. Human and machine activities, mediated by digital interfaces, generate a colossal volume of data that is collected, processed, and analyzed in real time to then inform, personalize, and optimize the very activities that produced them.

This transition from the static possession of information to the dynamic management of data flows marks the birth of the data economy, in which value lies not only in the content of the data itself but in its capacity to generate insights, predictions, and automations that drive efficiency and create new markets. The rise of data ecosystems is driven by three interdependent forces that together create an unprecedented cycle of concentration of power: datafication, network effects, and platform power.

Datafication refers to the process of transforming aspects of life and work that previously existed outside any quantitative formalization into data. Conversations, movements, social interactions, preferences, and even emotional states are converted into digital signals that can be analyzed. This process exponentially expands the universe of available raw material.

Secondly, network effects describe the phenomenon whereby the value of a service increases exponentially as more users join it. On a digital platform, more users generate more data; more data enables the enhancement of algorithms and the improvement of the service; a better service attracts even more users, creating a virtuous cycle of growth that favors the formation of natural monopolies or oligopolies.

It is the combination of datafication with network effects that culminates in the third force: the immense platform power. The companies that control the main digital platforms are not mere intermediaries; they become true private governance entities, defining the rules of interaction, controlling access to markets, and accumulating deep knowledge about the behavior of millions of individuals and businesses. This power is not merely economic, as it also shapes what we see, how we interact, and, ultimately, how society itself is organized.

This new paradigm, while driving disruptive innovations, is inherently dual and marked by profound tensions. On one hand, the ability to reuse data—that is, to apply a dataset collected for a specific purpose in entirely new and unforeseen contexts—is one of the greatest sources of innovation in the digital age.

Urban mobility data analysis can optimize public transportation while also predicting the spread of epidemics. Consumer data can personalize advertising and, at the same time, identify macroeconomic trends. Innovation driven by AI and automation, which rely on vast datasets, promises productivity and efficiency gains across all sectors of the economy. On the other hand, this same practice of massive and often opaque data reuse generates significant and multifaceted risks.

The violation of privacy, identity theft, algorithmic discrimination, manipulation of democratic processes, and the creation of systemic security vulnerabilities are just some of the negative externalities that arise from this model. This fundamental tension between innovative potential and inherent risks calls into question the very legitimacy of the current data regime. It raises the issue of the ethical and legal grounds on which platforms may appropriate and exploit such a fundamental resource as personal and collective data, often without clear, specific, and informed consent for each new use.

However, to fully understand how we arrived at this stage of economic and political centrality of data, it is necessary to go back several decades and revisit the moment when these transformations began to take shape. Before the consolidation of data-driven ecosystems and platform power, the debate was structured around the so-called information society, a context in which the expansion of computing, telecommunications, and, above all, the Internet began to reorganize the ways in which knowledge was produced, circulated, and consumed. It is in this formative period—when information gradually becomes an economic input and social infrastructure—that the historical, technological, and conceptual foundations of the contemporary digital economy are found.

In this context, a postindustrial revolution is reported, characterized primarily by the growth of wealth dissociated from the expansion of industrial production and by the service sector surpassing industry in terms of employment.[1] It is rightly stated that the ongoing transformations are of a magnitude comparable to those observed during the Industrial Revolution, when the transition to an industrial economy was consolidated.[2] The distinctive element of this new stage, however, lies in the central role of electronics and digitalization, which are reshaping not only production processes but also the forms of marketing, consumption, and communication.

The phenomenon of economic internationalization is also noteworthy, intensifying as wealth becomes dematerialized and assumes essentially intangible forms. If the market can be understood as the "invisible hand" guiding economic life, dematerialized wealth emerges as its most sublime expression,[3] reflecting the growing centrality of information and knowledge in value creation processes.

This revolution is fundamentally driven by technological advancement and the extraordinary expansion of telecommunications networks, especially the Internet,

[1] Galgano (2005), p. 13.

[2] Van Alstyne (2016).

[3] Galgano (2005), p. 13.

as a vehicle for the transmission and exchange of all types of information.[4] As addressed in the Bangemann Report,[5] the core of the revolution is information, which is, in itself, an expression of human knowledge.[6]

The economic value of information was initially outlined in the Plan for the Information Society, developed by the Japan Computer Usage Development Institute (JACUDI), at which point the term "Information Society" was introduced. In this economy, business models are based on information, which is no longer valued solely for the knowledge it provides but is now regarded as a tradable commodity in the market. The commercialization of information encompasses everything from data and knowledge to music and literature.[7]

In this economy, business models are based on information, which is not valued for the degree of knowledge it provides but rather as a tradable commodity in the market. Information becomes the object of commercial transactions, encompassing everything from data to knowledge, music, and literature.

Indeed, the decentralization of information is a consequence of this new era, representing an important window of opportunity for citizens, businesses, public administration, and others. This consequence, combined with the other characteristics outlined above, affects, in a more or less direct manner, virtually all spheres of human development,[8] which raises the need to reconsider important aspects related to social organization, democracy, technology, privacy, and freedom.[9]

In addition to permeating all spheres, it is undeniable that new communication and information technologies have taken a central place in our daily lives. There is an omnipresence or ubiquity of information technology (ubiquitous computing), especially due to smartphones, the semantic web, and cloud computing.[10]

As mentioned, the Internet is one of the main factors responsible for this new landscape. Manuel Castells[11] states that the creation and development of the Internet represent an extraordinary human endeavor, demonstrating how cooperation and freedom of information can foster innovation.

Indeed, the origins of the Internet can be traced back to ARPANET, a computer network established by the Advanced Research Projects Agency (ARPA)[12] in

---

[4] Pastor Sempere (2003), p. 22.

[5] The Bangemann Report is a document prepared at the request of the European Council by a group of experts on information infrastructure. The report describes the occurrence of a worldwide revolution driven by information and communication technologies, one as significant and profound as its predecessors. This revolution is based on information, which is the expression of human knowledge. European Commission (1994).

[6] European Commission (1994).

[7] Menéndez Mato (2005), p. 102.

[8] Menéndez Mato (2005), p. 29.

[9] Lorenzetti (2001), p. 9.

[10] Mendes and Doneda (2016), p. 37.

[11] Castells (2003), p. 13.

[12] ARPA was an agency established in 1958 by the United States Department of Defense with the mission of mobilizing research resources, particularly from the academic world, with the aim of achieving military technological superiority. Castells (2003), p. 13.

September 1969.[13] ARPANET emerged as a project proposal for interconnecting hosts through packet switching.[14] The next step in this project was to connect ARPANET with other computer networks, which led to the introduction of the concept of a network of networks.[15]

In the 1980s, ARPANET became ARPA-INTERNET, dissociating itself from the military context.[16] Subsequently, in the 1990s, with computer network technology in the public domain and telecommunications fully deregulated, the Internet was privatized, which enabled its rapid growth as a global network of computer networks.[17]

It is evident, therefore, that the Internet was not originally designed for commercial transactions or electronic commerce. The primary objectives of the Internet were to facilitate the circulation of scientific information and to simplify the interconnection of various networks and devices, initially disregarding security concerns.[18]

The Internet can thus be defined as a network of computers comprising dozens of interconnected networks, ranging from local networks that serve an organization by connecting its computers located in one or several buildings, to the aggregation of these into larger networks with regional or national reach, and, ultimately, through the interconnection of these, to the major networks that link the entire world.

It is important to emphasize that the Internet is not merely a means of communication. As a product of the combination of information technology and telecommunications, it serves as a platform on which an infinite number of applications can be developed, enabling the integration of various combined technologies such as radio, television, video streaming, DVD, and mobile telephony.[19]

From a technical perspective, the Internet represents the pinnacle of a process of interaction and cooperation among various technological systems originating from different fields of knowledge. To enhance user experience, information circulates through the three layers of the Internet: the physical layer, which is the infrastructure; the logical layer, which encompasses the standards and programs that translate information; and the content layer, which consists of information endowed with meaning for individuals.[20]

A peculiarity introduced by the Internet is the dynamism of the market, such that the cycle of technological developments can be measured not in days but in minutes

[13] Castells (2003), p. 12.

[14] Oppliger (2002), p. 12.

[15] Castells (2003), p. 14.

[16] Menéndez Mato (2005), p. 15.

[17] Castells (2003), p. 5.

[18] Pastor Sempere (2003), p. 23.

[19] Menéndez Mato (2005), p. 33.

[20] Lucero (2011), p. 39.

or even seconds.[21] One example is the drastic change in the way journalistic information circulates around the world, diminishing the relevance of daily journalistic content, which has also shifted in many markets to digital content updated in real time on websites or blogs.

When the most important books on computer law were just being published, the Internet was dominated by America Online (AOL), which today poses no competitive threat.[22] In the digital age of the twenty-first century, innovation can overnight transform a menacing giant gorilla into a small chimpanzee offspring.[23]

It is certain that online services play a significant role in the digital economy. Peculiarly, the majority of these services appear to be free of charge. In reality, however, payment is made through the provision of consumers' personal information.[24]

In the Brazilian context, the legal classification of seemingly "free" digital services has been addressed both by case law and consumer protection legislation. The Superior Court of Justice has established the understanding that the absence of direct monetary payment—as is the case with digital platforms, search providers, and online services—does not preclude the application of the Consumer Protection Code. This is because access to, collection, and processing of users' personal data constitute a form of indirect remuneration for the service, thus falling within the broad concept of consideration provided for under the Brazilian consumer protection regime.

National legal scholarship follows this perspective, emphasizing that, in the digital economy, the remuneration model is no longer necessarily monetary but has come to take on immaterial forms based on the transfer and economic exploitation of personal information. Claudia Lima Marques notes that the Consumer Defense Code does not require a direct payment but rather some form of remuneration for the service, so that digital services supported by data—even when offered free of charge to the user—remain subject to the protective rules of consumer law.[25,26]

In this context, data monetization ceases to be a mere side effect of the use of digital technologies and becomes a foundational element of a significant portion of the new products and services available on the market.[27] The consumer—as the holder of the information that fuels these systems—thus becomes the main source of the strategic asset that enables this economic model, as their personal, behavioral, and contextual data become central to the value generation process.

---

[21] Thierer (2010), p. 149.

[22] Thierer (2010), p. 151.

[23] Greenspan (2008), p. 480.

[24] Geradin and Kuschewsky (2013).

[25] Brazil. Superior Court of Justice. Special Appeal 1.444.008. Reporting Justice Nancy Andrighi. Judged on October 25, 2016.

[26] Marques et al. (2016), p. 201.

[27] National School of Consumer Defense (2010), p. 10.

This is, therefore, a profound reorganization of the logic of remuneration in the digital economy. Online services, often presented as free of charge, in reality operate through economic arrangements sustained by the massive collection, continuous processing, and analytical reuse of user data. These data are converted into economic value through practices such as targeted advertising, profiling, predictive inferences, and integration with broader informational ecosystems—mechanisms that ensure the financial sustainability of platforms and expand their informational power.

The consumer, therefore, ceases to be merely the recipient of the service and becomes the main source of informational assets that fuel the cycles of datafication, network effects, and platform power. In this dynamic, data come to structure actual markets, in which aggregation, correlation, and predictive analysis give rise to individualized and collective profiles capable of guiding commercial, political, and large-scale automated decisions.

Data thus becomes, simultaneously, a productive input and an instrument of power, creating opportunities for unprecedented innovation but also for informational asymmetries, decision-making opacity, and risks to individual autonomy. It is precisely this data economy—its markets and its mechanisms of value creation—that the next section will address, examining the legal, economic, and social contours of this new model of informational exploitation.

2.2 Datafication and Digital Platforms

Understanding this new economic-informational arrangement requires, before addressing its regulatory implications, a conceptual clarification of the categories that underpin it. If data simultaneously serve as both a productive input and a vector of power, it becomes essential to precisely distinguish what is meant by "data" and "information," as well as to define the boundaries of their legal protection and their circulation along the value chain.

This distinction is not merely terminological: it shapes the way the law perceives the processing of personal data, the extent of the risks involved, and the legitimate scope of action for public and private actors within the digital ecosystem. At this point, it is possible to draw a distinction between the terms "data" and "information," which are often used interchangeably and may at times result in terminological inaccuracy. Although both represent the same fact, each carries its own particular weight.[28]

The term "data" carries a more primitive and fragmented connotation and can be regarded as potential information or pre-information,[29] that is, simple facts, figures, or bits of information. In other words, "data" would be the records we can establish

[28] National School of Consumer Defense (2010), p. 10.

[29] National School of Consumer Defense (2010), p. 19.

regarding one of the attributes (names, addresses, measurements, monetary values, dates, etc.) of individuals, companies, or objects.[30]

On the other hand, information is the result of a process that uses data as its substrate, whether through processing, interpretation, organization, structuring, or presentation, and thus provides context to the data. Indeed, when data becomes information, it can be used in decision-making, often through automated means that enable its rapid retrieval.[31]

With the exponential advancement of computational capacity and large-scale data processing techniques, it is no longer sufficient to restrict legal protection solely to the level of information, that is, to the final result of processing. The contemporary landscape also demands the protection of raw data itself,[32] since the absence of such safeguards may render subsequent protection of the derived information ineffective.

In this context, the literature recurrently identifies four fundamental stages in the personal data value chain: (1) collection and access, (2) storage and aggregation, (3) analysis and circulation, and (4) use of the data. Throughout this process, various actors—individuals, companies, public agencies, civil society organizations, and, in particular, so-called data brokers—interact, negotiate, enrich, and recombine data, integrating them into increasingly complex informational markets.[33]

This trajectory demonstrates that data do not remain static: they are continuously enriched, recombined, and reinterpreted as they move between different agents, technologies, and purposes. Each stage of the chain expands their economic and decision-making potential but also multiplies points of risk—from massive and opaque collection to the creation of inferences and profiles that go beyond the information originally provided by the data subject. Raw data thus become a strategic informational asset, whose value derives less from their isolated content and more from the correlations produced by increasingly sophisticated analytical techniques.

From a legal perspective, this movement presents significant challenges to defining the object of protection. The boundary between "data" and "information" is no longer merely conceptual but has practical implications for the scope of regulatory protection, especially when inferences, profiles, or derived data begin to guide automated decisions, shape behaviors, or structure contractual and institutional relationships. Effective protection, therefore, cannot be limited to the initial moment of collection: it must accompany the data throughout the entire value chain, encompassing aggregation, circulation, and reuse operations, in which informational asymmetries and potential abuses are often consolidated.

At the same time, it is acknowledged that this dynamic creates significant opportunities for innovation, efficiency, and knowledge production, especially when guided by legitimate and socially relevant purposes. The contemporary challenge lies precisely in

---

[30] Gouvêa (1997), p. 41.

[31] Gouvêa (1997), p. 41.

[32] Veronese (2019), pp. 385–415.

[33] EDPS (2014).

developing regulatory and institutional frameworks capable of reconciling the economic and scientific exploitation of data with the preservation of informational autonomy, transparency, and the accountability of the agents operating within this ecosystem.

Thus, the consolidation of the personal data value chain, which encompasses the stages of collection, aggregation, analysis, circulation, and use, has ceased to operate solely on a technical level and has come to structure genuine informational markets. In these markets, data simultaneously serve as productive input, strategic asset, and mechanism of economic coordination.

In this context, digital platforms occupy a central position by organizing the flows of interaction among users, advertisers, content providers, and technological intermediaries, shaping an ecosystem in which the continuous circulation of data sustains the financial viability of services and redefines competitive dynamics.

Digital platforms can be understood as networks centrally organized by a controller—which may be a company, a state entity, or an academic institution—responsible for defining the rules of participation, moderating interactions, and structuring the flows that circulate within the digital environment. This orchestration occurs across multiple market sides (users, providers, advertisers, and developers, among others), through the control of access, terms of use, generated data, and the conditions of interaction established on the platform.

At the same time that they enable large-scale connections, transactions, and informational exchanges, platforms also impose technical and contractual architectures that guide—and often condition—the behavior of participants. These architectures incorporate mechanisms for continuous data collection, aggregation, mining, and redistribution, granting platforms a privileged position in the creation of economic value, the coordination of markets, and the production of inferences and profiles about individuals.

It is in this context that business models based on multisided markets (two-sided and multisided platforms) have emerged, in which "free" access for users is made possible by the monetization of data and the commercialization of highly targeted advertising spaces. Data thus ceases to be a mere by-product of digital interactions and comes to play a decisive role in value creation: it guides the personalization of services, enables the precise targeting of campaigns, fuels inference processes, and, above all, underpins the construction of behavioral profiles, which become the true operational unit of this economic model.

At the same time, this arrangement intensifies both the scale and depth of data processing, fostering ongoing practices of collecting, tracking, combining, and enriching information about individuals across multiple domains of daily life—consumption, mobility, work, leisure, and health. This creates an informational feedback loop in which the more data a platform acquires, the greater its capacity to generate new data, expand its analytical power, and consolidate competitive advantages—while simultaneously increasing the risks of decision-making opacity, algorithmic discrimination, and the asymmetric exploitation of users.

This chapter focuses on this economic and technological environment—in which data simultaneously function as "currency," commodity, and vector of power. In this model, most online services are two-sided. To attract users, providers offer their services (search or content) free of charge—the free side. To generate the revenue necessary to finance these services, providers engage in online advertising activities, which constitute the paying side.[34]

Personal data is essential on both ends, that is, on both sides. It enables online services to provide relevant and high-quality offerings that meet users' expectations. Furthermore, data is fundamental for search services, since when a user employs a search tool, they seek the answer that best satisfies their needs: if someone is looking for a service, they do not want just any provider but rather, for example, one that is closest to their location.[35]

Thus, personal data has come to serve, within the context of the contemporary digital economy, as a true currency of exchange, often constituting the main "payment" made by consumers in return for access to online services and platforms. Instead of direct financial transactions, the prevailing business model is based on the continuous collection of user information, which is subsequently used for economic, commercial, and analytical purposes.

As part of this arrangement, digital service providers employ a wide range of data collection, monitoring, and analysis mechanisms, structured with a focus on the individual—not merely on groups or broad segments—[36] in order to enable increasingly refined levels of precision, personalization, and targeting of content, products, and advertisements. This logic prioritizes the granular observation of user behavior, preferences, and interactions within the digital environment.

This scenario is largely driven by the combination of information asymmetry affecting the average user and the convenience offered by joining major platforms, whose use has become almost unavoidable in daily life. These factors contribute to the consolidation of economic and informational power by the entities operating these digital ecosystems,[37] enabling the expansion of broad—and often insufficiently transparent—practices of personal data collection, with significant implications for the protection of rights and for the governance of the digital environment.

Economic agents, therefore, employ a wide range of techniques to gain access to this resource, which are sometimes not aligned with data protection principles. Some recurring examples include the update of WhatsApp's privacy policy to allow data sharing with the Facebook group of companies for behavioral advertising purposes; new Uber terms, which permit the collection of data even when the app is not in use; and Spotify's privacy policy, which required users to waive their banking secrecy.[38]

In addition, data collection tools are increasingly efficient, as data can be stored without limitation and accessed at any time, regardless of distance or time constraints.[39] An example of this is the interconnection of systems and databases.

---

[34] Geradin and Kuschewsky (2013).

[35] Geradin and Kuschewsky (2013).

[36] Geradin and Kuschewsky (2013).

[37] Martins and Faleiros Junior (2020), p. 219.

[38] Bioni (2017).

[39] Doneda and Mendes (2017), p. 47.

In combination, there is the use of tools that enable the processing of an individual's data by combining fragments and primitive data, generating useful and valuable information for the company—a situation known as data mining.[40] It should be noted that this presents a concerning scenario, as these informational elements may not receive appropriate treatment, since they may initially appear insignificant.[41]

Furthermore, individuals increasingly have their data collected and processed repeatedly, in the various roles they assume: as taxpayers, patients, consumers, beneficiaries, etc. One of the defining characteristics of modern life is the emergence of technologies that make data collection and processing extraordinarily efficient.[42]

It is important to emphasize that large-scale data processing, if not properly regulated, can directly impact the private sphere of citizens, compromising their freedom, personality, privacy, and ability to control their own information. This situation is exacerbated by the installation of sensors or cameras by private entities in public spaces, often without adequate oversight or transparency. These devices, which may appear harmless, are capable of capturing and recording glances, faces, or bodily movements of individuals in response to the content displayed,[43] thereby revealing, through inference, extremely sensitive information.[44]

In this context, the relevance and importance of municipal regulation on the subject emerge, within the scope of local interest, to specify limits and obligations in the adoption of systems that collect and use personal data. As Danilo Doneda aptly points out, there is a tendency for municipal regulation to be highly significant in establishing limits and obligations regarding the use of systems that collect personal data by municipal entities, in public spaces, in concessionary services, and in other situations where it is necessary to guarantee citizens' rights over their data.[45]

To illustrate this scenario, we can take the city of Amsterdam as a reference. In 2021, after establishing a comprehensive public registry of all government sensors, the city implemented pioneering regulations requiring that all entities—whether public or private, companies, research institutions, or nonprofit organizations—that collect information through any type of sensory device in public spaces for professional purposes must disclose the use of these devices and specify the types of data collected or that may be collected.[46]

With the support of sensory data collection technologies in public spaces, it becomes possible to profile each individual. This is the technique known as

40 Mendes (2014), p. 109.

41 Doneda and Mendes (2017), p. 47.

42 Lessig (2006).

43 Kröger et al. (2020).

44 OECD (2023).

45 Doneda (2018).

46 Ordinance of the Council of the City of Amsterdam amending the General Local Bye-law 2008 in connection with the introduction of a notification obligation for sensors (Regulation on the Notification Obligation for Sensors).

profiling, which is the process of inferring[47] a set of characteristics (generally behavioral) of a person, which can be extremely useful to economic agents.[48]

In the Brazilian context, the debate surrounding the processing of personal data, and particularly the generation of inferences from collected data, can be illustrated by the case involving the Concessionaire of Line 4 of the São Paulo Metro S.A. (Via Quatro), adjudicated by the 8th Chamber of Public Law of the São Paulo Court of Justice (TJSP) in Appeal No. 1090663-42.2018.8.26.0100. In the public civil action brought against the company, the use of so-called Digital Interactive Doors was contested, through which images of metro users were captured for advertising and commercial purposes without prior notice or consent. The images served not only as visual records but also as the basis for extracting inferred attributes—such as physical and behavioral characteristics—with the aim of guiding advertising segmentation strategies.[49]

This Brazilian precedent is particularly relevant from a comparative perspective, as it demonstrates that data processing and the production of automated inferences—even without direct nominal identification—fall within the scope of legal protection for personal data and may give rise to liability when carried out without an appropriate legal basis, transparency, and respect for data subjects' rights.

The creation of these profiles can also be implemented through cookies, which allow providers to identify users' most common browsing paths and, thereby, ascertain their consumer preferences. Subsequently, the data may be used in targeted advertising campaigns directed at consumers whose profiles have been established.[50]

In this way, profiling has two facets: (a) profile generation, which consists of analyzing personal data in terms of patterns, sequences, and relationships in order to obtain a series of assumptions about the profile based on probabilistic reasoning, and (b) the application of the profile as an aid for research or for making a decision about a person or an entity.[51]

At times, such processing can even serve as a tool for abusive practices, such as consumer discrimination. For example, there have been reports of consumers being discriminated against by dynamic pricing systems in online purchases, where users of Apple's iOS system received higher-priced offers than users of the Android system. This situation may worsen with the advancement of the Internet of Things, enabling comprehensive cataloging of individuals.[52]

---

[47] Inference may result from the study of user behavior and does not require, for example, that a social network user be active and publish a large amount of content. Inference can arise from interactions such as "likes" on certain content, which may even reveal potential political or religious preferences.

[48] Mendes and Doneda (2016), p. 37.

[49] TJSP. ACF No. 15.997/2022 (JV Opposition) 8th Chamber of Public Law Appeal No. 1090663-42.2018.8.26.0100.

[50] Vega (2005), pp. 165–167.

[51] Bygrave (2001), p. 18.

[52] Bioni (2015), p. 5.

It is evident that the automated collection and processing of data have undergone significant advancements, both quantitatively (in terms of the large volume of data) and qualitatively, allowing each fragment of information about an individual to be cross-referenced, related, or aggregated with other information.[53] This is the distinguishing factor that computerization has brought to the processing of personal data.[54]

As a result, a new market comprising a wide range of sectors has emerged with the advent of automated personal databases. These databases are structured collections of information designed to maximize the utility of a given set of data.[55]

In this way, data serve as the main driving force of the digital market, which operates on a feedback cycle: the more data a company possesses, the more data it is likely to collect in future activities with the aim of providing better services. In the digital market, data play various roles, whether as input for social media, content-sharing platforms, and algorithms or as a product to be sold directly to third parties.[56]

From this perspective, it becomes evident that the shift from an information-centered logic to a data-driven economy redefines not only technological and economic flows but also the very institutional architecture of the digital environment. Platforms cease to be mere technical intermediaries and begin to function as infrastructures for economic and social coordination, capable of organizing interactions, extracting value from inferences and profiling, and influencing behavior through algorithmic mechanisms of ordering, recommendation, and targeting.

In this context, the processing of personal data becomes the structuring element of their business model, positioning platforms as central actors in the data value chain and, at the same time, as spaces where legal risks related to informational power, opacity, and asymmetry between users and economic operators are intensified. The conceptual framework developed here, therefore, is not merely descriptive: it provides the necessary analytical foundation to understand why platforms constitute a privileged locus where contemporary tensions between innovation, economic exploitation of data, and the protection of rights are manifested—a theme that will guide the in-depth analysis in the following chapters.

References

Bioni B (2015) Xeque-mate: o tripé da proteção de dados pessoais no jogo de xadrez das iniciativas legislativas no Brasil. GPoPAI/USP, São Paulo

Bioni B (2017) Privacidade e proteção de dados pessoais em 2017. Jota. https://www.jota.info/colunas/agenda-da-privacidade-e-da-protecao-de-dados/privacidade-e-protecao-de-dados-pessoais-em-2017-10012017

---

53 Doneda and Mendes (2017), p. 47.

54 National School of Consumer Defense (2010), p. 31.

55 National School of Consumer Defense (2010), p. 19.

56 OECD (2021).

Bygrave L (2001) Minding the machine: Article 15 of the EC Data Protection Directive and automated profiling. Comput Law Secur Rep 17:17–24
Castells M (2003) A galáxia Internet: reflexões sobre a Internet, negócios e a sociedade. Jorge Zahar, Rio de Janeiro
Doneda D (2018) Um panorama de proteção de dados para as cidades inteligentes. Jota
Doneda D, Mendes LSF (2017) Iniciativas legislativas sobre proteção de dados pessoais no Brasil. Rev Uruguaya Protección Datos Personales 2:44–52
European Commission (1994) Bangemann report: Europe and the global information society
European Data Protection Supervisor (2014) Privacy and competitiveness in the age of big data. https://edps.europa.eu/data-protection/our-work/publications/opinions/privacy-and-competitiveness-age-big-data_en
Galgano F (2005) La globalización en el espejo del derecho. Rubinzal-Culzoni, Santa Fe
Geradin D, Kuschewsky M (2013) Competition law and personal data: preliminary thoughts on a complex issue. https://papers.ssrn.com/sol3/papers.cfm?abstract_id=2216088
Gouvêa S (1997) O direito na era digital: crimes praticados por meio da informática. Mauad, Rio de Janeiro
Greenspan A (2008) A era da turbulência. Campus, São Paulo
Kröger JL, Lutz OHM, Müller F (2020) What does your gaze reveal about you? On the privacy implications of eye tracking. In: Friedewald M, Önen M, Lievens E et al (eds) Privacy and identity management. Data for better living: AI and privacy. IFIP Advances in Information and Communication Technology, vol 576. Springer, Cham
Lessig L (2006) Code: version 2.0. Basic Books, New York
Lorenzetti R (2001) Comercio electrónico. Abeledo-Perrot, Buenos Aires
Lucero E (2011) Governança de Internet: aspectos da formação de um regime global e oportunidades para a ação diplomática. Fundação Alexandre Gusmão, Brasília
Marques CL, Benjamin AH, Miragem B (2016) Comentários ao Código de Defesa do Consumidor. Revista dos Tribunais, São Paulo
Martins GM, Faleiros Júnior JLM (2020) O direito à portabilidade de dados pessoais e sua função na efetiva proteção às relações concorrenciais e de consumo. In: Lóssio CJB, Nascimento L, Tremel R (eds) Cibernética jurídica: estudos sobre direito digital, vol 1. EDUEPB, Campina Grande
Mendes LS (2014) Privacidade, proteção de dados e defesa do consumidor: linhas gerais de um novo direito fundamental. Saraiva, São Paulo
Mendes LS, Doneda D (2016) Marco jurídico para a cidadania digital: uma análise do Projeto de Lei 5.276/2016. Rev Direito Civil Contemporâneo 9:35–48
Menéndez Mato JC (2005) El contrato via Internet. Bosch, Barcelona
National School of Consumer Defense (2010) A proteção de dados pessoais nas relações de consumo: para além da informação creditícia. SDE/DPDC, Brasília
OECD (2021) Data portability, interoperability and digital platform competition. OECD Competition Committee Discussion Paper, Paris
OECD (2023) Global trends in government innovation 2023. OECD Publishing, Paris
Oppliger R (2002) Internet and intranet security. Artech House, Boston
Pastor Sempere MC (2003) Dinero electrónico. Nueva Imprenta, Madrid
Thierer A (2010) The case for internet optimism, part 2: saving the net from its supporters. In: Szoka B, Marcus A (eds) The next digital decade: essays on the future of the internet. TechFreedom, Washington, DC, pp 139–162
Van Alstyne M (2016) A platform strategy: creating new forms of value in the digital age. Capgemini Consulting
Vega JA (2005) Derecho de las nuevas tecnologías: contratos electrónicos y protección de los consumidores. Reus, Madrid
Veronese A (2019) Os direitos de explicação e de oposição frente às decisões totalmente automatizadas: comparando o RGPD da União Europeia com a LGPD brasileira. In: Tepedino G, Frazão A, Oliva M (eds) Lei geral de proteção de dados pessoais e suas repercussões no direito brasileiro, vol 1. Thomson Reuters Brasil, São Paulo, pp 385–415

Chapter 3
Foundations of Personal Data Protection in the European Union and Brazil

3.1 The Rise of Data Protection as a Fundamental Right

Understanding the legal and institutional conditions necessary to enable the safe, legitimate, and socially beneficial reuse of data requires, as a preliminary step, an examination of the normative foundations of personal data protection in the legal systems that serve as references for this study. In this context, the present chapter is dedicated to analyzing the conceptual and structural bases of data protection in the European Union and Brazil, providing the essential doctrinal foundation for the discussions developed throughout the book.

In addressing the research problem that guides this work—namely, how to design legal–institutional frameworks capable of reducing regulatory fragmentation, mitigating normative frictions, and providing legal certainty for data reuse—it becomes essential, above all, to understand the role played by personal data protection within these regulatory architectures.

The first subsection examines the rise of personal data protection to the status of a fundamental right, highlighting how this movement—particularly robust in the European context and progressively incorporated into Brazilian constitutionalism—redefines the boundaries and possibilities for data circulation. By recognizing data protection as an autonomous fundamental right, legal systems begin to structure protection mechanisms that not only impose restrictions but also guide the development of institutional solutions capable of reconciling protection, innovation, and the flow of information—a central element for reducing legal uncertainty and addressing regulatory fragmentation.

Subsequently, the second subchapter analyzes the normative frameworks of the General Data Protection Regulation (GDPR) and the Brazilian General Data Protection Law (LGPD), highlighting convergences, asymmetries, and regulatory choices relevant to the governance of data reuse. Examining these frameworks enables an understanding of how principles, legal bases, data subject

D. Copetti Cravo, *Law and the Digital Economy*,
https://doi.org/10.1007/978-3-032-36672-6_3

rights, and obligations of data controllers shape the environment in which instruments such as data portability may—or may not—function as effective mechanisms for interoperability and coordination among actors, sectors, and jurisdictions.

To begin this first subchapter, it is important to note that the protection of personal data, which extends beyond the defense of privacy,[1] has become a central issue in contemporary digital society, involving not only legal matters but also profound social and economic implications. In this context, the increasing economic value attributed to data demonstrates how the logic of profitability has become one of the main drivers behind the large-scale collection and processing of personal information.

Alongside profitability, which encourages the use of data, there is another concerning factor: users do not tend to choose services that invest in data protection. With the exception of services where security is truly essential, such as banking or medical services, consumers in general do not tend to select services that offer more secure personal data protection policies.[2] In fact, the public is largely unaware of the risks involved in providing their data, as well as the precautions that should be taken in this regard.

Furthermore, emerging developments in the digital society such as big data, the Internet of Things, and cloud storage present significant challenges to the protection of privacy and personal data. Especially with regard to big data, it must be remembered that although it includes aggregated and anonymous data, there is no guarantee that all the information used is completely and irreversibly anonymized.[3] In fact, it is argued that it is rare for data obtained from an active user to be completely and irreversibly anonymous.[4]

With these data collection mechanisms, companies can quickly profile users of the services provided and, based on this, personalize every aspect of the consumer experience. One key difference concerns the commercial approach: instead of waiting for the consumer to come to the *marketplace*, companies can reach their desired consumers at any time and in any place.[5]

As a result, companies may gain the advantage of understanding consumers' cognitive limitations and exploiting their vulnerabilities on an individual level. These situations place consumers in a state of extreme vulnerability, which may not be adequately addressed by the consumer protection regulations currently in force.[6]

It is worth considering that violations of personality rights often occur in this new digital economy. Many legal institutions were conceived in a different era, with

---

[1] Ruaro et al. (2012), p. 64.

[2] EDPS (2014).

[3] EDPS (2014).

[4] Geradin and Kuschewsky (2013).

[5] Calo (2014).

[6] Calo (2014).

physical boundaries that no longer exist and have been surpassed by the digital economy and the Internet.[7]

Thus, the protection of privacy and personal data has become a priority on the global agenda and was driven, in part, by espionage scandals involving world leaders, conducted by the United States National Security Agency. These events led to the adoption by the United Nations General Assembly of Resolution No. 68/167,[8] which expressed serious concern regarding the negative impact of espionage and the interception of communications on human rights.

The scandal involving Cambridge Analytica also sparked a discussion about the misuse of data and its impact on democratic relations. As a result, there was an opportunity to reconsider the existing data protection models, seeking modernization and the elimination of legal gaps,[9] as was the case in Brazil, which at the time did not have a General Data Protection Law.

According to Rafael Zanatta, the situation in Brazil was striking when compared to other Latin American countries, where there was a proliferation of general data protection laws, accompanied by specific mechanisms to ensure the enforcement of established rights and the creation of regulatory agencies.[10]

It is worth recalling that the right to personal data protection had one of its earliest manifestations with the establishment of the Special Subcommittee on Invasion of Privacy by the U.S. Congress in the 1960s. During this period, the first data centers played a decisive role in advancing personal data protection, as they not only enabled benefits related to efficiency and service improvement but also introduced significant risks to individual rights and freedoms. This prompted specialized legal scholarship to reflect on the subject.[11]

However, it was in the 1970s, in Europe, that the first laws on the subject emerged, such as the Hesse State Law in 1970 in Germany and the *Datalag* in Sweden in 1973. Thus, it was with the Hesse State Law that the development of an autonomous regulatory model for data protection was inaugurated.[12] It is worth noting that the Hesse Law was limited to addressing data collected and processed by public entities, whereas the Swedish law applied to both public and private entities.[13]

Following the trend set by such legislation, which established data protection as an autonomous right, the 1980s marked a period of consolidation for the protection of personal data. Among the main milestones of this decade are the OECD Guidelines on the Protection of Privacy and Transborder Flows of Personal Data, Convention 108 of the Council of Europe, and the decision of the German

---

[7] Lorenzetti (2001), p. 25.

[8] UN (2020).

[9] Zanatta (2015), p. 454.

[10] Zanatta (2015), p. 454.

[11] Gomes (2024).

[12] Doneda (2021), p. 8.

[13] Acocella and Sampaio (2020).

Constitutional Court, which examined the 1983 Census Act and affirmed the existence of a "right to informational self-determination."

In the following decades, the subject evolved significantly, particularly due to the digitalization of society and the economy, so that we can now observe the emergence of a new generation of personal data protection laws. In this regard, Directive 95/46/EC is noteworthy, having been replaced in 2016 by the General Data Protection Regulation (GDPR).

One of the main reasons for replacing the Directive was the different approaches adopted within the domestic law of the Member States. Furthermore, the Directive struggled to keep pace with the advances of the technological revolution witnessed in recent times, which compromised and jeopardized its effectiveness, since at the time of its creation the so-called digital age was only just beginning.[14] Additionally, the Regulation has an additional objective related to the consolidation of the digital single market. For its success, the existence of uniform rules and the removal of technical and legal barriers are essential.[15]

Such contemporary legislation, like the GDPR, goes far beyond informational self-determination and seeks to provide tools for collective protection, as well as risk management mechanisms, based on the recognition that the success of personal data protection depends on the prevention of information-induced harms[16] and on accountability. These risk management mechanisms are closely aligned with the understanding that data protection also encompasses the safeguarding of the confidentiality and integrity of technical and informational systems, as highlighted in a 2008 decision by the German Constitutional Court.[17]

Another aspect of these legislations concerns the emergence of new rights, which originally would not even appear to be related to data protection and which today have naturally found their place within this context. In this regard, data portability and the right to review automated decisions may be cited.[18,19]

Although some rights are not new to our legal system (consider the right of access and rectification, already implemented through *habeas data* since the 1988 Federal Constitution), it is certain that concern for the exercise of data subjects' rights takes on a new dimension with the entry into force of the General Data Protection Law (LGPD) in Brazil.

The introduction of habeas data by the 1988 Federal Constitution marked a significant milestone in the realization of rights related to data protection, in line with

---

[14] Edwards and Harbinja (2013), p. 130.

[15] Wubben et al. (2012).

[16] Purtova (2018).

[17] Sarlet (2021), p. 35.

[18] Doneda (2021), p. 5.

[19] Data portability is a global trend that encompasses several distinct initiatives. As Peter Swire points out, these initiatives revolve around the following perspectives: (1) data portability as an individual right, provided for in personal data protection laws such as the GDPR, (2) the debate on the regulation of large platforms, and (3) sector-specific regulations for data transfer. Swire (2020), p. 2.

the redemocratization movement that characterized the 1980s.[20] Nevertheless, despite the symbolic and legal importance of this instrument, it is necessary to acknowledge that its inclusion could not be presumed sufficient to comprehensively and exhaustively safeguard all the protections required for the effective defense of individuals in the contemporary informational context.[21]

In the other chapters of this book, we have examined certain risk situations faced by individuals arising from the digital economy, precisely due to its distinctive characteristic of being driven by data collection and processing. With this foundation, there is a significant incentive for economic agents to engage in a competition for data access, as well as to restrict access to this resource by competing companies.

In this context, data protection laws play a fundamental role by establishing legal boundaries for the access, processing, and sharing of personal information, serving as instruments to curb abusive and irregular conduct. Although primarily aimed at safeguarding the fundamental rights of data subjects, such regulations produce effects that go beyond the individual sphere, also contributing to the promotion of more ethical and transparent practices in the data market.

The benefits of this regulation are manifold. On the one hand, it ensures essential guarantees for the protection of individuals' personality and dignity; on the other, it curbs aggressive and anticompetitive practices based on the indiscriminate manipulation of personal information, fostering a more balanced and trustworthy economic environment. Thus, data protection emerges not only as a mechanism for safeguarding rights but also as a structuring element of a more responsible digital economy.

There is, therefore, no doubt as to the necessity of protecting personal data through appropriate regulatory frameworks. However, given that a significant portion of the services exposing individuals to risks operate in the digital environment, it is equally essential to consider the importance of broader regulation of cyberspace—one that is capable of coordinating data protection with the governance of the very infrastructures and dynamics of the Internet and how this connects with personal data protection regulations.

The debate on the regulation of the Internet and cyberspace has been characterized by the coexistence of different theoretical models, each reflecting distinct perspectives on who should exercise control over digital dynamics. Among these approaches, the model of regulation by *code*[22] stands out. This proposal recognizes that the Internet does not possess an intrinsically free or ungovernable essence; rather, it is shaped by the set of software, hardware, and protocols that structure its operation. Thus, the very technical architecture of these systems constitutes a powerful regulatory mechanism, capable of creating environments of greater freedom or, conversely, of strict control over behaviors.

At the same time, there has been the development of transnational and international institutions, based on the premise that cyberspace is an essentially global and

[20] Doneda (2021), p. 12.

[21] Rodriguez (2021), p. 181.

[22] Lessig (2006).

deterritorialized environment, existing beyond the isolated regulatory capacity of nation states. According to this perspective, Internet governance should be carried out by transnational bodies endowed with their own legitimacy, capable of formulating rules and coordinating interests on a global scale. In contrast, the national law model maintains that the Internet, although it possesses specific characteristics, remains an activity subject to state regulation, as is the case with other economic and social sectors.

There is also the proposal of self-regulation, based on the idea that the digital market itself can establish standards of conduct and best practices through the spontaneous emergence of codes of behavior and private governance mechanisms. Finally, the economic model describes the phenomenon of the Internet essentially as a large market for products and services, arguing that competitive dynamics and economic incentives are the main drivers of organization and regulation in this environment.

These different conceptions have materialized in concrete institutional initiatives. On the one hand, there are arrangements that, while recognizing the transnational nature of the Internet, preserve the centrality of states in its governance, as is the case within the International Telecommunication Union (ITU). As a member of the United Nations System and dedicated to issues related to Information and Communication Technologies, the ITU currently brings together 193 countries, constituting an intergovernmental forum of great relevance for the establishment of global standards and guidelines.[23]

On the other hand, an alternative model of multistakeholder governance has been consolidated, exemplified by the activities of the Internet Corporation for Assigned Names and Numbers (ICANN). Since its inception, the organization was conceived not as a private club but as an entity oriented toward public purposes, adopting a unique institutional format based on the principles of bottom-up, consensus-driven, and multistakeholder governance. This arrangement seeks to coordinate the participation of governments, the private sector, the technical community, and the civil society in the formulation of policies related to the core infrastructure of the Internet.[24] The significance of this model was reinforced in 2014, culminating in 2016 with the definitive transition of Internet Assigned Numbers Authority (IANA) functions to the global Internet community.

The analysis of these different models demonstrates that the regulation of cyberspace cannot be understood through a single normative logic. On the contrary, the protection of personal data and the regulation of digital activities require hybrid solutions that combine state legal instruments, technical mechanisms, transnational institutional arrangements, and self-regulatory practices. Only through this multifaceted approach is it possible to adequately address the challenges posed by the digital economy and the global flow of information.

---

[23] Lloyd (2014).

[24] Sundfeld and Rosilho (2015), p. 54.

In this context, it is recognized that the market alone is not capable of ensuring the protection of social values or fundamental rights related to human dignity.[25] Therefore, Internet regulation emerges as an essential instrument to safeguard these principles that underpin our society. However, it is necessary to make efforts to identify and develop the most appropriate way to structure an effective and balanced regulatory system.

Some of these values are undeniably linked to the intimacy, freedom, and privacy of Internet users, as well as to personal data. The regulation of these matters is of utmost importance, given the current paradigm, as previously discussed in this work.

In this regard, it is important to note that the protection of personal data originated as an extension of the safeguarding of the right to privacy. From the moment information gained significant relevance in general terms, the issue of privacy began to revolve around the subject of personal data.[26]

Thus, data protection pertains to personality rights, being directly related to the moral aspects of the individual. The foundation of privacy and the protection of personal data would be ontologically the same, grounded in the dignity of the human person.[27]

However, defining the concept of privacy has always proven to be a complex task, particularly because it is a notion deeply sensitive to temporal and cultural transformations. In its initial formulation, privacy was predominantly conceived as the "right to be left alone,"[28] emphasizing the protection of the individual against undue intrusions into their personal sphere. Over time, however, this understanding evolved into a postmodern facet, in which privacy becomes associated with each person's freedom to manage and choose under what circumstances and to what extent they wish to expose themselves in the social and informational sphere.

In the same vein, Ruth Gavison proposes a conceptual approach according to which privacy is structured around three fundamental elements: secrecy, anonymity, and solitude—dimensions that express different forms of individual control over third-party access to one's personal life.[29]

The limitations to the right to privacy, in turn, had already been outlined in the classic article by Warren and Brandeis,[30] a landmark in the legal reflection on the subject. According to the authors, the right to privacy is not absolute and allows for restrictions in certain circumstances, such as (1) when there is a relevant public interest in the information; (2) in cases of mere oral disclosure that does not result in actual harm; and (3) when the facts have been made public by the holder themselves or disclosed with their consent.

---

[25] Nadel (2000), p. 822.

[26] National School of Consumer Defense (2010), p. 25.

[27] Doneda (2008).

[28] Warren and Brandeis (1890), pp. 193–201.

[29] Gavison (1980), p. 421.

[30] Warren and Brandeis (1890), pp. 193–201.

In this evolutionary context, the contributions of German jurisprudence to the theoretical consolidation of privacy throughout the twentieth century deserve particular attention, especially through the so-called theory of spheres. As systematized by Robert Alexy, this theory proposes the division of private life into three spheres—intimate, private, and social—arranged in descending order of legal protection. This framework resulted from a process of balancing the principle of negative liberty with other constitutional values, seeking to establish more precise criteria for determining the appropriate levels of protection for each dimension of personality.

In this way, there is the innermost sphere, which represents the intangible and the most intimate aspects that are absolutely protected; the broad private sphere, in which the individual selectively chooses with whom to share certain aspects of their intimacy; and the social sphere, of a residual nature in relation to the other spheres, encompassing information that the individual wishes to exclude from the knowledge of third parties.

Wanderley de Paula Barreto[31] adds that the theory of spheres, however, has not been immune to criticism and counterarguments, particularly due to the existence of a "privacy within publicity," when someone seeks to withdraw into a special form of seclusion that cannot be defined *ex ante* but only subsequently by case law, which could ultimately benefit a potential violator of the right. As corroborated by Otávio Rodrigues Junior, this theory, in the current context, has been abandoned, as exemplified by the case involving Princess Caroline of Monaco.[32]

There are also discussions regarding the distinction between intimacy, privacy, and private life. According to René Ariel Dotti,[33] intimacy would be encompassed within private life, as a particular category thereof, but with a more limited scope.

Danilo Doneda,[34] in turn, suggests the use of the term privacy, given its broader scope and reach. According to this author, the terms private life and intimacy refer specifically to certain aspects of the development of privacy, whose importance was linked to a different context and historical moment.

It should be emphasized, finally, as a consequence of human development and evolution itself, that many questions are emerging regarding the core of privacy protection in light of the Internet and digital services. Some argue that, in contemporary times, privacy has assumed a new conception or, for the more skeptical, has even become an illusion.[35] In this context, it is important to weigh the values of postmodern culture, which directly influence legal science and its protective instruments, as elucidated by Erik Jayme,[36,37] which may lead to a new conception of privacy.

---

[31] Barreto (2010), pp. 135–159.

[32] Rodrigues Junior (2013), p. 118.

[33] Dotti (1980).

[34] Doneda (2009), p. 95.

[35] Miguel (2012).

[36] Jayme (2003), pp. 59–68.

[37] In this line of reasoning, according to the teachings of Erik Jayme, the core of the intersection between postmodern culture and Law consists of the values they share. These values can be summarized as (1) pluralism, not only of forms but also of styles, including autonomy with respect to

Personal data can be seen as an extension of the right to privacy, providing it with updated and distinct contours.[38] Although the regulation of personal data derives from the right to privacy, these rights cannot be regarded as identical.[39]

Privacy, in general, protects the individual against intrusion into their private sphere, while data protection regulates the processing of an individual's data, regardless of whether such data is considered private. The purpose of data protection is to prevent any potential association of this data from violating the individual's personality rights.[40]

It is noted that data protection must be ensured throughout all stages of data processing, such as collection, processing, storage, transfer to third parties, and others. Furthermore, this protection must focus on personal data regardless of the medium in which they are found. Additionally, protection should encompass both automated data records and those that are not.[41]

In this regard, the fundamental right to data protection grants individuals the power to control their personal data, its use, and its destination, with the aim of preventing its unlawful circulation and any harm to dignity and the affected right. Thus, it protects the data subject rather than the data itself.[42] In other words, the protection of personal data is intended to safeguard individuals (and not merely the data itself).

It is possible to observe in some regulations the recognition of data protection as an autonomous right, distinct from the rights to privacy and intimacy. In others, such protection remains an intrinsic aspect of privacy and intimacy[43] or arises from the analogous application of other intrinsically interconnected rights.[44]

As a human right, data protection can be found in the Universal Declaration of Human Rights, in Article 12, and in the International Covenant on Civil and Political Rights of 1966, in Article 17. In both cases, data protection is encompassed within the protection of privacy and intimacy.

Within the scope of regional human rights protection, data protection is also covered by the protection of privacy and intimacy. In the European context, reference is made to Article 8 of the European Convention on Human Rights, which—in

---

lifestyle, thereby recognizing the right to difference; (2) communication and the absence of boundaries, since, according to Erik Jayme, it is not only technological means that enable the rapid exchange of information and images but also the will and desire to communicate; (3) narration: "to communicate is also to describe, to recount, to narrate"; and (4) the return of feelings, evidenced by the appreciation of one's own identity, religion, and other expressions of individualism. These four values demonstrate the relationship between law and postmodern culture. Jayme (2003), pp. 59–68.

[38] National School of Consumer Defense (2010), p. 25.

[39] Kuner (2013).

[40] Kuner (2013).

[41] Kuner (2013).

[42] Vega (2005), p. 360.

[43] Kuner (2013).

[44] Privacy International (2015).

the interpretation provided by the European Court of Human Rights—includes data protection. According to the aforementioned Court, the term "private life" should not be interpreted restrictively. Thus, personal data receive such protection and are defined as any information relating to an identified or identifiable individual.[45]

In addition to these provisions on human rights, it is possible to identify international conventions that address the right to data protection as an autonomous matter. This is the case of the Council of Europe Convention for the Protection of Individuals with regard to Automatic Processing of Personal Data and the Supplementary Act on Data Protection adopted by the Economic Community of West African States (ECOWAS).[46]

In the Americas, there is a movement by the Organization of American States ("OAS") aimed at establishing detailed regulations in this area. In 2012, the Draft Declaration of Principles on Privacy and Personal Data Protection in the Americas was released, presenting 12 fundamental principles on the subject.[47]

Furthermore, the Inter-American Court of Human Rights, in its judgment of the case *Escher v. Brazil*, expressed concern over the increased risks to the right to privacy due to the fluidity of information in the context of new technological tools, especially the Internet. The Court emphasized that the growing use of these technologies imposes on the State the duty to strengthen its commitment to adapting traditional forms of privacy protection to these new models.[48]

Within Mercosur, there are already some initiatives, such as Decision 15/20, which sets forth provisions regarding data protection and its circulation within the regional bloc. Item 7 of this Decision states that the parties commit to applying an adequate level of protection to the personal data received. In the context of the European Union, the Charter of Fundamental Rights of the European Union (2000/C 364/01) expressly established, on December 7, 2000, a rule addressing the protection of personal data in its Article 8. The Treaty on the Functioning of the European Union also includes provisions on data protection in its Article 16.[49]

As a result of these two provisions, Directive 95/46/EC on Data Protection was enacted, which also applies to the Internet. It is important to note that this Directive represents a historic milestone in the field of data protection, with its main objectives being to ensure the promotion of the fundamental rights of privacy and individual intimacy and, at the level of regional integration, to guarantee the free flow of personal information within the European market.

One of the most paradigmatic cases involving the Directive was adjudicated by the Court of Justice of the European Union (CJEU),[50] which addressed the right to be forgotten and involved Google, the Spanish Data Protection Agency, and Mr. Mario

[45] Kokott and Sobotta (2013), p. 223.

[46] Kuner (2013).

[47] Article 19 (2016), p. 8.

[48] Inter-American Court of Human Rights. *Case of Escher et al. v. Brazil.*

[49] Kuner (2013).

[50] European Union. Court of Justice of the European Union. *Case C-131/12*. Judged on May 13, 2014.

Costeja González. In brief, the facts of the case are as follows: in 1998, the Spanish newspaper *La Vanguardia* published, in its print editions, notices regarding the auction of assets to be conducted by the Ministry of Labor and Social Affairs for the payment of debts owed to social security, one of which concerned the properties of Mr. Mario Costeja González. These editions were later made available on the Internet.

Although a substantial amount of time had passed since the publication of such advertisements, as well as the final sale of Mr. Mario Costeja González's property, every time Mr. Mario Costeja González's name was entered into Google, those reports, which had been digitized, would appear. When he requested that the newspaper remove this association, Mr. Mario Costeja González was informed that nothing could be done by the newspaper in this regard.

Thus, Mr. Mario Costeja González approached Google Spain, which also failed to resolve the issue, claiming that the indexing of his data had been carried out by Google Inc., located in the United States. Faced with this impasse, Mr. Mario turned to the Spanish Data Protection Agency (AEPD), which ordered Google Spain to remove the data.

As a result, Google appealed to the Spanish judiciary, arguing, among other points, that the activities of Google Inc. were not subject to the provisions of European regulations set forth in Directive 95/46/EC, since its operations were not conducted within the territory of the Member State. Consequently, as the matter involved European law, a preliminary reference was made to the Court of Justice of the European Union, which held that the activities of Google Search in the United States and those of its establishment in the Member State (Google Spain) were inextricably linked, thereby justifying the application of the data protection rules established by the European Union to the case.

It is important to note that, although the CJEU affirmed the principle of territoriality in the application of data protection rules (albeit broadening the scope of this territoriality), Alsenoy and Koekkoek argue that this expanded jurisdiction has acquired characteristics typical of extraterritoriality, supported by the effects doctrine.[51]

The case discussed above clearly illustrates the potential of the Directive. However, despite its achievements, its implementation has faced obstacles, particularly regarding the different approaches adopted within the domestic law of the Member States.[52,53]

Furthermore, the Directive struggled to keep pace with the advances of the technological revolution witnessed in recent times, which compromised and jeopardized its effectiveness, since at the time of its creation the so-called digital era was only just beginning.[54]

---

[51] Alsenoy and Koekkoek (2015).

[52] Fernández Rozas and Sánchez Lorenzo (2009).

[53] Despite the protection afforded, the Directive has faced criticism, even being described as follows: "the elephant has laboured and given birth to a mouse," especially due to the problems encountered in its implementation (Lloyd 2014).

[54] Edwards and Harbinja (2013), p. 130.

For these reasons, a regulation (General Data Protection Regulation (GDPR)) was enacted for data protection, presented by the European Commission to the Council in 2012 and published on May 4, 2016. Its application began on May 25, 2018. From this regulatory milestone, it becomes possible to understand not only the evolution of the European model but also its influence on other regulatory frameworks, such as the Brazilian one.

3.2 The Architectures of the General Data Protection Regulation (GDPR) and the General Data Protection Law (LGPD)

This section presents an in-depth comparative analysis of the two main legislative frameworks shaping data governance in the European Union and Brazil: the GDPR and the LGPD. The examination will begin with the European legislation, detailing the transition from Directive 95/46/EC to the General Data Protection Regulation.

The limitations of the Directive will be discussed, such as the fragmentation resulting from different national implementations and its inadequacy in light of technological advances. In contrast, the GDPR will be highlighted as a regulation with direct and uniform application, designed not only to protect individuals' rights but also to consolidate the digital single market. The main innovations introduced by the GDPR will be explored, including its broad extraterritorial scope, which extends to entities outside the EU that offer products or monitor the behavior of individuals within the bloc; the expanded definition of personal data, encompassing pseudonymized data; the broadened concept of sensitive data to include genetic and biometric data; stricter conditions for obtaining consent, including the right to withdraw consent and the requirement for specific consent for different purposes; protection rules for children and adolescents; and alternative legal bases to consent, such as contractual necessity and legitimate interests.

On the Brazilian side, the analysis will begin with the constitutional foundation, starting from the interpretation of Article 5, items X and XII, of the Federal Constitution by the Supreme Federal Court, moving through the recognition of the fundamental right to data protection in 2020, and culminating in its explicit enshrinement with Constitutional Amendment No. 115/2022. The process of developing the LGPD will be detailed, highlighting the maturation of public debate through consultations that led to Bill No. 5276/2016, up to the enactment of Law No. 13,709/2018.

The central features of the LGPD will be analyzed, such as the pursuit of uniformity and cross-sector applicability to address legislative fragmentation, its application to both the public and private sectors, and the establishment of a set of guiding principles in Article 6 and legal bases for processing in Articles 7 and 11. The comparison between the GDPR and the LGPD will highlight the notable convergences in fundamental concepts, such as the definitions of personal data, sensitive data, and the adoption of a risk-based approach, demonstrating the influence of the European model on Brazilian legislation and the alignment of both regimes with the highest international standards of data protection.

Beginning the analysis of the GDPR, and considering the previous examination of the Directive, it is possible to state that the shift to a regulation is highly commendable, particularly as a means to address fragmentation. In this regard, it should be noted that a regulation has significantly greater binding force than a directive, requiring its full and immediate adoption by Member States. In contrast, a directive, once it applies to a given factual situation, mandates the implementation of national laws by the Member States.[55]

The Regulation also has an additional objective, alongside the protection of individuals' privacy, which concerns the consolidation of the digital single market. For its success, the existence of uniform rules and the removal of technical and legal barriers are essential.[56]

The first noteworthy aspect of the Regulation is the broad scope of protection it provides, which may extend to entities that do not have a presence in the European Union, as long as the data of a resident of the European Union is processed as a result of the offering of a product or service. Another scenario is when the behavior of an individual within the European Union is monitored,[57] which demonstrates, in both cases, the possibility of the extraterritorial application of the Regulation.[58]

Furthermore, the Regulation applies to all data relating to an identified or identifiable natural person.[59] Notably, the Regulation provides that personal data which has been pseudonymized is still considered data of an identifiable person, as long as it is possible to attribute it to a natural person by means of additional information.[60]

With regard to sensitive data,[61] the concept has been broadened compared to the Directive, now including genetic and biometric data.[62] As an example of how such biometric data can be used in the digital market, one may cite the "Touch ID" system implemented in Apple's mobile phones, computers, and *tablets*.

This technology allows only those whose fingerprints are registered to unlock devices equipped with such embedded technology. This unlocking method has replaced the use of codes with the owners' fingerprints, enabling them not only to

---

[55] Fernández Rozas and Sánchez Lorenzo (2009).

[56] Wubben et al. (2012).

[57] Boardman et al. (2017), p. 1.

[58] Zeiter (2014).

[59] Boardman et al. (2017), p. 1.

[60] Pseudonymization was an innovation introduced by the GDPR, as the European Directive 95/46/EC only provided for the concept of anonymization. Luz (2021).

[61] Sensitive data are those that can be used for discriminatory purposes. In this regard, it is important to recall that one of the inherent purposes of the right to data protection is to prevent discrimination (Döhmann 2021, p. 112).

[62] Boardman et al. (2017), p. 1.

access their devices but also to purchase books and make transactions through enabled applications.[63]

The conditions for obtaining consent for use have become more stringent under the new Regulation. Indeed, individuals now have the right to withdraw their consent at any time, and different processing activities require separate consents.[64]

Adolescents and children under the age of 13 are not permitted to provide consent on their own for the processing of their personal data in online services.[65] For adolescents between 13 and 15 years old, parental consent is required, except where Member State legislation allows for independent consent from the age of 13. Adolescents aged 16 or older may provide the required consent on their own.[66]

Despite the stricter rules regarding consent, there are cases in which consent is not required to justify the processing of personal data, such as contractual necessity, compliance with legal obligations, or legitimate interests.[67]

With regard to transparency, organizations must provide individuals with extensive information about the processing of their personal data. The Regulation also introduces an obligation to notify[68] security breaches to supervisory authorities and to the respective victims of the incident.

Furthermore, the Regulation consolidates several rights such as the right to be forgotten, data portability,[69] and objection to certain processing activities and to decisions made by automated procedures. These are just some of the changes introduced by the Regulation.

Ultimately, the Regulation aims to ensure a high level of data protection by seeking to minimize the risk of data breaches.[70] One of the mechanisms to achieve the effectiveness of these objectives is precisely the imposition of severe fines, which may reach up to 20 million euros or up to 4% of the worldwide annual turnover (whichever is greater).[71]

---

[63] Such technology, however, has already been largely replaced by facial recognition (*Face ID*) of the device owner.

[64] Boardman et al. (2017), p. 5.

[65] Thus, the prevailing rule is that, in cases where services are directly offered to children and adolescents, prior consent from parents or guardians is required for minors under 16 years of age. However, Member States are allowed to set a lower age limit in their domestic law for this purpose, provided that the minimum age is not set below 13 years (Borelli 2021).

[66] Boardman et al. (2017), p. 1.

[67] Boardman et al. (2017), p. 1.

[68] Regarding the notification deadline, the GDPR establishes a period of 72 h and, if this is not possible, requires that justifications be provided for non-compliance with the deadline. Crespo (2021).

[69] According to Bárbara da Rosa Lazarotto, the right to data portability, introduced by the GDPR, was considered revolutionary due to its novelty and its potential to give data subjects control over their data and potentially alter the market landscape. Lazarotto (2024).

[70] In the event of noncompliance with the GDPR, it is possible to apply flexible and scalable measures, which may be corrective, preventive, or repressive, in order to encourage organizational diligence (accountability) in mitigating the occurrence of unlawful events (Vainzof 2022).

[71] Marko (2017), pp. 65–66.

The European data protection model, especially since the GDPR, has exerted significant influence on various legal systems. In this context, it is pertinent to examine how Brazil has structured its own regulatory response to the protection of personal data, as well as the extent to which it aligns with—or diverges from—the solutions adopted within the European Union.

In Brazil, the Federal Constitution (FC), in Article 5, item X, considers private life and intimacy to be inviolable and further establishes in Article 5, item XII, the confidentiality of correspondence and telegraphic, data, and telephone communications. In the latter case, confidentiality may be breached, provided there is a judicial order, in the circumstances and manner prescribed by law, for the purposes of criminal investigation or criminal procedural instruction.[72]

This language has raised numerous questions regarding the possible existence of an absolute right to the inviolability of correspondence, telegraphic communications, and data, given that the only circumstance for breach of confidentiality, according to the constitutional text, would be for telephone communications.

As is well known, there is no such thing as an absolute right,[73] and for this reason, inviolability cannot be absolute either. According to the Supreme Federal Court (STF), as can be inferred from the leading case, Extraordinary Appeal No. 418,416, reported by Justice Sepúlveda Pertence and adjudicated by the Plenary of the Supreme Federal Court on May 10, 2005,[74,75] the breach of confidentiality applies only to telephone communications, as this is the only form of communication that is instantaneous and leaves no trace, thus necessitating court-authorized interception. In contrast, data communications, correspondence, and telegraphic communications leave evidence or traces, which may, for example, be subject to search and seizure.

Thus, for the Supreme Federal Court, the protection referred to in Article 5, XII, of the Constitution concerns the "communication of data" and not the "data itself," even when stored on a computer.[76] On the one hand, the decision is correct in recognizing that absolute inviolability does not exist; on the other hand, there is a certain weakness regarding the protection of the data itself, which, in the current context, should not be left without any specific protection.

---

[72] Habeas data guarantees access to and rectification of personal data but is limited to public entities and is considered, according to Doneda, insufficient for effective protection in the information society. Doneda (2011), p. 103.

[73] According to Ingo Wolfgang Sarlet, it is almost universally accepted that, in principle, there is no absolute right, that is, there is no right that is entirely immune to any form of restriction. Sarlet (2002), p. 119.

[74] Brazil. Federal Supreme Court. Extraordinary Appeal No. 418,416. Reporting Justice Sepúlveda Pertence, Plenary Session, Judged on May 10, 2005.

[75] Brazil. Supreme Federal Court. Habeas Corpus No. 124322, Reporting Justice Roberto Barroso, First Panel, Judged on December 9, 2016.

[76] Brazil. Federal Supreme Court. Extraordinary Appeal No. 418,416. Reporting Justice Sepúlveda Pertence, Plenary Session, Judged on May 10, 2005.

It is evident, thus, that the Brazilian legal framework was far from providing the necessary protection. This scenario was often based on a binary perspective of secrecy/openness, public/private, failing to reflect the complexity inherent to information matters.[77]

Therefore, the interpretation given to the right to intimacy and privacy did not correspond to the underlying reality or to the breadth and importance that the issue of personal data currently holds. Fortunately, in recent years, this matter has advanced significantly in Brazil.

In 2020, the Federal Supreme Court (STF), in the judgment of ADIs 6389, 6390, 6393, 6388, and 6387,[78] recognized the existence of the fundamental right to the protection of personal data.[79] In 2021, Constitutional Amendment Proposal (PEC) No. 17/2019 was approved, with the purpose of including the protection of personal data as an expressly stated fundamental right in the Federal Constitution.[80]

As a result of the approval of Constitutional Amendment Proposal No. 17/2019, Constitutional Amendment No. 115/2022 was enacted in 2022. This Amendment included the protection of personal data as a separate item in Article 5 of the Federal Constitution, specifically item LXXIX.

At the infraconstitutional level, until 2018, there was no general legislation in Brazil regarding the protection of personal data that fulfilled the function of safeguarding individuals[81] against both public authorities and private entities.[82]

To address this omission, several legislative proposals were introduced, each offering distinct safeguards—or, conversely, posing different risks—to the rights to privacy and other fundamental freedoms, according to the human rights organization Article 19.[83]

According to Danilo Doneda and Laura Schertel Mendes,[84] among the legislative proposals, Bill 5276/2016 was the most detailed and thorough. This Bill was the

[77] Doneda (2011), p. 106.

[78] Brazil. Supreme Federal Court. *Referendum on the Preliminary Injunction in ADI 6387*. Rapporteur: Justice Rosa Weber, Judged on May 7, 2020.

[79] In this case, Provisional Measure 954/2020, which required telecommunications service providers to share user data with the IBGE for statistical production during the coronavirus pandemic, was suspended.

[80] The Proposed Constitutional Amendment (PEC) 17/2019, in addition to expressly providing for the protection of personal data in Article 5 of the Federal Constitution (CF), also established the exclusive competence of the Union to legislate on the matter.

[81] As Anderson Schreiber recounts, until 2018, the protection of personal data in our legal system was merely incidental, addressed only by scattered or sector-specific laws. Schreiber (2019), pp. 367–383.

[82] This symmetry between the public and private sectors regarding the use of personal data is a global trend and can be observed in the OECD guidelines on privacy protection and transborder flows of personal data, as well as in the Convention for the Protection of Individuals with regard to Automatic Processing of Personal Data (Wimmer 2020, pp. 27–36).

[83] Article 19 (2016), p. 3.

[84] Doneda and Mendes (2017), p. 45.

result of approximately 5 years of debate and stemmed from an initiative of the executive branch.

The project was developed through two public consultations, held in 2010 and 2015, respectively. On these occasions, more than 2000 contributions were received from a wide range of stakeholders, including academia, civil society, businesses, and the public sector.[85]

Indeed, it can be said that it was a highly developed text, even comparable to foreign legislation considered to be quite advanced, while still observing and remaining in harmony with the necessary protection of human dignity.[86]

In fact, it is evident that Bill No. 5276/2016 fully fulfilled the mission of protecting individuals and, if approved, would have served as a general regulatory framework for the protection of personal data, applicable to both the private and public sectors. The starting and ending point is always the individual, through the protection of their personality, ensuring privacy, freedom, and equality.[87]

It is interesting to note that Bill No. 5276/2016 proposed the enactment of a general and unified law. This would prevent the creation of legislative enclaves,[88] with varying levels of protection within the same legal system.[89]

It is evident that fragmented legislation, in addition to creating legal uncertainty for citizens and legal practitioners, could render protective regulations completely ineffective, given the well-known and common practice of data transfer across various sectors.[90] Precisely because of the cross-sectoral nature of data use, Bruno Bioni[91] argues that a general regulatory framework is necessary.[92]

In 2018, the Chamber of Deputies reviewed Bill 4060/2012, with Bill 5276/2016 and Bill 6291/16 attached to the main proposal. A substitute bill and amendments were proposed. These were ultimately set aside, and the Global Substitute Subamendment was approved in the end.

---

[85] Mendes and Doneda (2016), p. 46.

[86] Mendes and Doneda (2016), p. 46.

[87] Doneda and Mendes (2017), p. 46.

[88] Tepedino (2001), pp. 199–216.

[89] Even before the LGPD came into effect, it was already possible to discern a framework for data protection in Brazil (although it was not comprehensive), but its sectorization and fragmentation were among the main obstacles to its effectiveness. Oliveira and Lopes (2019), pp. 53–84.

[90] Doneda and Mendes (2017), p. 46.

[91] Bioni (2017).

[92] According to Laura Mendes, general personal data protection laws have established themselves as one of the most effective means of safeguarding privacy in developed countries, influencing, among others, the European Union, Canada, and Australia. Outside this trend, however, is the United States, which has a comprehensive law for the public sector and scattered, sector-specific laws for the private sector. Mendes (2014), p. 48.

Subsequently, the Bill was approved by the Senate and forwarded for presidential sanction. On August 14, 2018, with partial veto, Ordinary Law No. 13,709/2018 was enacted, known as the General Data Protection Law (LGPD).[93]

Thus, the LGPD introduced a series of innovations into the Brazilian legal system, among which the following stand out: the uniformity and cross-sectoral nature of the legal framework on the subject, in a clear attempt to ensure legal certainty and combat fragmentation, applying both to public administration and private entities, as well as the establishment of legal bases that legitimize the processing of personal data.

In this regard, the LGPD sets forth in Article 6 several principles that must guide data processing activities, such as free access, purpose limitation, transparency, necessity, data quality, security, and nondiscrimination. It is important to note that the significance of principles within the legal system and their normative character is already well established, extending beyond the mere function of normative guidelines. These principles are highly useful for regulating dynamic markets such as the technological and digital sectors, as they possess a more flexible normative structure, prescribing conduct in an indirect manner, linked to the achievement of specific objectives.[94]

The General Data Protection Law (LGPD) establishes a broad scope of application but provides for certain specific exceptions. These include processing carried out by a natural person for exclusively personal and noneconomic purposes; processing carried out exclusively for journalistic and artistic purposes; or academic purposes, in which case Articles 7 and 11 of this law apply; processing carried out exclusively for purposes of public security, national defense, state security, or activities of investigation and prosecution of criminal offenses; or data originating from outside the national territory that are not subject to communication, shared use with Brazilian data controllers, or international data transfer to a country other than the country of origin, provided that the country of origin offers a level of personal data protection adequate to that provided for in the LGPD.

These exceptions are relevant as they allow activities of public and social interest to be conducted appropriately. The specific nature of sectors such as public security, national defense, journalism, the arts, and academia requires a balance between the protection of personal data and the need to preserve the effectiveness of these activities. It should be emphasized, however, that such exceptions may only be applied for the exclusive use of their intended purposes and not for other ends.

Furthermore, the LGPD sets forth the circumstances under which data processing is lawful. These circumstances, also known as legal bases, are provided for in Articles 7 and 11 of the LGPD.

---

[93] As Cueva states, this law emerges to fill gaps in the Brazilian legal system and ensure an adequate level of protection. Cueva (2017), pp. 59–67.

[94] Humberto Ávila clarifies that, regarding the nature of the prescribed behavior, principles are teleological, being immediately associated with an ideal state of affairs and only mediately with conduct. Rules, on the other hand, prescribe conduct directly. Ávila (2014), pp. 95–101.

It should be added that the LGPD introduces important concepts, such as that set forth in Article 5, item I, which establishes that personal data is any information relating to an identified or identifiable natural person,[95] including identification numbers, location data, or electronic identifiers when these are related to an identified or identifiable person. It is evident that the LGPD adopts an expansive approach by including the characteristic of "identifiable" within the concept of personal data.

Item II of the same Article 5 provides for the characterization of sensitive data. According to this provision, these are personal data concerning racial or ethnic origin, religion, political opinions, party affiliation, membership in unions or participation in religious, philosophical, or political organizations, sexual life, health, genetic and biometric data.[96]

The creation of this special category of data results from an analysis that identified the significance of the information contained therein, as well as the distinct impact that the processing of such data may have on the data subject, given the potential for its use by third parties to serve discriminatory purposes against the individual[97] or to generate situations of inequality.[98] Thus, the importance of specific and stricter protection for sensitive data is recognized in order to safeguard the fundamental rights and freedoms of the data subject.[99]

These concepts are in line with international legislation, specifically the European General Data Protection Regulation, which presents similar concepts in its Article 4, item I.[100] Thus, the LGPD seeks to have the broadest possible scope of application. Its aim is to protect any data linked to an individual, even if such data do not pertain to more intimate or sensitive aspects.[101]

The LGPD, similarly to the European General Data Protection Regulation, provides special treatment for sensitive data, considering that the processing of such data may pose a greater risk to individual personality, including serving as a basis for discriminatory practices.[102]

As an example, the following provisions specifically dedicated to sensitive data can be cited: (1) the validity of consent regarding the processing of personal data

---

[95] Alexandre Veronese and Noemy Melo, while the Bill was still under discussion, argued for the need to further clarify the concept set forth in Article 5, item I. Veronese and Melo (2018), pp. 71–99.

[96] It is important to note that there is no consensus in legal scholarship regarding whether the list of sensitive data is illustrative or exhaustive. Some authors argue that it is an illustrative, rather than exhaustive, list: Mulholland et al. (2020), pp. 109–124; Konder (2019), pp. 445–463. In contrast, others advocate for an exhaustive list: "It is advisable that the concept of sensitive data be exhaustive and not merely illustrative" Leonardi (2021), p. 290.

[97] Teffé and Fernandes (2020), pp. 283–310.

[98] Negri and Korkmaz (2019), p. 63.

[99] Teffé and Fernandes (2020), pp. 283–310.

[100] Doneda and Mendes (2017), p. 47.

[101] Doneda and Mendes (2017), p. 47.

[102] The applicable criterion for classifying data into one category or another lies in its potential to socially stigmatize or discriminate against the individual, being considered sensitive data when there is the potential for qualified harm to the individual. Konder and Fajngold (2021).

must meet stricter requirements, so that the data subject must provide consent in a specific and highlighted manner, for specific purposes (see Article 11 of the LGPD); (2) arguments that the processing of such data arises from the legitimate interests of the controller or from the execution of a contract do not legitimize the processing of sensitive data; and (3) regulatory authorities must exercise much greater oversight in this area.[103]

The stricter treatment afforded to sensitive data may also be applied to other types of data when these are subject to a special processing procedure that could result in discrimination. This situation is known as sensitive data processing.[104]

It should be emphasized that merely classifying data as sensitive is not sufficient to prevent its processing, as this would hinder certain lawful activities in which the use of such data is legitimate and necessary, such as those whose very purpose would be compromised if information of this nature could not be obtained, for example, political or religious organizations. Therefore, in certain circumstances, the processing of sensitive data is possible and even natural, provided that such processing does not result in discriminatory use.[105]

Furthermore, the LGPD introduced a specific catalog of rights for data subjects in its Chapter III. While it is true that some of these rights already existed in our legal system, others are genuine innovations. Among these new rights, some stand out for their modernity and sophistication, representing a significant step forward in the pursuit of effective informational self-determination.

Thus, alongside the rights known as access, rectification, erasure, and objection (ARCO),[106] the LGPD introduces a series of other rights granted to data subjects. In this regard, we highlight (1) confirmation of processing, (2) access to data, (3) data correction, (4) anonymization, blocking, or deletion of unnecessary or excessive data, (5) data portability, (6) deletion of personal data (when processed with consent), (7) information about data sharing, (8) information about the possibility of withholding consent and its consequences, (9) withdrawal of consent, and (10) review of automated decisions (including the right to an explanation[107]).

Such a catalog of rights closely aligns with the list provided by the General Data Protection Regulation (GDPR). As Ingo Sarlet aptly explains,[108] "it is possible to observe a substantial symmetry between the catalogs of user rights under the LGPD and the GDPR (art. 17), so that the differences, as a rule, are limited to terminological variations."

For this reason, it is worthwhile to examine, in European practical experience, which rights are subject to greater judicialization or are more frequently exercised

---

[103] Doneda and Mendes (2017), p. 49.

[104] Doneda and Mendes (2017), p. 49.

[105] National School of Consumer Defense (2010), p. 27.

[106] Feigelson and Siqueira (2019), p. 119.

[107] Although the LGPD does not explicitly use the term "explanation," it is understood to enshrine a right to explanation, as analyzed by Carlos Affonso Souza, Christian Perrone, and Eduardo Magrani (Souza et al. 2021, p. 268).

[108] Sarlet (2021), p. 43.

by data subjects. In general, a significant portion of cases involves the right of access.[109] This is undoubtedly one of the most frequently exercised rights and plays a central role in the protection of personal data. Another noteworthy aspect concerns cases related to the charging of fees for the exercise of rights.[110]

A turning point concerns potential violations of the principles of the LGPD during the data subject authentication process for the exercise of any right. At this stage, it is important to avoid the unnecessary collection of additional personal data, as well as to prevent fraud by malicious individuals.

One possibility is the use of two-factor authentication or requiring the applicant to enter their password. Additionally, an email may be sent to the applicant's registered address so that they can confirm whether they truly wish to proceed with the request (and even prevent the transfer if they do not recognize the request[111]).

Based on experience with the GDPR, it has been observed that the speed of responding to requests and thorough verification of the applicant's identity cannot always be reconciled. In this regard, there is the case of a researcher who managed to obtain data about his fiancée through requests based on the rights provided for in the GDPR.[112]

By the way, the nonprofit organization NOYB-European Center for Digital Rights,[113] which is engaged in filing lawsuits and strategic petitions on personal data protection in the pan-European context and based on the GDPR, warns about the risk of the right of access generating the "boomerang effect."

According to the organization, which filed a complaint with the Austrian Data Protection Authority, Kreditschutz-verband von 1870 (KSV), the leading credit reference agency in Austria, has been processing identification data it requested from the data subject when the latter exercised their right of access in a distorted manner and for commercial purposes.

The situation would be as follows: a data subject who previously had no data processed by KSV has their data included in the company's databases after exercising their right of access. If the data subject was already present in the databases, KSV would use the data collected during the exercise of this right for the purpose of updating records. These scenarios, if proven through due legal process, may constitute a violation of the purpose limitation principle.

Indeed, it is established that authentication systems must collect only the minimum necessary data and process them for other purposes only if such purposes are compatible with the original intent. Furthermore, caution must be exercised regarding the type of data requested for authentication, especially if it is biometric data, which, due to its sensitive nature, requires even greater protection.[114]

---

[109] In this regard, see Republic of Austria. Vienna Higher Regional Court. 11 R 153/20f, 154/20b.

[110] The LGPD expressly provides, in paragraph 5 of Article 18, that requests by data subjects to exercise their rights must be fulfilled free of charge.

[111] Facebook (2020).

[112] Huddleston (2020).

[113] Noyb (2021).

[114] In this regard, a relevant case involving the Information Commissioner's Office (ICO), the United Kingdom's data protection authority, stands out. Her Majesty's Revenue and Customs

Such vulnerabilities in the exercise of data subjects' rights[115] underscore the need for the development of supplementary regulations or guidelines by the Brazilian National Data Protection Authority (ANPD). The rights of data subjects were initially included in Phase 3 of the Regulatory Agenda, with the regulatory process scheduled to begin in the first half of 2022.[116] In December 2023, the CD/ANPD resolution was published, establishing the regulatory agenda for 2023–2024 and moving data subjects' rights to Phase 1. At the beginning of 2024, a public consultation was opened about data subjects' rights.

Regarding the rights set forth in Chapter III, Eduardo Souza and Rodrigo da Guia Silva argue that the items in Article 18 do not introduce new rights for data subjects but rather remedies, as they establish measures and procedures.[117] Furthermore, the list provided therein would be merely illustrative.[118]

Regardless of the debate over whether the claims set forth in Article 18 constitute rights or remedies, it is certain that the list is indeed open-ended, as evidenced by the provision in Article 64 of the LGPD, which states: "The rights and principles expressed in this Law do not exclude others provided for in the national legal system relating to the subject matter or in international treaties to which the Federative Republic of Brazil is a party."

(HMRC) required taxpayers to register their voice as a password in its customer service system. According to the ICO, there was insufficient information provided about the processing of these data and no opportunity for data subjects to withhold consent. ICO (2019).

[115] Regarding the exercise of data subjects' rights, it is also important to consider their limits and potential abuses. The ICO provides guidance on manifestly unfounded or excessive requests, noting that the controller's assessment must always be conducted on a case-by-case basis. A request may be deemed manifestly unfounded if the individual does not have a clear intention to access the information or is acting in bad faith, such as when the sole purpose is to disrupt the organization without any genuine objective. Examples cited by the ICO include requests directed at a specific employee out of personal animosity, systematic or frequent requests intended to disrupt operations, or requests for the correction of nonexistent information. Excessive requests may occur when there is repetition of previous requests without a reasonable interval or when a new request overlaps with others already made. It is emphasized that the classification of a request as unfounded or excessive always depends on the specific circumstances of each case. ICO (2023). Although it is possible to refuse to comply with abusive requests from data subjects, the controller's assessment must always be conducted on a case-by-case basis, and a general policy of refusals is not permitted. Furthermore, any refusal must be reasoned and transparent, allowing for oversight by the data subject, the ANPD, and other authorized entities. In this regard, the controller must, pursuant to Article 18, §4, item II of the LGPD, indicate the factual and legal grounds justifying the refusal of the request. Such refusal, however, does not prevent the data subject from appealing to the ANPD, consumer protection agencies, or even the judiciary to challenge the decision, as provided in §§1 and 8 of Article 18 and Article 22 of the LGPD. Finally, it is important to highlight that data subjects' rights represent a significant advancement in promoting informational self-determination. Therefore, any refusal must be carefully substantiated in light of the specific case and should only occur in instances of excesses contrary to good faith, economic or social purposes, or good morals.

[116] Brazil. Ordinance No. 11, of January 27, 2021.

[117] Souza and Silva (2019), p. 264.

[118] Analyzing the rights provided for in the LGPD, Ingo Sarlet notes that the list in Chapter III is illustrative. Sarlet (2021), p. 43.

Similarly, there is consensus that data subjects also have rights arising from the principles of the LGPD, as set forth in Article 6.[119,120] A Brazilian precedent is the Cyrela case, in which, among other grounds, the court found that there had been a violation of the right to information.[121]

Another important point concerns the possibility of using data to assess individuals and make decisions regarding various aspects, such as their professional capacity, trustworthiness, or creditworthiness. The LGPD requires compliance with certain requirements for the lawful use of information obtained through automated processing, such as the right to review. The controller must also provide all information regarding the criteria and procedures used for automated decision-making while respecting commercial and industrial confidentiality.

Similar protection already existed in Law 12,414/2011,[122] which establishes in its Article 5, item VI, the right of the data subject to "request the consultant to review a decision made exclusively by automated means." On this subject, it is also necessary to mention the decision of the Superior Court of Justice (STJ)[123] regarding credit scoring.

On that occasion, the STJ held that credit scoring is lawful. Credit scoring is a method developed to assess the risk of granting credit, based on statistical models that take into account various variables and assign a score to the evaluated consumer (credit risk score).[124] A consumer's score may influence the creditor's decision to extend credit and determine its terms. In general, consumers with higher scores are more likely to obtain credit and on better terms (annual interest rate, grace period, number of installments, among others).

Considering that the Superior Court of Justice (STJ) has determined that credit scoring is a methodology for calculating credit risk, based on statistical models that seek information from registries and databases available in the digital market, and not itself a registry or database, the requirement for obtaining the consumer's prior and express consent (Article 4 of Law No. 12,414/2011) does not apply to it.

Despite such reservations, credit scoring must still comply with the other obligations established by the Consumer Defense Code and the positive credit registry law, such as providing consumers with clarification regarding the sources of the data considered, as well as the personal information taken into account by credit institutions.

---

119 Ana Frazão states that several of the rights of data subjects derive directly from the principles set forth in Article 6 of the LGPD. Frazão (2019), p. 35.

120 According to Priscilla Regina da Silva, the legislator's intention was merely to enumerate rights in Article 18, even though others could be derived from those listed and inferred from the principles and the duty of care. Silva (2020).

121 Court of Justice of the State of São Paulo. Case No. 1080233-94.2019.8.26.0100. Judgment. 13th Civil Court.

122 Supplementary Law No. 166/2019 amended Law 12,414/2011 to provide for the automatic inclusion of data in the positive credit registry.

123 Brazil. Superior Court of Justice. *Special Appeal No. 1419697*. Reporting Justice Paulo de Tarso Sanseverino. Third Panel. Judged on November 12, 2014.

124 Brazil. Superior Court of Justice. *Special Appeal No. 1419697*. Reporting Justice Paulo de Tarso Sanseverino. Third Panel. Judged on November 12, 2014.

Attention must be paid to the criteria used in credit scoring, as there are reports of a growing number of companies extracting consumer data from social networks such as Facebook, Instagram, and LinkedIn. One such company assigns credit scores based on information collected from users' social media profiles, taking into account their education and employment history, as well as the number of followers and friends.[125]

The subjectivity of these criteria cannot be overlooked, even though they are supported by mathematical models,[126] which suggest objective behavioral patterns, since they are not as clear and transparent as they should be, potentially causing serious harm to consumers, particularly with regard to elements of their personality.

The failure to observe this duty of care and to provide clarification regarding data sources may constitute an unlawful act subject to liability. Liability may also arise in cases of proven unjustified denial of credit due to the use of incorrect or outdated data.[127]

It should be noted that credit scoring is a specific type within the broader category of objective evaluation systems or simply scoring. In such systems, consumers who are more likely to generate economic or financial gains for a company are analyzed. Once identified, these consumers may be targeted, for example, with promotions and customer loyalty strategies.[128]

Another relevant point regarding data concerns security and the damages resulting from its absence, whether to the data subjects or to those responsible for processing. In this context, there are several concerns, such as those arising from unauthorized access to personal information stored in computerized systems,[129] as well as those related to security incidents that may cause significant harm or risk to data subjects.[130]

It is essential to establish policies to be adopted in the event of information leaks or breaches of security protocols. In the formulation and implementation of these policies, the participation of the regulatory body is required.[131]

It should be noted that security incidents are not a remote possibility; on the contrary, they are a present concern. A paradigmatic case was that of the company Uber, which suffered a major security breach resulting in the theft of information pertaining to 57 million users and drivers worldwide.

However, instead of disclosing the incident and notifying the competent authorities, the company chose to pay a ransom for the data in order to have it deleted. As

---

125 Wei (2014).

126 Wei (2014).

127 Brazil. Superior Court of Justice. *Special Appeal No. 1419697*. Reporting Justice Paulo de Tarso Sanseverino. Third Panel. Judged on November 12, 2014.

128 Mendes (2014), p. 112.

129 Doneda and Mendes (2017), p. 50.

130 Doneda and Mendes (2017), p. 50.

131 Article 19 (2016), p. 21.

a result, regulators from various parts of the world have launched investigations against the company, and class actions have already been filed. This highlights the need to regulate not only the procedures to prevent such incidents but, more importantly, the duties and measures to be adopted by providers when an event of this nature occurs.

Finally, the international transfer of data[132] also represents another critical issue in the field of data protection. As is well known, services inherent to the information society are cross-border in nature and involve an extremely large flow of personal information.[133]

Thus, the LGPD, in alignment with European Union legislation on the subject, establishes conditions to legitimize the international transfer of data, such as the adequacy requirement,[134] ensuring that the legal frameworks of the countries involved in the transfer provide adequate levels of data protection.[135]

If such adequacy is not present, the LGPD provides alternative conditions,[136] such as authorization granted by a competent authority, the data subject's specific consent, international cooperation, or the recognition of global corporate rules within a corporation. These alternative conditions offer the necessary flexibility for the development of social and economic relations.[137]

Finally, the LGPD also included in the text approved by the National Congress the establishment of the National Data Protection Authority (ANPD), an agency responsible, among other duties, for ensuring the protection of personal data, overseeing compliance, and imposing sanctions in cases of data processing carried out in violation of the legislation. However, the creation of this agency was vetoed by the President of the Republic on the grounds of a procedural defect.

Indeed, Provisional Measure 869/2018 was issued, which amended the LGPD and reinstated the creation of the ANPD. This Provisional Measure was approved by the National Congress, and on July 8, the Conversion Law of the Provisional Measure was enacted (Law No. 13,853, of July 8, 2019), which establishes the creation of the ANPD.

In August 2020, the ANPD's Regulatory Framework was approved through Decree 10,474, whose entry into force was contingent upon the publication of the appointment of the President-Director of the ANPD in the *Official Gazette of the Union*. This appointment took place in November 2020, marking the commencement of the ANPD's activities.

---

[132] For the purposes of being considered an international data transfer, the information must be deliberately made available to recipients in the third country; mere transit is not sufficient (Rodrigues Araújo 2017, p. 210).

[133] Doneda and Mendes (2017), p. 51.

[134] An equivalent level is not required, as long as protection is not compromised. Prata de Carvalho (2019), pp. 621–642.

[135] Doneda and Mendes (2017), p. 51.

[136] Leonardi emphasizes that there is no hierarchy among the transfer mechanisms provided for in the LGPD. Leonardi (2021), p. 291.

[137] Doneda and Mendes (2017), p. 51.

It is important to emphasize, finally, that even before the LGPD, there were already sector-specific laws regulating matters related to data protection. For this reason, it would be incorrect to claim that there were no personal data protection regulations in Brazil prior to the LGPD.[138]

Among these,[139] Article 43 of the Consumer Protection Code stands out, as it provides specific regulation for consumer-related databases and registries.[140] However, this protection is narrowly aimed at preventing abuses in the processing of credit data and does not extend to other areas of consumer relations.[141]

Indeed, even with the aim of extending data protection beyond the credit market, we must not overlook one of the proposed amendments to the Consumer Protection Code currently under consideration in the National Congress, namely, Bill No. 3514/2015,[142] appended to Bill 4906/2001. This proposal seeks to introduce into our legal framework the regulation of "the fundamental right to the protection of personal data and records, especially in remote and electronic communication media (computerized databases)."[143]

It is also important to mention the Brazilian Internet Bill of Rights (Marco Civil da Internet), Law 12,965/2014,[144] which also sought to address the issue of personal data. Despite criticisms directed at the new regulatory framework for the Internet in Brazil, the Internet Bill of Rights can be considered a victory for those who have long fought against the lack of regulation in the virtual space.[145]

The greatest merit of the Framework lies in being the result of an extensive national debate, with the participation of society and the conduct of public consultations.[146] It should be noted, however, that the national regulatory model, as one of the possible proposals for Internet governance, as previously discussed, is only one of the available modalities and not necessarily the best of all.[147]

---

[138] Bioni (2015), p. 2.

[139] An interesting example is Law 5878/73, which established the Brazilian Institute of Geography and Statistics (IBGE) and imposed confidentiality on the data collected, in order to prevent their use for purposes other than purely statistical ones (Article 6). This protection was recognized by the Superior Court of Justice (STJ) in Special Appeal No. 1353602. Brazil. Superior Court of Justice. Special Appeal No. 1353602. Reporting Justice Napoleão Nunes Maia Filho. Judged on December 7, 2017.

[140] Doneda (2011), p. 103.

[141] National School of Consumer Defense (2010), p. 12.

[142] This project, which addresses international trade and consumer contracts, with particular protection for consumers who purchase goods and services online, is one of two proposed amendments to the Consumer Protection Code. Marques and Vial (2017).

[143] Klee (2015), p. 131.

[144] Regarding the Brazilian Internet Bill of Rights (Marco Civil da Internet), it is important to highlight Theme 987 adjudicated by the Supreme Federal Court (STF).

[145] De Lucca (2015), p. 25.

[146] De Lucca (2015), p. 27.

[147] De Lucca (2015), p. 27.

The Framework serves as a model that may potentially be adopted by other countries and is internationally recognized as the Constitution of the Internet.[148] One of the positive aspects of the Framework was the establishment of principles, rights, and duties in a manner aligned with the value of democracy, seeking integrity at a time when the Internet is characterized by technical and legal fragmentation.[149]

With regard to the issue of personal data, the enactment of the Framework represented progress in recognizing the need to protect personal data and records. However, it is not a law specifically addressing this subject.[150]

Thus, although the Framework does not provide comprehensive and structured data protection, it does refer to certain relevant topics. In this regard, Article 3 is cited, which, in items II and III, sets forth the principles of privacy and data protection as established by law.

Article 7 also provides for certain rights related to privacy and private life, as well as the inviolability of the confidentiality of communications traffic and their storage, except by court order. Furthermore, the provision of personal data and records of connection and access to Internet applications may only occur with free, express, and informed consent or in other cases provided for by law.

Furthermore, it should be emphasized that consent for the collection, use, storage, and processing of personal data must be obtained separately from other contractual clauses, and all information must be clear and comprehensive. Data may only be used for specific and legitimate purposes that justify its collection, are not prohibited by law, and are clearly disclosed in service agreements or in the terms of use of Internet applications. Finally, the aforementioned Article 7 requires the definitive deletion of personal data upon request at the end of the relationship, except when record retention is mandatory.[151]

Decree No. 8771/2016, which regulates the Brazilian Civil Rights Framework for the Internet, provides supplementary provisions on this subject, particularly regarding the protection of records, personal data, and private communications. Article 11 specifically addresses the request for registration data. Article 12, in turn, requires public administration authorities to publish annual statistical reports on requests for registration data.

In the same vein, the Decree, in its subsequent section, establishes standards for the security and confidentiality of records, personal data, and private communications. Article 13 sets forth various obligations, such as strict control over data access, the requirement for authentication mechanisms for access to records, the creation of

---

148 Quesada (2014).

149 Lemos (2015), p. 79.

150 Klee (2015), p. 131.

151 Regarding the mandatory retention of records, Article 13 of the Brazilian Internet Civil Framework (Marco Civil da Internet) establishes that it is the responsibility of the autonomous system administrator, when providing Internet connection, to keep connection records confidentially, in a controlled and secure environment, for a period of 1 year, in accordance with the regulations.

detailed access logs, and the use of record management solutions employing techniques that ensure the inviolability of the data.

Furthermore, paragraph 2 of the aforementioned article stipulates that connection and application providers must retain the minimum amount of personal data, private communications, and records of connection and access to applications, which must be deleted as soon as the purpose of their use has been fulfilled or the period established by legal obligation has expired.

Article 14 introduces several important concepts, such as personal data and the processing of such data, as previously discussed. Article 15 establishes that data must be maintained in an interoperable and structured format to facilitate access resulting from a court order or legal requirement. Finally, Article 16 stipulates that information regarding the security standards adopted by application providers and connection providers must be disclosed in a clear and accessible manner to any interested party, preferably through their websites, while respecting the right to confidentiality concerning trade secrets.

Finally, alongside the Brazilian Internet Bill of Rights and the Consumer Protection Code, it is also possible to mention the Access to Information Law (LAI),[152] which contains specific provisions regarding the processing of personal information within the public sector.

In addition to the entire relationship between personal data and the protection of personality rights and human dignity, which led to the enactment of all the aforementioned regulations, there is an undeniable concern regarding anticompetitive practices involving personal data. Fabiano Menke's observation is particularly relevant in that data protection serves as a functional prerequisite for a market economy, as it prevents the use of data to manipulate consumers. Such measures ensure greater transparency and fairer competition.[153] Therefore, there is a need to create or implement mechanisms that prevent or inhibit anticompetitive situations that are detrimental to data subjects, the market, and society,[154] given the diffuse nature of free competition.

Throughout this chapter, it has been demonstrated that the protection of personal data, both in the European Union and in Brazil, is not limited to a set of defensive guarantees aimed at restricting the use of information but rather constitutes a structuring element of the legal and institutional frameworks that shape the circulation, access, and reuse of data. The elevation of data protection to the status of a fundamental right and the consolidation of comprehensive regulatory regimes, such as the GDPR and the LGPD, redefine the parameters within which it becomes possible to consider interoperability, regulatory coordination, and legal certainty.

The comparative analysis of the frameworks of these statutes reveals that, although there are significant convergences—particularly regarding the centrality of

[152] Têmis Limberger points out that while the administration has a need for transparency, it is also bound by the requirement to protect personal data (Limberger 2016, p. 209).

[153] Menke (2018).

[154] Ferraz Junior (2009), p. 174.

principles, the accountability of agents, and the assignment of rights to data subjects—important institutional and operational differences persist. These asymmetries are not merely technical: they influence the degree of regulatory fragmentation, the predictability of regulatory decisions, and the capacity for coordination among different sectors and jurisdictions.

This chapter, therefore, establishes the normative and institutional foundations essential for the subsequent analyses in the book. Based on this groundwork, it becomes possible to advance the investigation into how to design data governance models that promote the safe and legitimate reuse of information, reduce regulatory fragmentation, and strengthen legal certainty, with a more specific examination of the role of data portability and other coordination instruments within the Brazilian and European regulatory ecosystems. In this context, it is important to highlight that the intensive reuse of data constitutes one of the main drivers for the development of artificial intelligence systems, which introduces new challenges for data protection and the effectiveness of data subjects' rights—a topic that will be explored in the following chapter.

References

Acocella J, Sampaio R (2020) Impactos da LGPD sobre a atuação da administração pública: alguns desafios e sua efetividade. In: Dal Pozzo AN, Martins RM (eds) LGPD e Administração Pública. RT, São Paulo

Alsenoy B, Koekkoek M (2015) The extra-territorial reach of the EU's 'right to be forgotten'. ICRI Research Paper 20

Artigo 19 (2016) Proteção de dados pessoais no Brasil: análise dos projetos de lei em tramitação no Congresso Nacional. Artigo 19, São Paulo

Ávila H (2014) Teoria dos princípios. Malheiros Editores, São Paulo

Barreto W (2010) Os direitos da personalidade na jurisprudência alemã contemporânea. Rev Trimestral Direito Civil 41:135–159

Bioni B (2015) Xeque-mate: o tripé da proteção de dados pessoais no jogo de xadrez das iniciativas legislativas no Brasil. GPoPAI/USP, São Paulo

Bioni B (2017) Privacidade e proteção de dados pessoais em 2017. Jota. https://www.jota.info/colunas/agenda-da-privacidade-e-da-protecao-de-dados/privacidade-e-protecao-de-dados-pessoais-em-2017-10012017

Boardman R, Mullock J, Mole A (2017) Guide to the General Data Protection Regulation. Bird & Bird, London

Borelli A (2021) O tratamento de dados de crianças no âmbito do General Data Protection Regulation (GDPR). In: Blum RO, Maldonado VN (orgs) Comentários ao GDPR. Revista dos Tribunais, São Paulo

Calo R (2014) Digital market manipulation. Geo Wash Law Rev 82:995–1051

Crespo M (2021) Gestão de incidentes de violação de dados pessoais. In: Palhares F (coord) Temas atuais de proteção de dados. Revista dos Tribunais, São Paulo

Cueva RVB (2017) A insuficiente proteção de dados pessoais no Brasil. Rev Direito Civil Contemporâneo 13:59–67

De Lucca N (2015) Marco Civil da Internet: uma visão panorâmica dos principais aspectos relativos às suas disposições preliminares. In: De Lucca N, Simão Filho A, Lima CRP (coords)

Direito & Internet III, Tomo I: Marco Civil da Internet (Lei n.° 12.965/2014). Quartier Latin, São Paulo, pp 23–78
Döhmann ISG (2021) A proteção de dados pessoais sob o Regulamento Geral de Proteção de Dados da União Europeia. In: Mendes L, Doneda D, Sarlet I, Rodrigues Jr OL (coords) Tratado de proteção de dados pessoais. Forense, Rio de Janeiro, p 112
Doneda D (2008) Privacidade, vida privada e intimidade no ordenamento jurídico brasileiro: da emergência de uma revisão conceitual e da tutela de dados pessoais. Âmbito Jurídico 52
Doneda D (2009) A tutela da privacidade no Código Civil de 2002. Anima Rev Eletrônica Curso Direito Opet 1:89–100
Doneda D (2011) A proteção dos dados pessoais como um direito fundamental. Espaço Jurídico 12(2):91–108
Doneda D (2021) Da privacidade à proteção de dados pessoais, 2nd edn. Thomson Reuters Brasil, São Paulo
Doneda D, Mendes LSF (2017) Iniciativas legislativas sobre proteção de dados pessoais no Brasil. Rev Uruguaya Protección Datos Personales 2:44–52
Dotti RA (1980) A liberdade e o direito à intimidade. Rev Informação Legislativa 66:125–152
Edwards L, Harbinja E (2013) Protecting post-mortem privacy: reconsidering the privacy interests of the deceased in a digital world. Cardozo Arts Entertain Law J 32(1):101–147
European Data Protection Supervisor (2014) Privacy and competitiveness in the age of big data. https://edps.europa.eu/data-protection/our-work/publications/opinions/privacy-and-competitiveness-age-big-data_en
Facebook (2020) Comments to the Federal Trade Commission on data portability. Palo Alto
Feigelson B, Siqueira AHA (coords) (2019) Comentários a Lei Geral de Proteção de Dados Lei 13.709/2018. Thomson Reuters Brasil, São Paulo
Fernández Rozas JC, Sánchez Lorenzo S (2009) Derecho internacional privado. Civitas, Madrid
Ferraz Junior TS (2009) Concorrência como tema constitucional: política de Estado e de governo e o Estado como agente normativo e regulador. Rev IBRAC 16(1):169–186
Frazão A (2019) Direitos básicos dos titulares de dados pessoais. Rev Advogado 144:35
Gavison R (1980) Privacy and the limits of law. Yale Law J 89:421–471
Geradin D, Kuschewsky M (2013) Competition law and personal data: preliminary thoughts on a complex issue. https://papers.ssrn.com/sol3/papers.cfm?abstract_id=2216088
Gomes RDP (2024) Legítimos interesses na LGPD: trajetória, consolidação e critérios de aplicação. Foco, Indaiatuba
Huddleston J (2020) Comments regarding data to go: an FTC workshop on data portability. https://beta.regulations.gov/comment/FTC-2020-0062-0007
Information Commissioner's Office (2019) Enforcement notices. https://ico.org.uk/media/action-weve-taken/enforcement-notices/hmrc-en-201905.pdf
Information Commissioner's Office (2023) Manifestly unfounded and excessive requests. https://ico.org.uk/for-organisations/guide-to-data-protection/guide-to-law-enforcement-processing/individual-rights/manifestly-unfounded-and-excessive-requests/
Jayme E (2003) Direito internacional privado e cultura pós-moderna. Cad Programa Pós-Graduação Direito PPGDir/UFRGS 1(1):59–68
Klee A (2015) A regulamentação do uso da internet no Brasil pela Lei n.° 12.965/2014 e a proteção dos dados e dos registros pessoais. Direito Justiça 41:126–153
Kokott J, Sobotta C (2013) The distinction between privacy and data protection in the jurisprudence of the CJEU and the ECtHR. Int Data Privacy Law 3(4):222–228
Konder C (2019) O tratamento de dados sensíveis à luz da Lei 13.709/2018. In: Tepedino G, Frazão A, Oliva MD (orgs) Lei geral de proteção de dados pessoais e suas repercussões no direito brasileiro, vol 1. Thomson Reuters Brasil, São Paulo, pp 445–463
Konder C, Fajngold L (2021) O papel dos mecanismos de compliance e das políticas de proteção de dados para a proteção de dados sensíveis. In: Frazão A, Cueva RVB (orgs) Compliance e políticas de proteção de dados. Thomson Reuters Brasil, São Paulo

Kuner C (2013) Extraterritoriality and the fundamental right to data protection. EJIL: Talk!. https://www.ejiltalk.org/extraterritoriality-and-the-fundamental-right-to-data-protection/
Lazarotto BR (2024) The right to data portability: a holistic analysis of GDPR, DMA and the Data Act. Eur J Law Technol 15(1)
Lemos R (2015) Uma breve história do Marco Civil da Internet. In: De Lucca N, Simão Filho A, Lima CRP (coords) Direito & Internet III, Tomo I: Marco Civil da Internet (Lei n.° 12.965/2014). Quartier Latin, São Paulo, pp 79–100
Leonardi M (2021) Transferência internacional de dados pessoais. In: Bioni B, Doneda D, Sarlet IW et al (orgs) Tratado de proteção de dados, vol 1. Forense, São Paulo
Lessig L (2006) Code: version 2.0. Basic Books, New York
Limberger T (2016) Cibertransparência: informação pública em rede e a intimidade como um dos limites constitucionais uma abordagem a partir do tema 483 da Repercussão Geral examinada pelo STF. Rev Direito Adm Const 16(65):209
Lloyd I (2014) Information technology law. Oxford University Press, Oxford
Lorenzetti R (2001) Comercio electrónico. Abeledo-Perrot, Buenos Aires
Luz C (2021) Anonimização, venire contra factum proprium e relatório dos riscos de reidentificação. In: Palhares F (coord) Estudos sobre privacidade e proteção de dados. Revista dos Tribunais, São Paulo
Marko A (2017) The right to personal data protection. Palgrave Macmillan, London
Marques CL, Vial S (2017) O comércio eletrônico internacional e a proteção do consumidor. Revista dos Tribunais, São Paulo
Mendes LS (2014) Privacidade, proteção de dados e defesa do consumidor: linhas gerais de um novo direito fundamental. Saraiva, São Paulo
Mendes LS, Doneda D (2016) Marco jurídico para a cidadania digital: uma análise do Projeto de Lei 5.276/2016. Rev Direito Civil Contemporâneo 9:35–48
Menke F (2018) Fundamentos da proteção de dados. http://itsa-brasil.com.br/hotsite/artigos/fundamentos-da-protecao-de-dados/
Miguel C (2012) The transformation of intimacy and privacy through social networking sites. http://media.leeds.ac.uk/files/2013/07/Miguel_The-Transformation-of-Intimacy-and-Privacy-through-Social-Networking-Sites.pdf
Mulholland C, Martins G, Rosenvald N (2020) Responsabilidade civil por danos causados pela violação de dados sensíveis e a Lei Geral de Proteção de Dados Pessoais (Lei 13.709/18). In: Martins GM, Rosenvald N (orgs) Responsabilidade civil e novas tecnologias, vol 1. Foco, Belo Horizonte, pp 109–124
Nadel M (2000) Computer code vs. legal code: setting the rules in cyberspace. Fed Commun Law J 52:821–836
National School of Consumer Defense (2010) Personal data protection in consumer relations: beyond credit information. SDE/DPDC, Brasília
Negri S, Korkmaz MR (2019) A normatividade dos dados sensíveis na Lei Geral de Proteção de Dados: ampliação conceitual e proteção da pessoa humana. Rev Direito Gov Novas Tecnol 5:63
Noyb (2021) Right of access as a data protection boomerang? noyb.eu
Oliveira MAB, Lopes IMP (2019) Os princípios norteadores da proteção de dados pessoais no Brasil e sua otimização pela Lei 13.709/2018. In: Tepedino G, Frazão A, Oliva M (orgs) Lei geral de proteção de dados pessoais e suas repercussões no direito brasileiro, vol 1. Thomson Reuters Brasil, São Paulo, pp 53–84
Prata de Carvalho AG (2019) Transferência internacional de dados na lei geral de proteção de dados: força normativa e efetividade diante do cenário transnacional. In: Frazão A, Tepedino G, Oliva MD (orgs) A Lei Geral de Proteção de Dados e suas repercussões no direito brasileiro. Revista dos Tribunais, São Paulo, pp 621–642
Privacy International, Open Society Institute (2015) Privacy and human rights. http://gilc.org/privacy/survey/intro.html
Purtova N (2018) The law of everything. Broad concept of personal data and future of EU data protection law. Law Innov Technol 10:141–168

Quesada A (2014) Protección de dados en la convergencia de las telecomunicaciones. Dissertation, Universidad de Costa Rica

Rodrigues Araújo A (2017) As transferências transatlânticas de dados pessoais. Rev Direitos Humanos Democracia 5(9):201–236

Rodrigues Junior OL (2013) Do Príncipe Bismarck à Princesa Carolina de Mônaco: vida privada de pessoas célebres e as liberdades comunicativas no Código Civil. In: Estudos em homenagem ao Professor Carlos Alberto Dabus Maluf: 10 anos de vigência do Código Civil de 2002. Saraiva, São Paulo, pp 111–125

Rodriguez DP (2021) O direito fundamental à proteção de dados. Lumen Juris, Rio de Janeiro

Ruaro R, Rodriguez DP, Finger B (2012) O direito à proteção de dados pessoais e a privacidade. Rev Fac Direito (UFPR) 53:45–66

Sarlet I (2002) Dignidade da pessoa humana e direitos fundamentais. Livraria do Advogado, Porto Alegre

Sarlet I (2021) Fundamentos constitucionais: o direito fundamental à proteção de dados. In: Mendes L, Doneda D, Sarlet I, Rodrigues Jr OL (coords) Tratado de proteção de dados pessoais. Forense, Rio de Janeiro

Schreiber A (2019) Direito ao esquecimento e proteção de dados pessoais na Lei 13.709/2018: distinções e potenciais convergências. In: Tepedino G, Frazão A, Oliva M (orgs) Lei geral de proteção de dados pessoais e suas repercussões no direito brasileiro, vol 1. Thomson Reuters Brasil, São Paulo, pp 367–383

Silva PR (2020) Os direitos dos titulares de dados. In: Mulholland C (org) A LGPD e o novo marco normativo no Brasil. Arquipélago Editorial, Porto Alegre

Souza EN, Silva RG (2019) Direito do titular de dados pessoais na Lei 13.709/2018: uma abordagem sistemática. In: Tepedino G, Frazão A, Oliva MD (coords) Lei geral de proteção de dados pessoais e suas repercussões no direito brasileiro. RT, São Paulo, p 264

Souza CA, Perrone C, Magrani E (2021) O direito à explicação entre a experiência europeia e a sua positivação na LGPD. In: Mendes L, Doneda D, Sarlet I, Rodrigues Jr OL (coords) Tratado de proteção de dados pessoais. Forense, Rio de Janeiro, p 268

Sundfeld CA, Rosilho A (2015) A governança não estatal da Internet e o direito brasileiro. Rev Direito Administrativo 270:41–79

Swire P (2020) The portability and other required transfers impact assessment: assessing competition, privacy, cybersecurity, and other considerations

Teffé CS, Fernandes ER (2020) Tratamento de dados sensíveis por tecnologias de reconhecimento facial: proteção e limites. In: Tepedino G, Silva RG (orgs) O direito civil na era da inteligência artificial, vol 1. Revista dos Tribunais, São Paulo, pp 283–310

Tepedino G (2001) As relações de consumo e a nova teoria contratual. In: Tepedino G (coord) Temas de direito civil, 2nd edn. Renovar, Rio de Janeiro, pp 199–216

United Nations (2020) The right to privacy in the digital age. http://www.ohchr.org/en/issues/digitalage/pages/digitalageindex.aspx

Vainzof R (2022) O modelo sancionatário do GDPR (RGPD). In: Maldonado VN (coord) LGPD: sanções e decisões judiciais. Revista dos Tribunais, São Paulo

Vega JA (2005) Derecho de las nuevas tecnologías: contratos electrónicos y proteção de los consumidores. Reus, Madrid

Veronese A, Melo N (2018) O Projeto de Lei n.° 5.276/2016 em contraste com o novo Regulamento Europeu (2016/679 UE). Rev Direito Civil Contemporâneo 14:71–99

Warren S, Brandeis L (1890) The right to privacy. Harv Law Rev 4(5):193–220

Wei Y, Yildirim P, Van den Bulte C, Dellarocas C (2014) Credit scoring with social network data. Mark Sci. https://ssrn.com/abstract=2475265

Wimmer M (2020) Cidadania, tecnologia e governo digital: proteção de dados pessoais no Estado movido a dados. In: Barbosa AF (org) TIC Governo Eletrônico 2019: pesquisa sobre o uso das tecnologias de informação e comunicação no setor público brasileiro, vol 1. Comitê Gestor da Internet no Brasil, São Paulo, pp 27–36

Wubben M, Schermer B, Teterissa D (2012) Legal aspects of the Digital Single Market: current framework, barriers and developments. Considerati, Amsterdam

Zanatta R (2015) A proteção de dados entre leis, códigos e programação: os limites do Marco Civil da Internet. In: De Lucca N, Simão Filho A, Lima CRP (coords) Direito & Internet III: Marco Civil da Internet. Quartier Latin, São Paulo, pp 447–470

Zeiter A (2014) The new General Data Protection Regulation of the EU and its impact on IT companies in the U.S. Stanford Vienna

Chapter 4
Data Protection and Artificial Intelligence

4.1 Artificial Intelligence and Data Subjects' Rights

The expansion of artificial intelligence systems as central instruments of the digital economy has repositioned the legal debate on access, control, and reuse of data at a level of greater institutional complexity. As significant decisions become increasingly mediated by automated systems, the need for normative frameworks capable of ensuring the effective protection of the rights of affected individuals intensifies, without compromising innovation, the legitimate circulation of data, and the legal certainty required for the functioning of digital markets.

In this context, the rights to information, explanation, contestation, and review of automated decisions play a strategic role in the regulatory framework of artificial intelligence. These rights, traditionally developed within the scope of personal data protection, are expanding beyond this domain and are gradually being incorporated into specific regulatory regimes for artificial intelligence. The result is a normative ecosystem characterized by overlaps, complementarities, and potential regulatory frictions, especially when the exercise of these rights encounters limitations invoked on the grounds of protecting industrial and commercial secrets.

The manner in which these boundaries are drawn and enforced is decisive for the broader issue addressed by this book: regulatory fragmentation and legal uncertainty, which can inhibit legitimate access to and responsible reuse of data in the digital economy. An excessively broad invocation of trade secret protection can undermine the essential core of the rights of data subjects and individuals affected by artificial intelligence systems; on the other hand, a disregard for the protection of trade secrets may produce adverse effects on innovation and competitiveness, increasing regulatory costs and legal uncertainties.

This chapter analyzes, from a comparative perspective between Brazil and the European Union, how legal frameworks for data protection and artificial intelligence regulation can be coordinated to reduce normative frictions and provide

D. Copetti Cravo, *Law and the Digital Economy*,
https://doi.org/10.1007/978-3-032-36672-6_4

greater legal predictability. It argues that the reconciliation between data subjects' rights and the protection of trade and industrial secrets should not be understood as a zero-sum game but rather as an exercise in normative coordination guided by the dialogue of legal sources, proportionality, and the preservation of the essential core of fundamental rights, thereby contributing to a safer and more legitimate environment for data reuse in the digital economy.

The theoretical tensions described above are not merely abstract; they manifest concretely in recent cases involving the use of artificial intelligence systems. Concerns related to discrimination or manipulation are recurrent when the subject involves artificial intelligence. Certain scandals serve as warnings and indicate how the use of automated systems without proper safeguards and without adequate handling of personal data can lead to serious violations of fundamental rights.

In the Netherlands, the use of algorithms for risk profiling related to the detection of fraud in child welfare benefits caused irreparable harm to families who were erroneously identified as suspected fraudsters. Because the system was trained and fed with biased data, it ultimately produced discriminatory, inaccurate, and unjust results, which primarily affected minorities and financially vulnerable families.

As a result, some victims went so far as to take their own lives, and children were removed from their biological families. Situations such as these must lead to accountability. They should also serve as a warning and a point of reflection to prevent recurrence.

Concerned, therefore, with the risks and consequences of the improper use of new technologies,[1] legislators from various jurisdictions have advanced proposals for the regulation of artificial intelligence. In this context, the European Union has emerged as a leading actor, proposing the first comprehensive regulation of artificial intelligence.

In Brazil, several legislative proposals aimed at establishing guidelines for the development and application of artificial intelligence systems have been introduced. In this regard, mention should be made of Bill (PL) No. 2338/2023, currently under consideration in the Federal Senate, which is the result of the work of the Commission of Legal Experts established to analyze existing proposals and support the drafting of a substitute bill.[2]

A key aspect of artificial intelligence regulation concerns the rights of individuals affected by AI systems. Once regulatory frameworks are approved, these rights will become part of a system of rights protection, complementing those rights already in place and applicable to artificial intelligence, such as those established by the General Data Protection Law (LGPD).

---

[1] From the moment an electronic profile becomes the only aspect of a person's personality visible to others, behavioral pattern prediction techniques may lead to a reduction in their sphere of freedom. Doneda (2021).

[2] https://www12.senado.leg.br/noticias/materias/2023/05/12/senate-reviews-bill-to-regulate-artificial-intelligence.

However, the exercise of these rights may give rise, even if only apparently, to potential conflicts regarding the protection of information, particularly with respect to the safeguarding of industrial and commercial secrets.

According to Veronese, Silveira, and Lemos,[3] the regulation of artificial intelligence, in the strict sense, can occur in two ways: the first is through the regulation of the creation and modification of computer programs. The second concerns the regulation of part of the raw material used by computer programs, namely, data.

In both the first and second approaches, we observe a catalog of rights for natural persons. These rights not only can but must be applied systematically and complementarily in the pursuit of effective protection.

In this context, it is relevant to consider Doneda's interpretation,[4] in the sense that issues such as the limits of automated decision-making are increasingly finding a natural space for development within data protection legislation. Thus, it is undeniable that data protection regulations intersect with the subject of artificial intelligence.

In this regard, reference is made to the Preliminary Analysis of Bill No. 2338/2023 prepared by the National Data Protection Authority (ANPD),[5] which clearly outlines the relationship between data protection and the regulation of artificial intelligence, particularly with respect to the safeguarding of rights. In its analysis, the ANPD emphasizes the need for legal compatibility among the relevant regulations (especially those yet to be enacted, such as the proposal in Bill No. 2338/2023), both to avoid legal uncertainty and to ensure respect for the ANPD's authority to regulate matters within its remit.

Among the rights of individuals affected by artificial intelligence systems, the rights to information, explanation, contestation, and the right to request a review are particularly noteworthy, as provided for in Bill 2338/2023. These rights are related to the following data subject rights established in the General Data Protection Law (LGPD): the right of access (Articles 9 and 19 of the LGPD), the right to request a review of automated decisions (Article 20 of the LGPD), and the right to an explanation (Article 20, §1 of the LGPD).

As stated in the LGPD, the rights established in Article 20, §1, and Article 19, item II, must respect trade secrets.[6] It is clear, however, that the protection of trade secrets, as provided for, for example, in Article 20, §1, of the LGPD, must be carried

[3] Veronese et al. (2019), pp. 233–264.

[4] Doneda (2020).

[5] ANPD (2023).

[6] Within the European Union, Directive 943/2016 on Trade Secrets, in its Recital 35, establishes that the directive shall not affect the rights or obligations set out in Directive 95/46/EC, in particular, the rights of data subjects to access their personal data undergoing processing and to obtain the rectification, erasure, or blocking of data where such data are incomplete or inaccurate, nor, where applicable, the obligation to process sensitive data in accordance with Article 8(5) of Directive 95/46/EC. According to Noto and Sappa, regardless of the Directive's assumption that there will be no conflicts, trade secrets and the protection of personal data do and will indeed collide. Therefore, it is crucial to understand how to govern such conflicts. Noto La Diega and Sappa (2020), pp. 419–458.

out in an appropriate and balanced manner so as not to undermine the essential core of the rights guaranteed to data subjects.

It should be noted that this is not a conflict or an antinomy between the exercise of rights by the affected individuals/data subjects and the observance of trade and industrial secrets. Rather, it concerns a possible harmonization, consistent with the framework and principles established by the Federal Constitution.

In this regard, it is important to note that the legal phenomenon is characterized by a plurality of norms. Although this plurality is not a new development, it has become even more pronounced in the current context, where technological, social, and economic advancements have led to an intense process of norm production. This situation requires legal practitioners to skillfully coordinate values, objectives, principles, and rules, which—not only complex—can also result in legal uncertainty.

This scenario is particularly evident in the context of information protection, precisely due to the existence of laws that may appear to be in conflict. However, the approach most consistent with legal principles is one that seeks a harmonious and complementary dialogue among all these norms, aiming for solutions that do not undermine the essential core of the values at stake (such as data protection, the free development of personality, and the protection of trade secrets[7]).

To this end, a case-by-case analysis will always be required. Furthermore, the legal interest protected by trade secrets must possess economic value, and its content cannot be irrelevant in the market. It must constitute something that provides an advantage over competitors and is applicable to the company's business.[8]

In this context, the following question arises: how can the monopoly over intangible information, generally protected through trade secrets, be reconciled with the rights guaranteed to data subjects[9] and to individuals affected by artificial intelligence systems?

As highlighted by Noto and Sappa,[10] trade secrets are often considered a more viable option than patents, particularly in the field of information technology. As a result, the disclosure of information and transparency in the public interest may be more marginal than appropriate. Indeed, according to the aforementioned authors, the only way to counter this trend is through a balanced interpretation of the rules governing trade and industrial secrets, both in terms of the implementation of protection and its limits.

How, then, can industrial and commercial secrets contained in the technical details of artificial intelligence be protected without creating an obstacle to the exercise of the rights of individuals affected by artificial intelligence systems? The first step in answering this question would be to attempt to identify what may, in principle, be considered covered by secrecy.

---

[7] As Spiecker aptly points out, we are still far from establishing a uniform and balanced information law that fosters a functional information market suitable for both private and public decision-making. Spiecker (2018).

[8] Fekete (2003).

[9] Malgieri (2018), pp. 193–203.

[10] Noto La Diega and Sappa (2020), pp. 419–458.

In this regard, it should be noted that the text of the LGPD contains approximately 13 provisions concerning the necessary observance of industrial and commercial secrecy.[11,12,13] Despite the legislator's significant concern with the protection of trade secrets within the scope of personal data protection, this remains one of the most neglected and underexplored topics in Brazil,[14] with no precise definition of its content, and it is still subject to the practice of unfair competition.

Bill No. 2338/2023 also contains references to industrial and commercial secrets. Article 20, item V, stipulates that artificial intelligence agents who provide or operate high-risk systems must adopt technical measures to enable the explainability of the results produced by artificial intelligence systems, as well as measures to provide operators and potentially affected parties with general information about the functioning of the artificial intelligence model employed, specifying the logic and relevant criteria for the production of results. Furthermore, upon request by an interested party, they must provide adequate information that allows for the interpretation of the results actually produced while respecting industrial and commercial confidentiality.

Article 26 of Bill No. 2338/2023 provides that the conclusions of the impact assessment shall be made public while ensuring the protection of industrial and commercial secrets. Article 43 also refers to the obligation of the competent authority to respect industrial and commercial secrets when creating and maintaining a publicly accessible high-risk artificial intelligence database containing the public documents from the impact assessments.

Considering, therefore, that there is no precise definition of the content of a trade secret, which is contingent upon the practice of unfair competition, the provisions on this subject set forth in the LGPD and in the forthcoming regulatory framework for artificial intelligence in Brazil will need to be applied with caution, whether due to the lack of tradition and consensus on the matter or the absence of interpretative guidelines in both the LGPD and Bill No. 2338/2023, which neither define what may be considered a secret nor specify to what extent or degree this interest should be observed.

---

[11] In this regard, the following provisions are cited: Article 6, item VI, on the principle of transparency; Article 9, item II, on the right of access; Article 10, § 3, which addresses the data protection impact assessment; Article 18, item V, which establishes the right to data portability; Article 19, item II, and § 3 (confirmation and access to personal data); Article 20, §§ 1 and 2, which concern the right to review automated decisions; Article 38 (impact assessment); and Article 48, regarding the notification of security incidents (§ 1, item III). There were also provisions in Article 56, which was ultimately vetoed.

[12] Provisional Measure (MP) 869/2018 sought to establish that the competent data protection authority would be held liable if it failed to safeguard trade secrets. Upon review of the MP by the legislative branch, the measure was converted into Law 13,853/2019, which did not confirm the liability provision. However, Article 55-J, item II, and § 5 of the LGPD stipulate that the authority must ensure the preservation of trade secrets and regulate the forms of disclosure while respecting business confidentiality (item X).

[13] The provisions regarding trade and industrial secrets were introduced by EMP9, received in Plenary during the consideration of Bill 4060/2012 by the Chamber of Deputies, with Bill 5276/2016 and Bill 6291/16 appended to the main proposal.

[14] Pela (2018), pp. 546–550.

In this context, it should be considered that if the protection of industrial and commercial secrets is conditioned upon an act of unfair competition, the mere acquisition of a copy of the data for personal use and the exercise of the right of access by the data subject cannot, *prima facie*, be denied on the grounds of trade secrets, since, as a rule, such exercise does not have the potential to cause unfair competitive harm to the company.

Another critical issue involving trade secrets concerns inferences, which are obtained through the processing of "raw" data, generally carried out using artificial intelligence. These inferences reveal the tastes, preferences, and positions of a given individual. The creation of profiles and rating systems also falls under the category of inferences.

Since they are produced by companies through their investments in technologies, could inferences be protected as trade or business secrets? Answering this question is not an easy task, especially because it would require a thorough investigation into the nature of inferences in order to determine whether they are considered personal data.

It can be argued that knowledge generated from the use of data, when such data can no longer be associated with the original data in a way that would allow the identification of the data subject—thus preventing backtrace—may, provided that all other legal requirements are met, be protected as a trade secret. Similarly, the techniques and algorithms employed in obtaining such information and knowledge may also fall within the concept of trade secret, provided that the applicable conditions are observed.[15,16]

Whenever the exercise of any right by the data subject compromises trade secrets—understood here as technique or anonymized knowledge and not the inferences themselves—the controller may justify any eventual denial or limitation of these rights, provided this is done transparently and explicitly, demonstrating the internal investment made to protect the secret. In this context, the role of the ANPD and/or the future authority on artificial intelligence becomes essential, with the aim of systematizing and clearly regulating industrial and commercial secrets, as well as exercising oversight over possible denials or restrictions of rights on the grounds of protecting trade secrets.

At the European level, and based on the proposed Artificial Intelligence Regulation, Mylly[17] points out that trade secrets may not pose as significant an obstacle to algorithmic transparency as might initially be assumed.[18]

This assertion is relevant to the subject of the present study and may be applied by analogy, since the rights to explanation and access are directly related to

[15] Wachter and Mittelstadt (2019), p. 79.

[16] However, there is the possibility of mitigating algorithm protection in favor of the data subject, for example, *metamorphic algorithms*, which, when processing personal data, end up modifying themselves.

[17] Mylly (2023), pp. 1013–1043.

[18] In the context of data protection, Noto and Sappa argue that trade secrets cannot limit the rights to be informed, to rectification, to erasure, to restrict processing, to object, and not to be subject to automated decision-making. Noto La Diega and Sappa (2020), pp. 419–458.

algorithmic transparency. The primary basis for this conclusion is that, even if an explanation is not exhaustive, it may still be sufficient to achieve meaningful oversight.

In other words, it is possible to provide information that is meaningful to individuals affected by intelligence systems without disclosing or compromising trade secrets. Transparency does not necessarily mean "total transparency"; rather, what is required is that the explanation be appropriate to the intended purposes, even if it is not necessarily complete.[19]

It is also important to note that the development of artificial intelligence systems may rely on a large number of basic science components and preexisting software modules. Additionally, there is the development of systems based on standards, which, in order to fulfill their role, must be open. Furthermore, artificial intelligence systems contain many components that use data collected from publicly available sources.

In such cases, it seems reasonable to conclude that situations like those described above may not meet the requirements for the protection of industrial and trade secrets. These characteristics of artificial intelligence system development apparently reduce the scope of protection for industrial and trade secrets. However, the specific manner in which these generally known components are assembled may be considered to fall within the scope of the secret.[20]

Ultimately, considering that issues related to industrial and commercial secrets are still widely neglected and underexplored in Brazil, in addition to the absence of a precise definition of such protection, it is concluded that their application must be approached with caution. The role of the ANPD and/or the future authority on artificial intelligence will be essential in exercising oversight over potential denials or restrictions of rights based on claims of protection of trade secrets.

Overall, transparency fosters trust, ensuring that technology serves humanity responsibly. Therefore, the proper balance between the exercise of the rights of individuals affected by artificial intelligence systems and the observance of trade secrets is key to a society where innovation thrives without compromising the dignity and freedom of each individual.

Still on the topic of AI and data subject rights, it is important to note the evolution of agentic AI and its relationship with data portability. The advancement of artificial intelligence (AI) has been marked by successive waves of innovation, each redefining the boundaries of what is possible and profoundly impacting the economy and society. The most recent and perhaps most transformative of these is the rise of so-called agentic AI, a technological paradigm that moves away from reactive and generative models to embrace systems endowed with the autonomy to plan, decide, and execute complex tasks with limited human supervision.

Despite market enthusiasm, which projected 2025 as the year in which this technology would become widely adopted, there is still no unequivocal definition of

---

[19] Mylly (2023), pp. 1013–1043.

[20] Mylly (2023), pp. 1013–1043.

what constitutes agentic AI, with the concept situated along a spectrum of autonomy and capability.[21] Analogous to the classification of levels of autonomy in vehicles proposed by the Society of Automotive Engineers, AI systems can be organized on a scale of "agenticity," ranging from tools that support human decision-making to agents capable of autonomously performing tasks in complex and dynamic environments.[22]

AI agents, therefore, represent a qualitative evolution of digital assistants, distinguished by their ability to integrate user preferences, employ multimodal communication, and interact with multiple systems to proactively achieve high-level objectives.[23] The defining feature of agentic AI lies precisely in its capacity to make decisions and execute complex actions in a not fully supervised manner. These agents incorporate learning, adaptation, and long-term planning, shifting from a merely assistive function to an active role in anticipating needs and automating processes.[24]

This ability to act on behalf of the user requires a high level of trust and marks the beginning of a new era in human–machine interaction. However, this same technological disruption, which creates rare opportunities for new competitors to enter the digital economy, also raises concerns about the recurrence of market concentration dynamics already observed in other sectors. In particular, the concentrated power in foundational models, combined with vertical integration with user access platforms, can create closed ecosystems—the so-called walled gardens—limiting consumer choice and restricting competition.

In the context of agentic AI, among the various existing challenges, three factors stand out that directly impact informational self-determination and consumers' right to choose. The first concerns concentration at the infrastructure layer, associated with foundational models; the second relates to vertical integration at the interface layer, linked to the distribution and operation of AI agents with end consumers; and the third involves the dependency among specialized agents, whose full functionality can only be achieved in ecosystems that allow for their free combination.

At the foundation of this ecosystem, foundational models represent a critical element. Adler[25] emphasizes that the development and operation of foundational models require intensive resources—such as capital, data, and computational power—which has contributed to the strong concentration of this market in a few large technology companies. This concentration at the infrastructure layer is not merely an isolated issue: it can create a strategic bottleneck and platform power capable of fostering vertical integration, connecting the base model, agent, and user interface.

---

[21] Adler (2024).

[22] Adler (2024).

[23] Heikkilä (2024).

[24] Martins and Mucelin (2025).

[25] Adler (2024).

The second dynamic is manifested precisely in this vertical integration between AI agents and user access platforms, such as operating systems and smart devices. Bostoen and Krämer[26] point out that incumbent companies can use this integration—through preinstallation, default setting, and the absence of effective choice mechanisms (*choice screens*)—to erect significant entry barriers. This integration increases friction for the adoption of third-party agents, reduces interoperability, and restricts the alternatives available within the dominant ecosystem, thereby reproducing a model of competition "for" the market rather than "in" the market.

The most visible consequence of these two forms of concentration is the creation of so-called walled gardens, closed ecosystems in which AI agents developed on a specific base model communicate and interact optimally only with other agents within the same environment. Although such ecosystems may offer apparent advantages in terms of technical integration, security, and user experience, they do so at the cost of drastically limiting consumer choice, reducing competitive pressure, and stifling third-party innovation.[27]

Frazier and Joseph[28] argue that practices such as *lock-in*—resulting from restrictions on agent portability—create high switching costs and hinder users from migrating to competing solutions. They also highlight the risk of *bundling*, in which the AI agent is offered as part of a package of services, making its stand-alone use or combination with external products more difficult and thereby favoring market dominance.

The ability for users to freely choose their preferred AI agent provider, as well as to combine different solutions through interoperability, is a key factor in preventing the consolidation of monopolies and oligopolies.[29] In practical terms, this means that consumers must be able to migrate their AI agent and the entire history of their interactions when switching mobile device ecosystems or, even more fundamentally, to replace the default, preinstalled AI agent provided by the manufacturer (*default bias*) with an alternative of their choice.[30] This freedom is what enables new and innovative agents to compete on equal footing with solutions offered by major players.

Therefore, the active reduction of frictions in consumer choice is an essential public policy measure.[31] To this end, coordinated action among the various spheres of protection—consumer, competition, and personal data—is fundamental, applying a true "dialogue of sources" to ensure that continuous competitive pressure disciplines the market power of incumbents and fosters innovation throughout the sector.

[26] Bostoen and Krämer (2024).

[27] Adler (2024).

[28] Frazier and Joseph (2025).

[29] Bostoen and Krämer (2024).

[30] Bostoen and Krämer (2024).

[31] Bostoen and Krämer (2024).

Finally, regarding the combination of specialized agents, recent advances and increasing investments in artificial intelligence agents have driven their integration into composite systems, fostering the development of multi-agent systems. These systems consist of networks of autonomous agents that collaborate with each other to achieve complex objectives, often in a decentralized manner.

An intelligent agent is defined by its autonomy, ability to react to the environment, act proactively, and interact. In turn, a multi-agent system consists of several autonomous agents operating within the same environment, which may cooperate or compete, thus requiring efficient mechanisms for communication and coordination.[32]

The logic of task specialization—historically associated with increased productivity and economic efficiency—finds a clear parallel in the emerging architecture of artificial intelligence systems.[33] In the AI development market, there is a gradual transition from monolithic models, designed to perform a wide range of tasks, to systems composed of multiple specialized agents that collaborate in carrying out complex activities.

This approach enables the enhancement of collective efficiency, as each agent can be trained, optimized, and improved independently, without the need to restructure the entire system. It follows the same logic that established the assembly line as the foundation of industrial production: divide to specialize and thus produce more and better.

The potential of this specialization is prominently manifested in the growth of multi-agent systems (MASs), which consist of networks of autonomous agents cooperating to achieve complex objectives without the need for direct supervision by a centralized manager. Platforms developed by major technology companies have already demonstrated the expansion of corporate solutions based on MASs, highlighting the market's growing interest in exploring collaborative AI to optimize processes and increase productivity.[34]

However, the full realization of the benefits promised by this "digital division of labor" is intrinsically dependent on the structure of the market in which these agents operate. In this regard, the benefits of composite agentic AI systems can only be fully achieved in an ecosystem that allows for the free combination of specialized agents. This fundamentally depends on the removal of barriers that generate high switching costs and the consequent lock-in effect.

Data portability is widely recognized as a fundamental competitive tool in the digital economy, as it reduces switching costs and, consequently, lowers barriers to entry for new providers. Although this principle is essential across the entire digital sector, in the context of agentic AI it must be expanded in an even broader and deeper manner, going beyond the mere transfer of files in technically readable formats.

---

[32] Botti (2025).

[33] Adler (2024).

[34] Adler (2024).

The true utility of an AI agent lies in its accumulated knowledge of the user's preferences, context, and behavioral patterns—a set of information that can be metaphorically described as its "memory."[35] This data framework constitutes the individual's very "digital identity," an extension of their personality in the virtual environment, the control of which is a direct corollary of the fundamental right to informational self-determination. The effectiveness of portability, therefore, depends not only on technical compatibility but also on the new agent's ability to semantically and contextually interpret the transferred data in order to continue providing a personalized service.

This is where the most complex challenge lies. Even if data portability is guaranteed by law, as provided for in the General Data Protection Law (LGPD) and the European GDPR, the mere transfer of a dataset may not be sufficient if each competing agent interprets the data differently. Incumbent providers may create artificial barriers to importation, making the migration process frustrating and ineffective.[36]

This scenario raises a debate about the need for more sophisticated regulatory measures that go beyond a structured, machine-readable format. One approach would be to standardize the structuring of agents' "memories" (the previous agent could transmit not only facts but also context, patterns, and nuances to the new agent), by imposing interoperable formats.

A more advanced alternative, suggested by Frazier and Joseph,[37] would be to require providers to allow knowledge transfer between agents, whereby the former agent would be obligated to "teach" the new agent. Such a mechanism would create strong market incentives for effective portability, but it also raises new regulatory challenges, including the protection of confidential information and trade secrets during the transfer and the allocation of responsibilities in the event of failures. This would require a careful balancing of rights and the involvement of regulatory authorities to ensure that the protection of trade secrets does not undermine the core essence of the right to portability.

In light of the above, it can be concluded that the convergence between the rapid development of artificial intelligence and the protection of the fundamental rights of data subjects requires a sophisticated legal hermeneutic, guided by the dialogue of sources and the harmonization of seemingly conflicting values. The transition from reactive systems to agentic AI and multi-agent systems represents not only a technological leap but also a reconfiguration of informational self-determination itself, requiring that the right to data portability go beyond the mere technical transfer of files to achieve the interoperability of digital "memories" and contexts.

In this context, the protection of industrial and commercial secrets should not be construed as a carte blanche for algorithmic opacity or for maintaining walled gardens that stifle competition and consumer autonomy. On the contrary, a systematic

---

[35] Frazier and Joseph (2025).

[36] Frazier and Joseph (2025).

[37] Frazier and Joseph (2025).

interpretation of the LGPD and Bill No. 2338/2023 indicates that the essential core of the right to explanation and access must be preserved, allowing innovation to flourish without compromising human dignity.

Therefore, the proactive role of regulatory bodies will be crucial to ensure that the "digital division of labor" and the autonomy of AI agents operate within a transparent, competitive ecosystem that is, above all, centered on the protection of individual rights and the mitigation of discriminatory risks, thereby ensuring that technological progress remains subordinate to the imperatives of the democratic rule of law.

On the one hand, these transformations affect how data are structured, accessed, and shared within the internal environment of digital ecosystems; on the other hand, they have direct effects on the cross-border flow of such information. In this context, the increasing complexity of artificial intelligence systems also places pressure on the legal frameworks governing the international transfer of data.

4.2 Artificial Intelligence and International Data Transfer

The logic of continuous and interconnected data circulation, which underpins artificial intelligence systems, transcends the boundaries of digital ecosystems and becomes embedded in transnational flows, making international data transfer a central element of its regulation. AI systems, in order to function effectively, rely on large volumes of information, often collected in one country and processed in another, with effects that extend across multiple jurisdictions.

In this context, the limits and requirements established by personal data protection regulations for cross-border data flows directly impact both the development and application of these technologies. This is, therefore, a field in which traditional legal challenges related to sovereignty and jurisdiction are heightened, demanding innovative solutions capable of reconciling the protection of fundamental rights with the global circulation of data essential to AI.

However, the decentralized nature of the Internet and the "information highways" transcend national borders, expanding the locations where violations may occur. Data can be collected in one country and processed in another, producing effects across multiple jurisdictions. This digital environment challenges classical concepts of jurisdiction and state sovereignty, raising complex questions: which court should be approached? Which law should be applied? Are the traditional criteria of sovereignty and territorial boundaries sufficient to address the new dynamics imposed by the global circulation of data[38]?

In this context, it is evident that the European Union, while responding to the growing demand for data access in the race for artificial intelligence and adopting a new paradigm of digital sovereignty in the current geopolitical landscape, has begun

[38] Martins (2018).

to impose restrictions on the transfer of nonpersonal data outside the bloc. Examples of this include the provisions of the Data Act, the Data Governance Act, and the data localization requirements established by the European Health Data Space Regulation.[39]

Furthermore, the Data Act requires *data holders*, regardless of the country in which they are based, to provide users and recipients located in the European Union with information related to the use of connected devices. At the same time, initiatives aimed at strengthening European digital sovereignty and reducing dependence on transfers to centralized foreign platforms are gaining momentum.[40]

State jurisdiction, broadly speaking, refers to the authority granted by international law to a state to enact its own laws, apply them, and enforce them. These powers are described in legal doctrine as legislative or prescriptive jurisdiction, adjudicative or judicial jurisdiction, and executive jurisdiction.

This authority and competence for the creation and application of norms is, as a rule, guided by the principle of territoriality. This is the position of João Grandino Rodas and Gesner de Oliveira, who emphasize that international law upholds territoriality as a principle, allowing extraterritoriality only as an exception.[41]

This issue is, incidentally, one of the subjects of private international law. It is the role of this field to regulate the potential applicability of more than one legal system, preventing overlap or possible absence of rules, as well as to establish jurisdiction.[42]

While it was once uncontroversial to assert that jurisdictional limitation was restricted to the spatial scope of a state's territory—with the principle of nonintervention in the internal affairs of other states being one of the cornerstones of international relations since classical times—today, with globalization, technological development, and the reduction of distances, there is a relativization of the concept of sovereignty and of the very limitation of state jurisdiction.

One of the main drivers of such changes is undoubtedly the Internet: it is the source of an unprecedented level of innovation, enabling market development, the elimination of borders, the advancement of education and knowledge, and the exercise of the right to freedom of expression and access to information.[43]

Orin Kerr,[44] discussing the application of the Fourth Amendment of the American Constitution to Internet users, notes that at the beginning of the digital era it was still possible to support this application based on domestic territoriality. In the 1980s and 1990s, most services, companies, and users were US based.

[39] Kuner and Zanfir-Fortuna (2025).

[40] Kuner and Zanfir-Fortuna (2025).

[41] Oliveira and Rodas (2013).

[42] Ramos (2025).

[43] Braet et al. (2013).

[44] Kerr (2015), pp. 285–329.

However, this conception is now completely obsolete, emphasizes Orin Kerr.[45] According to the author, the past 20 years have witnessed a dramatic globalization of the Internet, so that by the end of 2013, less than 10% of digital traffic could be attributed to US-based users.

It is undeniable, in this context, that the global Internet and a digitalized world have brought renewed prominence to the extraterritorial protection of rights such as privacy. In the case of the European Union, its regulations have sought to establish criteria that define its "territoriality" in order to justify the application of its rules.

Prior to the enactment of the current GDPR, Directive 95/46/EC was in force. This directive, which was also applicable to the Internet, was a development of the provisions established in the Charter of Fundamental Rights of the European Union (2000/C 364/01) and in the Treaty on the Functioning of the European Union.

This Directive represents a historic milestone in the field of data protection, with its main objectives being to ensure the promotion of the fundamental rights of privacy and individual intimacy and, at the level of regional integration, to guarantee the free flow of personal information within the European market.

Based on this, a "territorial" application of data protection rules was advocated, which, according to the Court of Justice of the European Union (CJEU) itself, constituted a "particularly broad scope of application" (CJEU, Case C-131/12, 2014).

Hon, Hörnle, and Millard,[46] analyzing the provisions of the former Directive, report that the purpose of its jurisdictional provisions, set forth in Article 4, was to ensure the application of obligations concerning personal data that were in some way connected to the Union environment, even if the data processing was not established within its territory.

To determine the applicability of the Directive's provisions, one of these three requirements must be present in the data processing: the existence of an establishment carrying out the processing in the context of its economic activities, regardless of the physical location of the processing—as established by case law in the Google case; the application of national legislation by virtue of public international law in extended territories, such as vessels and aircraft, which poses regulatory challenges for cloud computing in international waters;[47] and the use of specific means or equipment within the territory for the collection of information, thereby

[45] Kerr (2015), pp. 285–329.

[46] Hon et al. (2012), pp. 1–44.

[47] Regarding the possibility of the deterritorialization of digital infrastructure, Hon, Hörnle, and Millard highlight a perspective that, although it may sound futuristic, is already supported by factual evidence in industrial property records. They cite as an example a patent obtained by Google in the United States for the implementation of data processing centers installed on vessels. According to the authors, such a configuration would allow these data centers to be anchored in international waters, beyond the reach of traditional territorial jurisdictions, enabling the strategic use of flags of convenience with the deliberate aim of circumventing or selecting less stringent data protection laws. This scenario poses new challenges to the effectiveness of privacy protection regulations. Hon et al. (2012), pp. 1–44.

consolidating a framework that seeks to prevent jurisdictional gaps and ensure the effectiveness of the regulation in the digital economy.[48]

These were the criteria used for the application of the Directive, which was attributed a "broad territorial scope." However, despite the achievements of the Directive, its implementation faced obstacles due to the different approaches adopted within the domestic law of the Member States.[49] Furthermore, the Directive struggled to keep pace with the advances of the technological revolution witnessed in recent times, which compromised and jeopardized its effectiveness, since at the time of its creation the so-called digital age was only just beginning.[50]

For these reasons, a regulation on data protection was issued, presented by the European Commission to the Council in 2012 and published on May 4, 2016. Its application began on May 25, 2018.

The change to be implemented through a regulation is highly commendable, particularly as a means to combat fragmentation. In this regard, it is worth noting that a regulation has a much stronger binding force than a directive, requiring its full and immediate adoption by Member States simultaneously. In contrast, a directive, once it applies to a certain factual situation, mandates the application of the national laws of the Member States.[51]

The Regulation also has an additional objective, alongside the protection of individuals' privacy, which concerns the consolidation of the digital single market. For its success, the existence of uniform rules and the removal of technical and legal barriers are essential.[52]

The key aspect of the Regulation relevant to this article is the scope of protection, which may extend to entities that do not have a presence in the European Union, provided that the data of a resident thereof is processed as a result of the offer of a product or service. Another scenario is when the behavior of an individual within the European Union is monitored,[53] which demonstrates the possibility of the extra-territorial application of the Regulation.[54]

In addition, Article 3 of the GDPR expressly provides for its application to the processing of personal data carried out in the "context of the activities" of an establishment located within the territory of the Union, regardless of whether the processing takes place inside or outside the Union. The GDPR is also applicable in cases where the law of a Member State applies by virtue of public international law.

Thus, the General Data Protection Regulation places even greater emphasis on its scope of application, which many have explicitly referred to as the

---

[48] Hon et al. (2012), pp. 1–44.

[49] Despite the protection granted, the Directive faced criticism, even being described as follows: "the elephant has laboured and given birth to a mouse," especially due to the problems encountered in its implementation (Lloyd 2014).

[50] Edwards and Harbinja (2013), p. 130.

[51] Fernández Rozas and Sánchez Lorenzo (2009).

[52] Wubben et al. (2012).

[53] Boardman et al. (2017).

[54] Zeiter (2014), pp. 1–34.

extraterritorial application of the Regulation. In other words, while up until now the European Union has enforced its data protection laws based on an "expanded territoriality," the future now appears to promise the establishment of extraterritoriality.

The rationale for adopting extraterritoriality was to ensure the effective protection of personal data, regardless of the geographical location of the data subjects. Thus, the expansion of the scope provided by the GDPR seeks to impose rules on the processing of data by those who have an establishment in the European Union or by those who use data belonging to individuals located within the territory of the Union.[55]

In fact, jurisdiction based solely on the principle of territoriality is becoming increasingly less evident in the digital age,[56] which even leads us to consider the need for harmonization or the adoption of an international legal instrument, such as a convention.

An example of this extraterritorial trend, in addition to the GDPR, is the Brazilian General Data Protection Law (LGPD), which not only establishes its applicability to processing carried out within Brazilian territory but also provides that its rules will apply to processing activities aimed at offering or supplying goods or services within its territory or when the data being processed has been collected within the national territory or pertains to individuals located here.

It should be noted, however, that this does not constitute a "pure" or extreme form of extraterritoriality. As a rule, extraterritoriality is limited to cases where there is a certain connection with the European Union—whether through the offering of goods or services or in the context of activities.[57]

This also applies to the criteria adopted by the LGPD, which are, in summary, those set forth in Article 3: (1) the collection of data within national territory; (2) the Brazilian geographic location of the data subject or the recipient of goods and services; or (3) the processing of data within national territory, except in the case provided for in §2 of Article 3 of the LGPD.[58]

In other words, there is also a certain degree of reasonableness in Brazil regarding the selection of criteria for the application of the law, which may, under certain circumstances, result in the extraterritorial application of data protection law.

The criteria for the applicability of data protection legislation are based on the coexistence of different connecting factors, notably the existence of an establishment that carries out processing in the context of its economic activities, regardless of the physical location of the processing—as established by case law in the Google case; the application of national legislation by virtue of public international law in extended territories, such as vessels and aircraft, which poses regulatory challenges for cloud computing in international waters; and the use of specific means or equipment within the territory for the collection of information, thereby consolidating a

[55] Fonseca (2019).

[56] De Hert and Czerniawski (2016), pp. 230–243.

[57] Kuner (2019), pp. 15–19.

[58] Menezes and Colaço (2019), pp. 157–195.

framework of protection aimed at preventing jurisdictional gaps and ensuring the effectiveness of the regulation in the digital economy.

The extraterritorial application of the GDPR exerts a significant influence on various sectors of the Brazilian economy, imposing compliance challenges that affect not only information technology companies acting as processors on behalf of controllers established in the European Union but also the tourism and logistics sectors, including airlines and digital platforms that manage information of European residents traveling to Brazil.

Similarly, the regulatory scope directly affects e-commerce companies and application developers that use tracking tools and automated profiling techniques to provide personalized services to users located in Europe. This consolidates a scenario in which the processing of personal data, even when carried out by Brazilian entities, must comply with the strict European standards of privacy protection whenever goods are offered or the behavior of individuals residing in the bloc is monitored.[59]

Therefore, although the actual effectiveness and enforcement of this extraterritorial application of the GDPR may be debatable, it is certain that data controllers whose processing activities fall within the scenarios provided for in the Regulation, even if the processing takes place in Brazil, will be subject to the duties and responsibilities set forth therein.

Furthermore, the extraterritoriality of European law regarding data protection has direct effects on businesses worldwide.[60] This situation has led to the European Union being referred to as a global regulator.[61] It involves the exportation of European Union law and its internal policies to other markets and legal systems.[62]

This reality, although not without criticism and raising serious doubts regarding its effectiveness—especially in relation to classic issues of private international law, such as difficulties in the enforcement of decisions or the recognition of foreign judgments—creates a level playing field for companies, regardless of their location. Companies with ties to the European market are required to comply with the same standards and levels of data protection demanded of European companies. Furthermore, this approach encourages companies to proactively extend rights and benefits to all their users, even if some do not have these rights guaranteed by the legislation of their country of residence.

In other words, there is an incentive to adopt best practices (or privacy-friendly measures), even if these are not yet mandatory under other legislations outside the European Union. In this regard, it is worth noting the tendency of a data protection regulation (such as the GDPR) to exert exogenous influence on another system.[63]

---

[59] Oliveira et al. (2018).

[60] Svantesson (2013), pp. 278–286.

[61] Young (2015).

[62] Fonseca (2019).

[63] Doneda (2006).

Another way to view this phenomenon is to emphasize the positive effects of harmonizing legislation. Through such harmonization, the free flow of data would be possible, which would ultimately benefit international trade.[64]

In the Brazilian context, it is understood that the provision contained in Article 3 of the LGPD can be classified as a rule of immediate application. According to Nádia de Araújo,[65] rules of immediate application are those whose entirety is considered part of state regulation and must be observed by all in order to safeguard the country's political, social, or economic organization. These rules do not require the mediation of general conflict-of-law rules, as they define their own scope of application in space.

According to Amanda Martins,[66] Article 3 of the LGPD qualifies as a rule of immediate application strictly linked to the territorial incidence scenarios described therein and is capable of overriding traditional private international law methods, especially in cases involving unfulfilled legal obligations or contractual relationships lacking forum selection or choice of law clauses.

However, this immediate application is not absolute, as it encounters insurmountable limits in the autonomy of the parties' will, which prevents the prevalence of national law in cases where there is a valid choice of foreign forum or different legislation, as well as in scenarios of noncontractual civil liability in which the damage does not occur on Brazilian soil and the company does not have its headquarters in the country. In such cases, the jurisdictional limits established by the Code of Civil Procedure are observed, as well as the exceptional absence of a consumer relationship that could trigger the application of the Consumer Protection Code.

The extraterritoriality of data protection regulations is also related to the issue of international data transfers. Taking the European Union as an example, its robust legal framework establishes guarantees for adequate data protection during such transfers, effectively serving as a means of exporting its legal standards. This means that, by requiring third countries to ensure adequate levels of data protection, EU legislation not only regulates data processing within its own borders but also exerts influence over the legislation of other jurisdictions.

This approach represents an extraterritorial application of the European Union's data protection legislation.[67] Furthermore, in the long term, it also promotes harmonization and convergence of protections worldwide, a necessary prerequisite for the purposes of international data transfers.[68]

In this regard, Articles 44–50 of the GDPR are cited, which establish the guidelines for international transfers of personal data.[69] Article 44 sets forth the general

[64] Fonseca (2019).

[65] Araújo (2023).

[66] Martins (2018).

[67] Kuner (2015), pp. 235–245.

[68] Bioni and Mendes (2019), pp. 797–819.

[69] It is worth noting that the transfer of personal data occurs when such data are or will be processed after the transfer. Therefore, it does not apply to the mere transit of data (Rodrigues Araújo 2017, p. 210).

principle of transfers, stipulating that any transfer of personal data to a third country is only permitted if the conditions established by the GDPR are strictly observed by the data controller and the processor.

The essential condition is that the level of protection ensured by the GDPR is not compromised during the transfer process.[70] This requirement underscores the importance of ensuring that individuals' rights remain protected, even when their data is processed outside the European territory, thereby consolidating the extraterritorial application of data protection legislation.

The international transfer of personal data, as established by the General Data Protection Law (LGPD), is regulated by Article 33, which sets forth guidelines to ensure the protection of data subjects' rights. The LGPD permits the transfer of data to countries or international organizations that provide an adequate level of protection, as determined by the National Data Protection Authority (ANPD).

On this subject, RESOLUTION CD/ANPD No. 19, of August 23, 2024, issued by the ANPD,[71] approves the Regulation on International Data Transfers and the content of standard contractual clauses, establishing clear parameters for such transfers. This regulation aims to ensure that international transfers of personal data occur securely and in compliance with the data protection standards established by the LGPD. It is important to note that, in addition to transfers to countries that already have a recognized protection standard, the LGPD provides for other mechanisms for the transfer of personal data, as set forth in Article 33 of Law No. 13,709, of August 14, 2018.

Within the scope of Mercosur, the Agreement on Electronic Commerce, established by CMC Decision No. 15 of 2020,[72] addresses the cross-border transfer of information by electronic means. This agreement stipulates that the parties undertake to apply an adequate level of protection to personal data received from another party, whether through general rules or specific autonomous regulations, mutual agreements—which may be general or specific—or through broader international frameworks. Additionally, for the private sector, the implementation of contracts or self-regulatory mechanisms that ensure such protection is permitted.

Ultimately, the extraterritorial application of data protection regulations encourages the extension of rights to data subjects who would not otherwise be entitled to certain protections while simultaneously impacting international data flows by subjecting them to specific requirements and conditions. Indeed, this creates a

[70] Prata de Carvalho (2019), pp. 621–642.

[71] Brazil. Official Gazette of the Union, Brasília, DF, Aug. 23, 2024. Edition 163, Section 1, p. 123. Ministry of Justice and Public Security/National Data Protection Authority/Board of Directors. Resolution CD/ANPD No. 19, of August 23, 2024. Approves the Regulation on International Data Transfers and the content of standard contractual clauses.

[72] Brazil. Official Gazette of the Union, Brasília, DF, Aug. 23, 2024. Edition 163, Section 1, p. 123. Ministry of Justice and Public Security/National Data Protection Authority/Board of Directors. Resolution CD/ANPD No. 19, of August 23, 2024. Approves the Regulation on International Data Transfers and the content of standard contractual clauses.

favorable environment for the adoption of a harmonized data protection system, which may, in turn, promote international trade with respect to the free flow of data.

Furthermore, the growing reliance of artificial intelligence on large volumes of data places international data transfers at the center of the regulatory agenda. While current data protection regulations already significantly condition cross-border data flows, this impact is likely to become even more pronounced as AI systems grow more sophisticated and require diverse, up-to-date, and globally accessible information bases. At this juncture, the tensions between digital sovereignty, technological competitiveness, and the protection of fundamental rights become particularly acute.

At the same time, the global race for AI intensifies the relevance of data flow regulations: the European Union is committed to its notion of digital sovereignty, China seeks to project its regulatory influence through multilateral initiatives (including within the BRICS - Brazil, Russia, India, China, and South Africa framework), and the United States reinforces selective barriers based on national security. The result is a fragmented landscape, in which the regulation of international data transfers becomes directly linked to the future of artificial intelligence.[73]

The future, therefore, appears to point toward a dual requirement: on the one hand, regulatory frameworks capable of ensuring security, transparency, and fundamental rights in international data flows; on the other, international cooperation mechanisms that prevent excessive fragmentation and allow AI to flourish as a global technology. Instruments such as contractual clauses tailored to AI use, adequacy criteria that consider not only privacy but also algorithmic ethics, and multilateral frameworks for data sharing in sensitive sectors (such as health and the environment) may represent promising pathways.

Ultimately, the regulation of international data transfers and the regulation of AI are not merely interconnected fields but rather facets of the same challenge: how to reconcile technological innovation on a global scale with the protection of fundamental rights in increasingly interdependent digital societies. The manner in which the international community responds to this challenge will determine not only the trajectory of artificial intelligence but also the legal framework of the digital age.

The convergence of artificial intelligence and personal data protection and the regulation of cross-border data flows create a uniquely complex scenario, requiring a reorientation of how law approaches the digital economy. The central objective of reducing regulatory fragmentation and the frictions that currently inhibit innovation should not be pursued through deregulation but rather through a more coordinated, predictable, and integrated normative framework, guided by systemic harmony and the dialogue between legal sources.

The analysis undertaken throughout this chapter demonstrates that the protection of data subjects' fundamental rights—especially the rights to information, explanation, objection, and portability—is fully compatible with the safeguarding of industrial and trade secrets, provided that the notion of a "zero-sum game" is set aside. The essential core of personality rights must be preserved, while the protection of

[73] Kuner and Zanfir-Fortuna (2025).

business secrets should be strictly defined, preventing the generic invocation of confidentiality from becoming a cloak for algorithmic opacity or a tool for maintaining "walled gardens" that stifle competition. The actions of regulatory authorities will be decisive in transforming the protection of trade secrets into a transparent mechanism, grounded in technical and legal reasoning, thereby aligning innovation with the principles of the democratic rule of law.

With regard to the rise of agentic AI, the transition to autonomous and collaborative systems underscores the urgency of rethinking the right to data portability. The effectiveness of this prerogative in the age of artificial intelligence requires that the concept of portability go beyond the mere migration of structured files, advancing toward the semantic and contextual interoperability of agents' "memories." Only by removing lock-in barriers and fostering open ecosystems will it be possible to ensure effective competition, where the market power of incumbents does not stifle the creativity of new entrants.

Finally, the international dimension of the issue requires that digital sovereignty and data protection imperatives be addressed from a global cooperation perspective. The phenomenon of extraterritoriality, led by the European model and reflected in the Brazilian legal framework, while signaling the export of high protection standards, creates significant challenges of fragmentation if not accompanied by mechanisms for convergence. The future challenge does not lie in jurisdictional isolation but in building an international consensus that facilitates the secure flow of data, harmonizing adequacy criteria and algorithmic ethics.

It can thus be concluded that the creation of a prosperous and equitable digital environment depends on an ongoing effort of regulatory coordination. The ability of the law to act as a facilitator of innovation—rather than a source of uncertainty—will depend on its capacity to establish clear guidelines that balance the protection of human dignity with the need for a global flow of information. By harmonizing the protection of data subjects' rights with the promotion of competitiveness and cross-border data flows, the legal framework can mitigate the frictions of the digital economy, ensuring that technological progress effectively serves the development and freedom of all individuals.

References

Adler B (2024) Interoperable agentic AI: unlocking the full potential of AI specialization. Tech Policy Press, 18 September 2024

ANPD (2023) Análise preliminar do Projeto de Lei n° 2338/2023, que dispõe sobre o uso da Inteligência Artificial. ANPD, Brasília

Araújo N (2023) Direito internacional privado. Revista dos Tribunais, São Paulo

Bioni B, Mendes L (2019) Regulamento Europeu de Proteção de Dados Pessoais e a Lei Geral Brasileira de Proteção de Dados: mapeando convergências na direção de um nível de equivalência. In: Frazão A, Tepedino G, Oliva MD (orgs) Lei Geral de Proteção de Dados e suas repercussões no direito brasileiro, 1st edn Thomson Reuters Brasil, São Paulo, pp 797–819

Boardman R, Mullock J, Mole A (2017) Guide to the General Data Protection Regulation. Bird & Bird, London
Bostoen F, Krämer J (2024) AI agents and ecosystems contestability. Issue paper. CERRE, Brussels
Botti V (2025) Agentic AI and multiagentic: are we reinventing the wheel? arXiv preprint https://arxiv.org/abs/2506.01463. https://arxiv.org/abs/2506.01463. Accessed 7 June 2026
Braet O, Graef H, Jacquemins M et al (2013) Étude portant sur la neutralité du réseau (Internet) et les mesures de gestion du trafic. Interdisciplinair Centrum voor Recht em Informatica, Belgium
De Hert P, Czerniawski M (2016) Expanding the European data protection scope beyond territory: Article 3 of the General Data Protection Regulation in its wider context. Int Data Privacy Law 6(3):230–243
Doneda D (2006) Da privacidade à proteção de dados pessoais, 1st edn. Renovar, Rio de Janeiro
Doneda D (2020) Panorama histórico da proteção de dados pessoais. In: Mendes LS, Bioni BR, Doneda D, Sarlet IW, Rodrigues OL (eds) Tratado de proteção de dados pessoais. Forense, Rio de Janeiro
Doneda D (2021) Da privacidade à proteção de dados pessoais, 2nd edn. Thomson Reuters Brasil, São Paulo
Edwards L, Harbinja E (2013) Protecting post-mortem privacy: reconsidering the privacy interests of the deceased in a digital world. Cardozo Arts Entertain Law J 32(1):101–147
Fekete EK (2003) O regime jurídico do segredo de indústria e comércio no Direito Brasileiro. Forense, Rio de Janeiro
Fernández Rozas JC, Sánchez Lorenzo S (2009) Derecho internacional privado. Civitas, Madrid
Fonseca MG (2019) A extraterritorialidade do regime geral de proteção de dados pessoais da União Europeia. Dissertation, Universidade Nova de Lisboa
Frazier K, Joseph J (2025) With AI agents, memory raises policy and privacy questions. Tech Policy Press, 29 September 2025
Heikkilä M (2024) Artificial intelligence: what are AI agents? MIT Technology Review, 5 July 2024
Hon WK, Hörnle J, Millard C (2012) Data protection jurisdiction and cloud computing: when are cloud users and providers subject to EU data protection law? Int Rev Law Comput Technol 26(2–3):1–44
Kerr OS (2015) The Fourth Amendment and the global internet. Stanford Law Rev 67:285–329
Kuner C (2015) Extraterritoriality and regulation of international data transfers in EU data protection law. Int Data Privacy Law 5:235–245
Kuner C (2019) The GDPR and international organizations. AJIL Unbound 114:15–19
Kuner C, Zanfir-Fortuna G (2025) Geopolitical fragmentation, the AI race, and global data flows: the new reality. Future of Privacy Forum, Washington, DC
Lloyd IJ (2014) Information technology law, 7th edn. Oxford University Press, Oxford
Malgieri G, Beslay L, Sanchez I (2018) The right to data portability in the GDPR: towards user-centric interoperability of digital services. Comput Law Secur Rev 34(2):193–203
Martins ACMS (2018) Privacidade, proteção de dados e danos transnacionais: aspectos do direito internacional privado brasileiro. Dissertation, Universidade de São Paulo
Martins GM, Mucelin G (2025) IA agêntica, comando e controle: oito medidas de governança para mitigar riscos e prevenir danos. Rev Direito Consumidor 160:281–310
Menezes JB, Colaço H (2019) Quando a Lei Geral de proteção de dados não se aplica? In: Tepedino G, Frazão A, Oliva MD (orgs) Lei Geral de Proteção de Dados Pessoais e suas repercussões no Direito Brasileiro. Thomson Reuters Brasil, São Paulo, pp 157–195
Mylly UM (2023) Transparent AI? Navigating between rules on trade secrets and access to information. IIC 54:1013–1043
Noto La Diega G, Sappa C (2020) The internet of things (IoT) at the intersection of data protection and trade secrets: non-conventional paths to counter data appropriation and empower consumers. Eur J Consum Law/Revue européenne de droit de la consommation 3:419–458
Oliveira G, Rodas JG (2013) Direito e economia da concorrência. Revista dos Tribunais, São Paulo
Oliveira DTN, Machado DC, Polido FBP, Brandão LCC (2018) GDPR and its effects on the Brazilian law: first impressions and a comparative analysis. IRIS, Belo Horizonte

Pela JK (2018) The Brazilian regulation of trade secrets. A proposal for its review. Gewerblicher Rechtsschutz und Urheberrecht - Internationaler Teil 6:546–550

Prata de Carvalho AG (2019) Transferência internacional de dados na lei geral de proteção de dados: força normativa e efetividade diante do cenário transnacional. In: Frazão A, Tepedino G, Oliva MD (orgs) A Lei Geral de Proteção de Dados e suas repercussões no direito brasileiro. Revista dos Tribunais, São Paulo, pp 621–642

Ramos AC (2025) Direito internacional privado. In: Enciclopédia Jurídica da PUC-SP, 1st edn. PUC-SP, São Paulo

Rodrigues Araújo A (2017) As transferências transatlânticas de dados pessoais: o nível de proteção adequado depois de Schrems. Rev Direitos Humanos Democracia 5(9):201–236

Spiecker I (2018) Direito à proteção de dados na internet em caso de colisão. Direitos Fundamentais & Justiça 12(38)

Svantesson D (2013) A "layered approach" to the extraterritoriality of data privacy laws. Int Data Privacy Law 3:278–286

Veronese A, Silveira A, Lemos ANLE (2019) Inteligência artificial, mercado único digital e a postulação de um direito às interferências justas e razoáveis: uma questão jurídica entre a ética e a técnica. In: Frazão A, Mulholland C (orgs) Inteligência artificial e direito: ética, regulação e responsabilidade, 1st edn. Thomson Reuters Brasil, São Paulo, pp 233–264

Wachter S, Mittelstadt B (2019) A right to reasonable inferences: re-thinking data protection law in the age of big data and AI. Columbia Bus Law Rev 2019:79

Wubben M, Schermer B, Teterissa D (2012) Legal aspects of the Digital Single Market: current framework, barriers and developments. Considerati, Amsterdam

Young A (2015) The European Union as a global regulator? Context and comparison. J Eur Public Policy 22(9)

Zeiter A (2014) The new General Data Protection Regulation of the EU and its impact on IT companies in the U.S. Stanford Vienna Transatlantic Technology Law Forum, pp 1–34

Chapter 5
Competition, Consumer Choice, and Structural Lock-In

5.1 Data, Competition, and Consumer Choice in Digital Markets

In data-driven digital markets, competition is structured not only by prices or productive efficiency but also by the ability of economic agents to collect, control, and exploit large volumes of data. These informational assets directly influence entry conditions, competitive dynamics, and the actual degree of user freedom, impacting consumer choices, innovation, and the distribution of economic power.

In this regard, it is undeniable that the free flow of personal data stimulates competition[1,2] and, consequently, enables the consumer's right of choice, thereby undeniably safeguarding their well-being. This constitutes consumer protection implemented through competition law,[3] reinforcing and giving effect to the principles of the economic order, notably the principle of free competition (Art. 170, item IV, of the Federal Constitution) and consumer protection (Art. 170, item V, of the Federal Constitution).

According to Egon Bockmann Moreira,[4] the principle of free competition upholds the freedom of entry, exercise, and management. Through this, the aim is to achieve an ideal outcome regarding the distribution of resources within society. Meanwhile, the principle of consumer protection reveals that "the human being

[1] Some argue, in fact, that the free flow of data would constitute the fifth fundamental freedom of the European Union.

[2] Article 29 Data Protection Working Party (2016), p. 3.

[3] In this regard, the Joint Note from SENACON and CADE states that competition policy and consumer policy share the same objective, namely, consumer welfare. Brazil. Ministry of Justice. Joint Note No. 8/SENACON-CADE. *Analysis of the interface between consumer protection policy and competition policy.*

[4] Moreira (2006), p. 109.

D. Copetti Cravo, *Law and the Digital Economy*,
https://doi.org/10.1007/978-3-032-36672-6_5

must be considered in their entirety and with paramount value in economic relations."

It is noteworthy that the recognition of consumer protection as one of the objectives of antitrust has been the subject of debate throughout the evolution of the economic theories that underpin competition law. From the Harvard School to the Chicago School, there has always been a concern for the consumer, albeit in different ways.

The Harvard School emerged in the mid-twentieth century, concerned with market structure, hence its designation as the structuralist school. As the name suggests, the school's focus was on the number of agents operating in the market and their respective sizes,[5] which led to the development of the structure–conduct–performance (SCP) paradigm.

This school exerted a strong influence in the United States until the 1970s, focusing on the cause-and-effect relationship between basic conditions (technology, cost curve, consumer preferences, among others), structure (barriers to entry, degree of concentration on the supply and demand sides, product differentiation), conduct (firm behavior including competition, pricing, advertising, etc.), and market performance (outcome, price, quality, and quantity).

The application of this school, in the 1950s and 1960s, led to the introduction of a series of rules containing *per se* prohibitions of business conduct that rarely produced anticompetitive effects in practice. Furthermore, there was strong state intervention in business practices and structures, which disregarded any efficiency arguments.[6]

Given that this school placed significant emphasis on the protection of small businesses (*small is beautiful*)[7] and, therefore, on competitors, the Harvard School became the target of a series of criticisms.[8,9] As a result, the Chicago School emerged,[10] introducing a new concept of competition focused on productive and allocative efficiency.[11] This marked the end of *per se* protection for small businesses and the beginning of the pursuit of efficiency elements within the scope of competition.

---

[5] Piraino Jr. (2007), p. 348.

[6] In this regard, Robert Pitofsky notes that, during the 1950s and 1960s, small mergers that could not seriously be seen as an obstacle to a competitive market were constantly blocked and curtailed (with the classification of *per se* illegality), despite rarely producing anticompetitive effects or being detrimental to consumer welfare. There was a complete disregard for efficiency claims. Pitofsky (2008), pp. 4–5.

[7] Forgioni (2008), p. 169.

[8] Pfeiffer (2015).

[9] One of the criticisms, by way of illustration, is that intervention as proposed by the Harvard School may even be inappropriate, since, even in markets with large companies, there may be competitive dynamics. Whish (2001), p. 18.

[10] The basic characteristics of the Chicago School are attributable to the work of Aaron Director in the 1950s. Posner (1979), p. 925.

[11] Frazão (2015), p. 182.

The major challenge within this school was how to ensure consumer satisfaction, as aptly noted by Guilhermo Cuevas.[12] As a result, and following the historical sequence, post-Chicago movements emerged,[13] whose main characteristic was to align the efficiency studied by the Chicago School with the promotion of an environment conducive to innovation and consumer choice. The cold view of the rational economic man was set aside, and greater value was placed on state intervention, entrusting the state with the task of intervening in the presence of market failures. All of this was supported by economic analysis.

Thus, even without providing an extensive descriptive framework of competition law, it can be stated that consumer welfare is one of the objectives pursued by antitrust law, although its content has undergone changes across different schools,[14] as discussed above. In any case, this work adopts the approach that seeks to recentralize competition law, following studies such as those by Robert H. Lande,[15] which argue that competition law should be guided by the consumer's right to choose.

Robert H. Lande[16] argued that the United States was already moving in this direction. As an example, the author cites the Microsoft case, in which consumer choice should be guided by the factor of innovation. For this reason, the resolution of the case did not focus solely on the prices charged by Microsoft for its operating system or web browser.[17]

Neil Averitt and Robert H. Lande[18] propose that a decision based on consumer choice power should be guided by the following premises: "i) that there is a range of options available to the consumer, made possible by competition; and ii) that consumers must be able to freely choose among these options." It would thus be the role of competition law to ensure competition in the market, addressing the external failures of this environment from the supply-side perspective. In this way, a reasonable range of options is preserved, over which the consumer may exercise their power of choice.[19]

In this regard, Robert H. Lande[20] argues that consumer welfare is much better protected by the choice model than by the price theory or the theory of economic efficiency. To support this premise, the author[21] cites markets in which prices are regulated by the state and yet competition remains a central point, as it allows for an increase in the quality level of the products or services offered. In such cases, the

12 Cabanellas de las Cuevas (2005), p. 45.
13 American Antitrust Institute (2017).
14 Salomão Filho (2003).
15 Lande (2010).
16 Lande (2010).
17 Lande (2010).
18 Lande and Averitt (2003), pp. 26–50.
19 Lande and Averitt (2003), pp. 26–50.
20 Lande (2010).
21 Lande (2010).

shortcomings of adopting the price theory become evident, as occurred in the neo-classical theory (Chicago School).[22]

Furthermore, with regard to the right of choice, it is worth noting Patrícia Regina Pinheiro Sampaio's observation[23] that "a society that upholds the principle of free competition is ensuring the freedom of individual choice: competition decentralizes decision-making centers and, therefore, favors the right of individuals to choose." On the other hand, if decision-making power is concentrated in small economic or political groups, individual freedom is diminished or even suppressed.

However, the realization of this right of choice should not be interpreted as merely ensuring the greatest number of options but rather, as interpreted by Ana Paula Martinez,[24] by achieving a "balance between the pursuit of economic efficiency and the maintenance of a range of effective options for the consumer."

For the full effectiveness of this model, it is imperative to ensure the simultaneous and effective implementation of consumer law, which must act to guarantee that "consumers can effectively choose among those options without having their critical faculties impaired by violations such as fraud or the withholding of material information.[25]" This action would be directed at internal market failures.

In this context, it can be concluded that consumer law, by acting on the demand side, aims to enable consumers to make free, informed, and qualitative choices. To achieve this, consumer law is guided by the promotion of education and information, as well as the protection of consumers' economic interests, health and safety, and physical and psychological integrity, in addition to ensuring access to justice and the protection of collective interests.[26]

Indeed, it is necessary to apply these two branches simultaneously and reciprocally, as they exert mutual influence. This interaction must prevail even though consumer protection and competition enforcement are carried out by different agencies, as is the case in Brazil.[27]

---

[22] Carpena (2005), p. 157.

[23] Sampaio (2013), p. 27.

[24] Martinez (2004), p. 73.

[25] Lande and Averitt (2003), pp. 26–50.

[26] Bourgoignie (1993), p. 52.

[27] Currently, at the federal level, there is National Consumer Secretariat (SENACON), an agency of the Ministry of Justice responsible for consumer protection, and the Administrative Council for Economic Defense (CADE), an independent authority responsible for competition defense. There was an attempt to create a single agency for both areas, namely, the Consumer and Competition Defense Agency (ANC), which did not come to fruition. After extensive discussions, public consultations, and working groups, the decision was made to strengthen CADE and create SENACON. It is worth mentioning, however, that prior to this change and the adoption of the SENACON and CADE model, consumer and competition protection were jointly handled by the Secretariat for Economic Defense (SDE) of the Ministry of Justice. By way of comparative law, it should be noted that the model followed by Australia and the United Kingdom is that of a single agency; in this regard, one may cite, respectively, the Australian Competition and Consumer Commission (ACCC) and the Office of Fair Trading (OFT, the Competition and Consumer Authority of the United Kingdom). OECD (2008).

Finally, it is reaffirmed, with support from Augusto Jaeger Junior,[28] the "necessary correlativity, interdependence, inseparability, and indivisibility" of the relationship between competition and consumer matters.[29] It is within this correlation that the importance of the dialogue of sources emerges, as conceived by Erik Jayme[30] and further developed by Claudia Lima Marques.[31]

Thus, it can be said that consumers are indeed among the interests protected, alongside other constitutional values. This does not, however, mean that competition can render the specific protection of consumers unnecessary.

To advocate a hypothesis in this regard would be almost an exaggeration, in the words of Ricardo Lorenzetti,[32] especially since consumer law is focused within the realm of private law, whereas competition is a matter of public policy.[33] Thus, the two approaches are complementary and function as communicating vessels while still observing their own inherent and distinct logics and rationales.[34]

Therefore, it is undeniable that, first, consumer welfare is one of the objectives pursued by competition, and, second, that synergy between competition law and consumer law is necessary, as both are influenced by and dependent on these reciprocal interactions. It can be stated that there is a systematic dialogue of complementarity and subsidiarity between them.[35]

However, such interdisciplinary interaction is not limited to consumer law and competition law. These areas also share a zone of intersection with the subject of personal data protection.

Explaining this intersection, it can be observed that, in the context of digital markets, the increase and maintenance of market power are achieved through the massive volume of data collected from users of online services, without regard or care for privacy. Exceptions to this rule are services related to medical treatment, finance and banking, security, and luxury tourism, which are businesses that compete on the level of privacy protection, since any failure in this regard can cause reputational damage to the companies and affect their market power.[36]

However, in addition to the general rule being the absence of competition between services in terms of data protection quality, consumers are not inclined to choose services that adopt more diligent privacy policies, resulting in the digital

[28] Jaeger Junior (2006), p. 172.

[29] In this regard, Daniel Frimato de Almeida Glória aptly points out that competition would make no sense without the consumer perspective. Glória (2003), p. 116.

[30] Jayme (2003), pp. 59–68.

[31] Marques (2012), pp. 17–66.

[32] Lorenzetti (2001), p. 222.

[33] Lorenzetti (2001), p. 222.

[34] Meledo-Briand (2000), p. 39.

[35] Marques (2010), p. 160.

[36] EDPS (2014).

market being characterized by a race to the bottom in terms of privacy protection.[37]

Thus, the violation of data protection regulations and the use of anticompetitive methods to acquire such data have become a clear symptom of market power.[38] If consumers do not adopt behaviors that encourage a commitment to privacy and data protection, economic agents have no incentive to implement measures that safeguard these interests.

At this point lies the first interaction between privacy, competition, and the consumer. Effective enforcement of data protection regulations can ensure greater competition in the digital market, fostering better practices, products, and services and preventing an environment where companies compete aggressively to collect user data.

Similarly, the converse is also true: if the market is extremely competitive, dynamic, and innovative, companies will have to strive to offer better proposals to consumers. Indeed, competition would promote data protection, as it would become an element of competitiveness.

The regulatory agencies involved in the subject matter at hand did not always previously recognize this necessary intersection or how it should be addressed. An example of this can be seen in two commercial partnership cases analyzed by the Administrative Council for Economic Defense (CADE): the first between the Oi group and Phorm[39] and the second between Telefônica and Phorm,[40] both for the purpose of online advertising.

In both cases, CADE acknowledged that privacy concerns were implicated; however, it did not engage in a substantive assessment of such issues, as they fell outside its institutional mandate.[41] Currently, however, there is a discernible trend toward progress in antitrust analysis in Brazil regarding data access, although it remains very incipient and gradual. For example, reference can be made to the opinion of Commissioner Paula Farani in the merger review involving the acquisition of Hortigil by IF Capital Ltda. (Grupo LASA).[42]

Abroad, a case similar to those mentioned above (Oi/Phorm and Telefônica/Phorm) was analyzed in connection with Google's acquisition of the company DoubleClick. This transaction was approved by the *Federal Trade Commission* (FTC, the competition authority of the United States)[43] in 2007 and by the European Commission in 2008.[44]

---

[37] EDPS (2014).

[38] EDPS (2014).

[39] Mattiuzzo (2014), p. 60.

[40] Mattiuzzo (2014), p. 60.

[41] Mattiuzzo (2014), p. 60.

[42] Brazil. Administrative Council for Economic Defense. Merger Filing No. 08700.004481/2021-80.

[43] Federal Trade Commission. Federal Trade Commission Closes Google/DoubleClick Investigation, 2007.

[44] European Commission. *Mergers: Commission clears proposed acquisition of DoubleClick by Google.*

Regarding this latest approval, it was argued that the Commission had failed to consider important aspects, such as the effects of the corporate transaction on the users of the acquired company, whose data would be processed by both companies, even though their consent had not encompassed both entities. The consequences for the well-being of thousands of consumers were also allegedly not taken into account.[45]

On the other hand, in the case involving the company ReverseAuction.com Inc.,[46] which registered as an eBay user to collect information from other users, such as email addresses and feedback ratings, the FTC expressed its commitment to protecting consumers' online privacy, stating that it would act swiftly against those who violate data protection policies. For the FTC, privacy is an important factor in the decision-making process of American consumers.

Another recent precedent that demonstrates a shift in antitrust analysis is the case involving Facebook and the German competition authority.[47] According to Caio Henrique Wisniewski,[48] "on February 6, 2019, the German antitrust authority, Bundeskartellamt, prohibited the data processing policy imposed by Facebook on its users, ordering the cessation of this conduct." Thus, the company would only be allowed to collect data outside its own website if there was specific consent for such collection.

Such a decision, despite its pioneering nature, was not exempt from criticism and even revision.[49] What stands out from the criticism is that a mere competitive advantage through greater access to data (*data advantage*) does not, in itself, constitute an antitrust violation.

In fact, data advantage alone cannot, by itself, constitute an antitrust violation, not least to avoid sanctioning conduct that is pro-competitive and fosters innovation. However, competition authorities need to be more vigilant regarding potential market dominance through mergers and acquisitions (such as Facebook's acquisition of WhatsApp)[50,51] or through anticompetitive practices such as refusal to deal or tying

---

45 EDPS (2014).

46 Federal Trade Commission. Online Auction Site Settles FTC Privacy Charges, 2000.

47 Bundeskartellamt. *Bundeskartellamt prohibits Facebook from combining user data from different sources*, 2019.

48 Wisniewski (2019).

49 Oberlandesgericht Düsseldorf Decision. *VI-Kart 1/19 (V)*.

50 As noted by Caio Henrique Wisniewski, the acquisition of WhatsApp by Facebook, Inc., (...) a $19 billion US dollar transaction, did not meet the notification criteria in most countries worldwide, including the Administrative Council for Economic Defense itself, due to WhatsApp's low revenue. Wisniewski (2019).

51 The case brought by the Federal Trade Commission (FTC) against Facebook (now Meta) in 2025 marks a significant shift in the approach of US competition authorities toward Big Tech. The lawsuit comes many years after the acquisitions of Instagram (2012) and WhatsApp (2014), which were approved by competition authorities at the time. Now, the FTC alleges that these acquisitions, combined with the imposition of restrictions on software developers, formed part of a long-term strategy to illegally maintain Facebook's monopoly in the personal social networking market. The case (Civil Action No. 20-cv-3590) remains pending before the District Court for the District of

arrangements, which constitute abuse of dominant position in relation to data, in order to avoid under-enforcement.

Another point of interaction concerns the identification, by competition authorities, of the use of data in distinct markets, since it is standard antitrust practice to delineate and define relevant markets. This would be the case, for example, of a supplier who collects data on a large scale in one market and then sells it for use in a second market. Indeed, antitrust analysis could lead to the conclusion that, from the perspective of data protection, processing by the second market is being carried out without the data subject's consent.[52]

Another issue faced concerns the overlap of the three important areas (data, consumer, and competition), which is related to the discrimination suffered by consumers. This discrimination arises not only from violations of privacy regulations but also from a jurisdictional gap in the application of competition law.[53] To a large extent, this occurs not due to intent or negligence on the part of antitrust authorities but rather because the competition protection model does not directly focus on consumers' internal vulnerabilities.[54]

Furthermore, one must not overlook the role of information in this analysis. The better informed consumers are, the more capable they will be of choosing among competing online services and effectively driving competition.[55]

Thus, a competitive market is not capable of producing all its positive effects if there are informational problems, which results in an economic performance below expectations. Furthermore, it can be stated that the exercise of the right to information by the consumer provides for the enforcement of competition rules.[56]

In the digital market, consumer access to information has a particular characteristic related to the consumers' ability to understand the information provided to them. An example of this is multiservice companies, where consumers may have difficulty understanding and foreseeing that the data provided for the use of a specific service will later be processed by the same company and used in other services not originally anticipated.[57]

The difficulty of comprehension is further compounded by the excessive length of privacy policies. According to studies, a user would need 244 h per year to read the privacy policy of every website visited, which represents more than 50% of the average time spent using the Internet. As if these were not enough to undermine the

Columbia. Federal Trade Commission. *FTC v. Facebook, Inc.* FTC Matter/File Number 191 0134. Civil Action Number 20-cv-3590. Federal Court District of Columbia.

[52] EDPS (2014).

[53] EDPS (2014).

[54] Regarding CADE's approach to consumer issues, José Reinaldo de Lima Lopes acknowledges that CADE is open to consumers but not to provide them with immediate satisfaction. CADE's role is, in fact, to maintain a more favorable environment, with allocative and productive efficiency, lower prices, more abundant products, and more alternatives. Lopes (2000), pp. 79–87.

[55] Kisyombe (2012), p. 4.

[56] Cseres (2006), p. 4.

[57] EDPS (2014).

right to information, these policies are generally written in small print, using vague terms and open-ended clauses that allow data to be used to "improve the customer experience."[58]

A brief observation should be made regarding the practices implemented by suppliers in the online market, who often resort to this escape valve referred to as "improving the customer experience." An example of such practices is advertising, which many platforms and services claim to be useful and beneficial to Internet users.

As Marcela Mattiuzzo points out,[59] this premise is highly questionable. First, it overlooks the fact that advertisements can be misleading or abusive, in addition to being partial and targeted (especially considering modern techniques of data collection and use, including profiling). Second, the sheer volume of advertising can make browsing overwhelming and difficult, potentially causing irritation or annoyance to users. Thus, the way advertising is currently conducted on the Internet can even be considered a disservice to users.[60]

Although information is indispensable, an even more essential factor is the ability to terminate the use of a service and transfer all provided and stored data to another platform or application. In this regard, it is asserted that the more difficult it is for an individual to move their data, the greater the market power held by the provider, which creates barriers and hinders the success of new entrants.[61]

In light of these peculiarities that hinder the functioning of digital markets, there is a recurring presence of mechanisms capable of sustaining dominant positions of an exclusionary or exploitative nature, limiting consumers' and competitors' access to effective alternatives.[62] Such dynamics undermine market contestability, reinforce barriers to entry, and reduce the ability of traditional competition and consumer protection instruments to produce sufficient corrective effects, especially when economic power is rooted in the control and retention of data.

To understand these phenomena, the concepts of consumer lock-in and switching costs are central. In digital environments, users tend to remain tied to certain services not due to genuine preference or competitive superiority but out of fear of losing data accumulated over time, usage history, contacts, reputation, or specific investments.[63] This risk acts as a factor of economic inertia, making migration to competing services costly or virtually unfeasible,[64] even when potentially more efficient or privacy-respecting alternatives exist. As a result, mechanisms that are often invoked as safeguards for consumer interests fail to operate effectively.[65]

[58] EDPS (2014).

[59] Mattiuzzo (2014), p. 61.

[60] Mattiuzzo (2014), p. 21.

[61] EDPS (2014).

[62] EDPS (2014).

[63] Diker Vanberg and Ünver (2017).

[64] Geradin and Kuschewsky (2013).

[65] Yosifon (2012), p. 1454.

It is precisely based on this diagnosis that a deeper examination of the specific mechanisms sustaining these dynamics becomes necessary. Accordingly, the following section will be dedicated to the analysis of switching costs and consumer lock-in, examining how these factors operate in digital markets, how they reinforce network effects and user dependency, and why they are central elements for understanding market power in the digital economy.

5.2 Structural Lock-In in Digital Markets: Switching Costs and Network Effects

In digital markets, there are several types of costs, such as searching costs and switching costs,[66,67] which create barriers to the free movement of consumers among the available options in the market, preventing them from exercising their right of choice due to the lock-in effect. These costs are a distinguishing factor in the supply of homogeneous products[68] and may be the reason why effective competition does not exist in certain markets.

As a result, consumers may begin to tolerate price increases, including the imposition of supra-competitive prices, or violations of their privacy. The consequence is that consumers may rely on heuristics instead of being guided by rationality.[69]

These costs, with the exception of those related to emotional, cognitive, and psychological issues, arise from certain commercial practices. When such costs occur, consumers—even if willing or eager to switch to new providers—are unable to do so due to circumstances that are generally deliberate and created in accordance with economic interests.[70]

An example of this is the very commercialization of durable goods, which began at the same time as modern companies. When a consumer purchases such a product, they become "bound" for a substantial period of time, to the point that the consumer can almost be compared to an investor, except with regard to the protection of their future interests, since the protection afforded to the former in this respect is much less than that granted to the latter.[71]

In terms of market structure, it can be said that in business models where there are switching costs for suppliers, competition occurs *ex ante* in order to secure full power *ex post*. In this competitive dynamic, suppliers resort to penetration pricing, introductory offers, and price wars (including predatory pricing), thereby

66 Kisyombe (2012), p. 4.

67 In the literature, there is also reference to communication costs. Eurich and Burtscher (2014), p. 3.

68 Dzhain (2014), p. 11.

69 Cseres (2006), p. 4.

70 Sanne (2002), p. 287.

71 Yosifon (2012), p. 1452.

establishing—thus—a "competition for the market" or a "competition for the lifecycle."[72]

Although there is *ex ante* competition, this is not sufficient to offset the harm. Studies indicate that such situations lead to reduced efficiency and consumer harm, particularly due to the obstruction of consumer access to other suppliers, which may even be more efficient.[73]

Thus, *ex ante* competition often fails to promote *ex post* competition, thereby generating oligopoly rents and returns for those who engage in practices that create switching costs for consumers.[74] Furthermore, a pricing system based on the "bargain-then-rip-off" model is employed, which typically distorts the quality of consumer choice and creates confusion through artificial incentives.[75]

Thus, when the supplier is dealing with a new consumer, attractive prices and bargains are offered. However, once this consumer becomes a returning customer, bound by the imposition of a switching cost (which, in addition to being imposed, may be consequential or incidental, as will be discussed later), prices tend to increase,[76] sometimes even to offset the initial bargains.

It is important to note that, at times, the practices employed to initially attract and subsequently retain consumers may exceed the boundaries of legality.[77] Pei-yu Chen and Lorin Hitt[78] assert that there is evidence of companies specifically investing in the creation of switching costs. They add that companies have considerable control over these costs through a variety of business practices.

This situation is observed in all markets, including digital ones, even though search costs are reduced and there is some access to information in these environments. In addition, consumer behavior resulting from their vulnerability—sometimes exacerbated by emotional shortcomings—further amplifies the harmful effects of such practices.

Regarding consumer behavior, according to David Yosifon,[79] there is a tendency for individuals to evaluate and weigh present gains much more heavily than future gains (or even losses), prioritizing the former. This phenomenon is known as "hyperbolic discounting," which suggests that we are much better at assessing the present, based on the costs and desires immediately before us, than the future. As a result, consumers may fail to anticipate the impact of future costs.

This situation further highlights the vulnerability of consumers. If their choices are generally based on immediate gains, considering switching costs, future

---

[72] Farrell and Klemperer (2007), p. 1970.

[73] Farrell and Klemperer (2007), p. 1972.

[74] In a similar vein, Nikita Dzhain argues that the presence of high switching costs can create an *ex post* monopoly, even if there is *ex ante* competition. Dzhain (2014), p. 11.

[75] Farrell and Klemperer (2007), p. 1970.

[76] Dzhain (2014), p. 11.

[77] Chen and Hitt (2018), p. 17.

[78] Chen and Hitt (2018), p. 17.

[79] Yosifon (2012), p. 1452.

problems may become even more severe.[80] As is well known, these costs will bind the consumer to their initial choices, even if the future consequences of those choices are disastrous.

It often happens that consumers are unable to assess the future costs they will incur in order to weigh them against the present offer. Suppliers do not always provide a comprehensive contract that considers the product's life cycle and specifies all current and future prices. In most cases, contractual relationships, although long term, are governed by short-term terms or provisions with only immediate effects.[81]

Specifying the costs that give rise to the situations described above, it is important to note that there are transaction costs and search costs. These share many similarities, and the model of effects applicable to one can often be applied to the other. Some studies do not even distinguish between these two types of costs.[82]

In any case, search costs can be defined as the time and effort spent researching various possible alternatives prior to making a purchase decision.[83] Additionally, search costs indicate the level of complexity consumers face in acquiring information about alternative sellers or service providers.[84]

Specifically regarding technological information platforms, it can initially be argued that search costs would be reduced, given that information would be readily available to consumers as one of the advantages of the Internet. However, this premise is not entirely accurate, since the vast volume of available information may have the opposite effect on consumers, causing them to spend a considerable amount of time processing information, which, consequently, ends up increasing search costs.[85]

Search costs give rise to a situation that has been referred to as a "confusopoly," that is, the power of a given supplier is determined by the poor quality of information provided to consumers rather than by the market structure itself. This situation is exacerbated in markets where there is substantial product differentiation, as consumers will face difficulties in comparing alternatives. An example of this is the banking sector, where there is an abundance of service packages.[86]

Switching costs, on the other hand, are those costs that arise when one wishes to change suppliers, which do not occur when remaining with the current supplier. As a result, suppliers have the opportunity to engage in anticompetitive behavior, regardless of the number of firms operating in the market.[87]

The classic switching cost occurs when the buyer repeatedly purchases the same product or service and, upon making a new purchase, finds it costly to switch from one

---

[80] Farrell and Klemperer (2007), p. 1970.

[81] Farrell and Klemperer (2007), p. 1973.

[82] Farrell and Klemperer (2007), p. 1978.

[83] Dzhain (2014), p. 16.

[84] Dzhain (2014), p. 14.

[85] Dzhain (2014), p. 14.

[86] Brazil. Ministry of Justice. Joint Note No. 8/SENACON-CADE. *Analysis of the interface between consumer protection policy and competition defense.*

[87] Brazil. Ministry of Justice. Joint Note No. 8/SENACON-CADE. *Analysis of the interface between consumer protection policy and competition defense.*

supplier to another. In addition to the classic case, there is the cost that arises from the need to purchase complementary products or services, such as maintenance or repair. In this case, the costs are related to changing suppliers in the complementary or secondary market, opting for a supplier different from that of the original product.

Furthermore, it is possible to identify six categories of switching costs, which are (a) transaction costs, including the opportunity costs of searching for a new supplier; (b) contractual costs,[88] among which are loyalty programs that induce the consumer not to switch suppliers under penalty of losing future discounts;[89] (c) informational costs, which include the learning costs associated with using a new product;[90] (d) compatibility costs, which prevent the use of products and services in combination with those of a competitor—a recurring situation in the technology market and across different platforms; (e) uncertainty costs, since it is not known whether the new product or service will be satisfactory or fulfill the offer; (f) psychological costs, as frequent use of a product or service by the consumer may generate sentimental value.[91]

In summary, switching costs may arise from the trust enjoyed by the supplier, brand loyalty, or even convenience. This effect is also reinforced by the use of specific technology, the desire not to lose a particular status, product customization, accommodation, habit, or familiarity.[92] Costs may also result from certain specific investments that are not transferable to a new supplier, such as equipment, training,[93] or warranties for latent defects.

An interesting example regarding the characteristics of training, adaptation, habituation, or familiarization is the QWERTY keyboard. As it was the first to appear on the market, most people learned to type using its layout.[94] Later, much superior keyboards such as the Dvorak were developed, which supposedly required less effort from the hands and fingers and resulted in fewer typing errors by touch than the QWERTY layout. However, since people were already accustomed to QWERTY, Dvorak was unable to gain a foothold in the consumer market.[95]

With regard to data, a fundamental product in the digital market, the easier it is for a consumer to transfer their data from one platform to another, the lower their switching costs.[96] A specific aspect of the digital market is that consumers often

---

[88] An illustrative example of the category of contractual costs is when someone wishes to close their account at one bank and open an account at another, fees may be charged for closing the original account. Dzhain (2014), p. 14.

[89] An example would be frequent-flyer programs. Farrell and Klemperer (2007), p. 1978.

[90] Learning costs are measured in terms of the time, money, and effort required to learn how to use a new product. If there is a future switch to another provider, these learning costs will be considered sunk costs. An example of this is switching devices that use different platforms such as iOS, Android, Symbian, and Windows. Dzhain (2014), p. 14.

[91] Yosifon (2012), p. 1454.

[92] Eurich and Burtscher (2014), p. 3.

[93] Office of Fair Trade (2003), p. 11.

[94] Yosifon (2012), p. 1457.

[95] Yosifon (2012), p. 1457.

[96] Engels (2016).

wish to use multiple platforms simultaneously (*multihoming*), which creates an additional need to facilitate the reduction of switching costs.[97]

Associated with the switching cost (and also with search costs) is the lock-in effect,[98] which refers to the situation in which the consumer becomes dependent on a supplier of a product or service and is unable to switch to another without substantial transaction costs or inconveniences, such as the costs specified above.

Therefore, *lock-in* refers to the effect whereby the consumer remains with the original provider even when there is a desire to switch, which may arise from price increases, failures, defects in the supply of the product or service, data breaches, or lack of privacy.[99] However, when the consumer weighs the cost-benefit of a potential switch, they realize that changing to an alternative provider would be more costly—whether financially, emotionally, or in terms of convenience.[100]

Furthermore, the effect may also be present in businesses that provide services in the aftermarket, which may include parts, maintenance, consulting, and upgrades. Generally, the company offering the service in the aftermarket is the same owner of the equipment requiring the service and may even be the sole provider of such service.[101] Coercion of the consumer in this secondary market can be subtle or even implemented through abusive and anticompetitive practices, such as tying arrangements.

Some examples can be found that are quite close to our daily lives. For instance, Nespresso sells a combination of coffee machines and coffee capsules, which ensures a steady stream of revenue over a long period through the sale of the capsules. Similarly, manufacturers sell printers at low prices but benefit in the long term from the sale of ink cartridges, which are not so inexpensive.[102] A famous case was that of Kodak,[103] a manufacturer and seller of copiers as well as replacement parts for them, some produced by Kodak itself and others by third parties at its request. However, in order to purchase the parts, consumers were required to use Kodak's own maintenance services, making it impossible for third parties to provide such services. This situation was deemed abusive and anticompetitive by the US Supreme Court.[104]

A similar case, but pertaining to Brazilian territory, was the Xerox case, adjudicated by CADE in 1993, in administrative proceeding no. 23/91. The subject of the case concerned market dominance and the elimination of competition through the

---

97 Engels (2016).

98 The literature reviewed for this study reveals different approaches to the relationship between lock-in and switching costs. While some authors regard lock-in as a consequence or development of switching costs, others treat the two concepts as synonymous. The latter view is reflected, for example, in the study by Eurich and Burtscher (2014), p. 3.

99 Eurich and Burtscher (2014), p. 3.

100 Murray and Häubl (2007), p. 2.

101 Borenstein et al. (1995), p. 2.

102 Eurich and Burtscher (2014), p. 3.

103 United States of America. *Eastman Kodak Co. v. Image Technical Servs. Inc.*, 504 U.S. 451, 458 (1992).

104 United States of America. *Eastman Kodak Co. v. Image Technical Servs. Inc.*, 504 U.S. 451, 458 (1992).

practice of tying sales. In its defense, Xerox argued that the actions it allegedly undertook were aimed solely and exclusively at protecting its property, brand, concept, reputation, and the quality of its products and services.[105]

These actions concerned the imposition of contractual clauses that prevented its clients from using competitors' parts, such as toners and developers, in Xerox copiers. As this restriction lacked technical justification, CADE found the conduct to be abusive and detrimental to competition, which led to Xerox's conviction by the Tribunal.

This decision by CADE was challenged in court, and in 2013 the Federal Regional Court of the 1st Region[106] ruled that the contractual clause in question, supported by the evidence in the case records, constituted tying, which is expressly prohibited under our legal system.

In addition to these, another paradigmatic case was the United States v. Microsoft Corporation,[107] which concerned the accusation brought by the Department of Justice against Microsoft Corporation for tying practices, specifically favoring the Internet Explorer browser to the detriment of competitors such as Netscape Navigator and Opera. In this case, Microsoft manipulated application programming interfaces, imposed contractual licensing clauses requiring the use of only original equipment developed by Microsoft Corporation, and engaged in boycott practices, such as deliberately slowing down downloads for competitors' browsers.

In response to this accusation, Microsoft Corporation argued that the operating system and the web browser had become a single product as a result of an innovation process. The case was subsequently settled through an agreement that imposed a series of obligations on Microsoft Corporation in order to prevent the recurrence of the reported practices.

Another business model that fits the lock-in effect pattern is the so-called *Freemium*, which combines *free* and *premium* services. In this model, there is a segment of free services and additional ones that are charged. The free component attracts a large user base and, when interconnected with the premium offering, increases demand for the latter.[108]

The model developed by Skype is an example of what is known as "Freemium." Using the voice over Internet Protocol (IP), its users can make video and voice calls for free. By adding the premium service, it is possible to call landlines or mobile phones using a debit account.[109] Other examples include Evernote and Dropbox,[110] each with its own unique features.

Well, the lock-in effect in the "Freemium" model operates as follows: the more users utilize the product, the more value it acquires in the market, thereby

[105] Brazil. Administrative Council for Economic Defense. *Case No.* 23/91. Decided in 1993.

[106] Brazil. Federal Regional Court of the 1st Region. Civil Appeal No. 0031266-06.2001.4.01.0000. Rapporteur: Judge Selene Maria de Almeida. Judged on 07/01/2013.

[107] United States of America. *United States District Court for the District of Columbia.* United States v. Microsoft Corporation, 2002.

[108] Eurich and Burtscher (2014), p. 3.

[109] Eurich and Burtscher (2014), p. 3.

[110] Shmilovici (2011).

increasing the dependency of its users, who often exchange information with individuals who, in turn, must also use the service. This is exemplified by a telecommunications tool where everyone needs to be a user of the intermediary application.

As a result, any potential change incurs switching costs, which will influence the consumer to remain with the same service,[111] since for a change to make sense, the other users with whom they interact would also need to switch services. When an entire group adopts the model, leaving becomes virtually unfeasible, resulting in a lock-in effect.

Hence, users remain with the original service and consequently exceed the free tier, becoming paying premium users. As stated, this new status arises essentially due to the lock-in effect, because if this effect did not exist, when the user reached the limit, instead of becoming a premium user, they could migrate to another provider.[112]

Furthermore, when analyzing the lock-in effect resulting from switching and search costs, it is essential to address network effects. The interaction between these effects and switching costs is a central topic in the new economy comprised of information technology industries,[113] a situation referred to as *network lock-in* or *path dependence.*[114]

These effects are related to (i) compatibility[115] among users, enabling them to interact, trade with each other, or use the same add-ons, which creates an economy of scope among different users,[116] or (ii) the situation in which increased consumption of a product or service raises its value,[117] thereby attracting new and future users who will find the business more appealing.[118]

Network effects can be compared to the effect experienced when we acquire a certain utility, such as learning a second language: it becomes increasingly useful as more people also speak it. The same applies to communication devices: mobile phones and fax machines were not as useful before the number of owners of these devices multiplied. Thus, utility increases as the number of consumers using them grows.[119] In the technological sphere, to offer another example, a messaging application only becomes relevant if there are other people using the service.[120]

---

111 Shmilovici (2011).

112 Shmilovici (2011).

113 Farrell and Klemperer (2007), p. 1971.

114 Yosifon (2012), p. 1456.

115 Email services provide a clear example of this phenomenon. Users not only seek a service that is easy to use or free of charge but also derive value from the fact that other people use email and that different email services are mutually compatible. Afuah (2013), p. 257.

116 Farrell and Klemperer (2007), p. 1971.

117 Chen and Hitt (2018), p. 17.

118 Engels (2016).

119 Farrell and Klemperer (2007), p. 2007.

120 Balfour (2012).

The most diverse industries, ranging from banks to telecommunications companies, benefit from these network effects. These industries have become dependent on such effects.[121]

For Google, to give an example, it is necessary to connect the indicated websites and the users of the search engine. On the Airbnb hosting platform, there is a relationship between guests and hosts;[122] on eBay, between buyers and sellers; on Visa, between merchants and credit card holders.[123]

It should be noted that network effects are so significant that they enable the maintenance of market power over an extended period, even when the product or service performs poorly or there are other competitors.[124] As a result, even if there is a more efficient competitor with superior technology or more attractive prices, a change of provider will not necessarily occur, since the migration of the majority of users would be required, given that the user experience depends on the collective participation of these users[125] or on compatibility.

Thus, it is evident that the service only performs adequately and as expected because of the number of its users.[126] As a result, a problem is recognized: new entrants will face significant difficulty in achieving a network effect and will ultimately encounter the "chicken and egg" problem: their service has no market value because it lacks a substantial user base; on the other hand, the service lacks users because it has no value.[127]

The issue of competition in products and services that follow this pattern is peculiar, as there is typically an all-or-nothing competition. In this market structure, consumers do not seek products that perfectly match their personal preferences but rather those products or services that emerge as winners, with the entire market going to the victor (*the winner takes it all*).[128]

Ultimately, variety—an important driver for the exercise of consumer choice—is undermined in markets characterized by network effects and switching costs, which arise from the inability of a new provider to offer a service compatible with the mainstream.[129] In other words, it is difficult for a provider to make available a competing service that enables interoperability between its users and those of the dominant services.

In this context, it is intuitive to state that the entry of new players into markets characterized by network effects and switching costs is highly unlikely, which constitutes a social cost of incompatibility. This difficulty stems from the absence of an installed user base for potential entrants and from consumers' lack of interest in

---

[121] Afuah (2013), p. 257.

[122] Van Alstyne (2016).

[123] Parker and Van Alstyne (2005), p. 1504.

[124] Balfour (2012).

[125] Chen and Hitt (2018), p. 15.

[126] Chen and Hitt (2018), p. 15.

[127] Balfour (2012).

[128] Farrell and Klemperer (2007), p. 1975.

[129] Farrell and Klemperer (2007), p. 1975.

contracting with new companies, especially given the "all or nothing" competition pattern and the "winner takes it all" dynamic,[130] as previously mentioned.

Another point of utmost relevance concerns the activity of data collection in markets where network effects are present. The more consumers are attracted by the value of the product or service, the more data can be collected, which in turn enhances the other side of the market—namely, advertising services in two-sided market models[131]—and generates a competitive advantage.

In most cases, users' data cannot be extracted when they wish to migrate to a competitor, as switching platforms is only possible at the cost of leaving and consequently losing their data.[132] This highlights the situation faced by users: if there is an increase in service price, a reduction in privacy protection, and a decline in quality, among other scenarios, the user is left completely unprotected, as their bargaining power is diminished. Thus, they must either remain and accept the new conditions imposed or leave without the data accumulated over time.[133] This, therefore, constitutes a form of lock-in, in which switching costs are related to the retention of data.

To further exacerbate the situation, it is reported that the risk of lock-in is the rule rather than the exception when it comes to online platforms. Companies have incentives and interests in keeping their systems closed, which creates access barriers for other companies that require user data to compete or to offer complementary services and products.[134]

In the search service, which is the one where the consumer seeks information—examples being Google, Yahoo, and Bing—the switching costs between mechanisms are high. It is worth noting that user lock-in is desirable for these companies, since the more users a search service has, the more attractive it becomes for advertising. There have even been reports of exclusive contracts between search services and their advertisers, as well as restrictions on the portability of advertisements.[135]

In this regard, reference is made to Administrative Proceeding No. 08700.005694/2013-19,[136] which was conducted before CADE, initiated following a complaint filed by Microsoft Corporation. This proceeding concerned the possible abuse of market power by Google Inc. and Google Brasil Internet Ltda., through the imposition of restrictions in the provision of services on Google's online advertising platform (AdWords). The contested practice involved the imposition of contractual clauses that prevented multihoming,[137] that is, the simultaneous use of multiple platforms.

---

[130] Farrell and Klemperer (2007), p. 1972.

[131] EDPS (2014).

[132] Engels (2016).

[133] Engels (2016).

[134] Engels (2016).

[135] Engels (2016).

[136] Brazil. Administrative Council for Economic Defense. *Case No. 08700.005694/2013-19*. Available at <http://sei.cade.gov.br/>.

[137] Carol Elizabeth Conway defines *multihoming* as the use of more than one sponsored search platform by the same advertiser. Conway (2015), p. 246. Conway (2015), p. 246.

It was thus argued that Google hindered the development of cross-platform campaign management software tools, making it difficult to compare performance and usage. Furthermore, it was contended that advertisers' data could not be used on other sponsored search platforms,[138] thereby undermining competition from rival platforms.

However, in an extraordinary judgment session, the Administrative Council for Economic Defense (CADE) decided to close the case. The agency concluded that the contractual clauses used by Google, although common in licensing and adhesion contracts, did not exhibit anticompetitive characteristics.

Similarly, in online marketplaces, which are platforms where consumers buy, sell, and share products and services, there are switching costs, particularly on the sellers' side of the commerce platform. In this regard, reputation and reviews of sales can be considered a platform-specific investment, as they depend on the number of transactions already completed.[139]

For consumers, although switching costs are generally low in online *marketplaces*, such costs may be imposed through the charging of an exit fee. Furthermore, familiarity with the platform's rules and its mode of use can create a lock-in effect.[140]

With regard to social networks, whose main sides are users and advertisers, switching costs are high. Although it is possible to obtain copies of certain data, transferring a profile to a competing service requires time and effort, given that there is no possibility of extracting data in a format that can easily be imported by another corresponding social network.[141]

Furthermore, contacts and shared information, such as messages, comments, and photographs, as a rule, cannot be transferred to other platforms. It is important to note the incompatibility that generates *network lock-in*: users cannot communicate across different platforms (inter-platform communication), which encourages them, as a rule, to use the largest networks in order to interact fully with the greatest possible number of users.[142] Such concerns could, however, be mitigated if social networks were to provide mechanisms that facilitate data export, as pointed out by Christopher Yoo.[143]

In the cloud services market (*cloud computing*), which is defined as a model that enables ubiquitous, convenient, and on-demand access to a pool of configurable computing resources, such as infrastructure, software, and platform resources,[144] switching costs are markedly high, making interoperability and portability necessary for users to be able to utilize other cloud services.[145]

---

138 Conway (2015), p. 246.

139 Engels (2016).

140 Engels (2016).

141 Engels (2016).

142 Engels (2016).

143 Yoo (2012), p. 1155.

144 Wang and Shah (2017).

145 Engels (2016).

Thus, in general terms and regardless of the market as discussed above, if a user wishes to switch platforms or services, they will need to make additional and substantial investments to provide the data again,[146] when this is possible. In such cases, the costs incurred may be considered *sunk costs*,[147] which are those unrecoverable costs incurred in the past.[148]

The effects of this situation can be observed not only among direct competitors (substitutes) but also in complementary services. In both scenarios, the number of users is positively correlated with the volume and quality of data.[149] Moreover, the volume and quality of data are related to the variety and quality of products and services, since companies are able to offer better products by more effectively analyzing user behavior and extracting data obtained through the provision of the service.[150]

Digital markets are characterized by structural mechanisms that limit consumer mobility and undermine effective competition over time. Search costs, switching costs, and network effects operate in combination to create situations of lasting lock-in, in which users' continued engagement with certain services results less from free and informed choices and more from economic, informational, and behavioral constraints. Even when there is ex ante competition, commercial strategies such as penetration pricing, introductory offers, and the subsequent exploitation of a captive user base tend to weaken ex post competitive discipline, enabling the extraction of supra-competitive rents and leading consumers to tolerate price increases, loss of quality, or violations of privacy.

The interaction between switching costs and network effects reinforces this scenario by consolidating cumulative competitive advantages, hindering the entry of new players, and favoring market structures characterized by a winner takes all logic. The centrality of data intensifies structural lock-in, as its accumulation and retention increase the market power of incumbent agents and reduce users' bargaining power. In this context, variety, innovation, and the right to choose are progressively restricted, demonstrating that structural lock-in constitutes a recurring failure of the digital economy and a central challenge for the legal and regulatory analysis of data-driven markets.

References

Afuah A (2013) Are network effects really all about size? The role of structure and conduct. Strateg Manag J 34:257–273

American Antitrust Institute (2017) The post-Chicago school. http://www.antitrustinstitute.org/content/post-chicago-school

---

[146] Dzhain (2014), p. 74.

[147] Dzhain (2014), p. 74.

[148] Wang and Yang (2001).

[149] Engels (2016).

[150] Engels (2016).

Article 29 Data Protection Working Party (2016) Guidelines on the right to data portability. European Commission, Brussels

Balfour B (2012) Achieving the network effect: solving the chicken or the egg. https://brianbalfour.com/essays/the-network-effect-marketplaces

Borenstein S, MacKie-Mason J, Netz J (1995) The economics of customer lock-in and market power in services. Springer, Dordrecht

Bourgoignie T (1993) Droits des consommateurs et marché économique: une perspective doctrinale. Story-Scientia, Brussels

Cabanellas de las Cuevas G (2005) Derecho antimonopólico y de defensa de la competencia. Heliasta, Buenos Aires

Carpena H (2005) Consumidor no direito da concorrência. Renovar, Rio de Janeiro

Chen P-Y, Hitt L (2018) Information technology and switching costs. http://citeseerx.ist.psu.edu/viewdoc/download?doi=10.1.1.458.1995

Conway CE (2015) Concorrência: a Lei 12.529/2011 e os e-mercados. In: Carvalho VM (ed) A Lei 12.529/2011 e a nova política de defesa da concorrência. Singular, São Paulo, pp 255–268

Cseres KJ (2006) The impact of consumer protection on competition and competition law: the case of deregulated markets. Amsterdam Center for Law & Economics Working Paper No. 05

Diker Vanberg A, Ünver M (2017) The right to data portability in the GDPR and EU competition law: odd couple or dynamic duo? Eur J Law Technol 8(1)

Dzhain N (2014) Impact of switching costs and network effects on adoption of mobile platforms. Dissertation, Aalto University School of Business

Engels B (2016) Data portability among online platforms. Internet Policy Rev 5(2)

Eurich M, Burtscher M (2014) The business-to-consumer lock-in effect. University of Cambridge, Cambridge

European Data Protection Supervisor (2014) Privacy and competitiveness in the age of big data. EDPS, Brussels

Farrell J, Klemperer P (2007) Coordination and lock-in: competition with switching costs and network effects. In: Armstrong M, Porter R (eds) Handbook of industrial organization, vol 3. Elsevier, North-Holland, pp 1968–2072

Forgioni PA (2008) Os fundamentos do antitruste. Revista dos Tribunais, São Paulo

Frazão A (2015) A análise de eficiências em atos de concentração sob o enfoque do princípio retributivo. In: Carvalho VM (ed) A Lei 12.529/2011 e a nova política de defesa da concorrência. Singular, São Paulo, pp 181–200

Geradin D, Kuschewsky M (2013) Competition law and personal data: preliminary thoughts on a complex issue. https://papers.ssrn.com/sol3/papers.cfm?abstract_id=2216088

Glória DFDA (2003) A livre concorrência como garantia do consumidor. Del Rey, Belo Horizonte

Jaeger Junior A (2006) A liberdade de concorrência na União Europeia e no Mercosul. LTR, São Paulo

Jayme E (2003) Direito internacional privado e cultura pós-moderna. Cad Programa Pós-Graduação Direito PPGDir/UFRGS 1(1):59–68

Kisyombe M (2012) Emerging issues in consumer protection: complementarities and areas of tension. UNCTAD, Geneva

Lande RH (2010) Consumer choice as the best way to recenter the mission of competition law. Edward Elgar, Academic Society for Competition Law

Lande RH, Averitt NW (2003) A escolha do consumidor: uma razão prática para o direito antitruste e o direito de defesa do consumidor. Rev Direito Consumidor 45:26–50

Lopes JRL (2000) Direito da concorrência e direito do consumidor. Rev Direito Consumidor 34:79–87

Lorenzetti R (2001) Comercio electrónico. Abeledo-Perrot, Buenos Aires

Marques CL (2010) Superação das antinomias pelo diálogo das fontes: o modelo brasileiro de coexistência entre o Código de Defesa do Consumidor e o Código Civil de 2002. In: Azevedo AJ, Tôrres HT, Carbone P (eds) Princípios do novo Código Civil brasileiro e outros temas: homenagem a Tullio Ascarelli, 2nd edn Quartier Latin, São Paulo, pp 129–167

Marques CL (2012) O diálogo das fontes como método da nova teoria geral do direito: um tributo a Erik Jayme. In: Marques CL (coord) Diálogo das fontes: do conflito à coordenação de normas do direito brasileiro. Revista dos Tribunais, São Paulo, pp 17–66
Martinez AP (2004) A defesa dos interesses dos consumidores pelo direito da concorrência. Rev Ibrac 11(1):67–99
Mattiuzzo M (2014) Propaganda online e privacidade: o varejo de dados pessoais na perspectiva antitruste. Prêmio SEAE, Brasília
Meledo-Briand D (2000) A consideração do interesse do consumidor e o direito da concorrência. Rev Direito Consumidor 35:39–59
Moreira EB (2006) Os princípios constitucionais da atividade econômica. Rev Fac Direito UFPR 45:109–120
Murray K, Häubl G (2007) Explaining cognitive lock-in: the role of skill-based habits of use in consumer choice. J Consum Res 34:1–12
OECD (2008) Enhancing competition in telecommunications: protecting and empowering consumers. https://www.oecd.org/sti/consumer/40679279.pdf
Office of Fair Trading (2003) Switching costs. OFT, London
Parker G, Van Alstyne M (2005) Two-sided network effects: a theory of information product design. Manag Sci 51(10):1494–1504
Pfeiffer RAC (2015) Defesa da concorrência e bem-estar do consumidor. Revista dos Tribunais, São Paulo
Piraino TA Jr (2007) Reconciling the Harvard and Chicago Schools: a new antitrust approach for the 21st century. Indiana Law J 82:346–409
Pitofsky R (2008) Introduction: setting the stage. In: Pitofsky R (ed) How the Chicago school overshot the mark: the effect of conservative economic analysis on U.S. antitrust. Oxford University Press, Oxford, pp 4–5
Posner R (1979) The Chicago school of antitrust analysis. Univ Pa Law Rev 127:925–948
Salomão Filho C (2003) Direito concorrencial: as condutas. Malheiros, São Paulo
Sampaio PRP (2013) Regulação e concorrência. Saraiva, São Paulo
Sanne C (2002) Willing consumers or locked-in? Policies for a sustainable consumption. Ecol Econ 42:273–287
Shmilovici U (2011) The complete guide to freemium business models. TechCrunch. https://techcrunch.com/2011/09/04/complete-guide-freemium/
Van Alstyne M (2016) A platform strategy: creating new forms of value in the digital age. Capgemini Consulting
Wang Y, Shah A (2017) Supporting data portability in the cloud under the GDPR. http://alicloud-common.oss-ap-southeast-1.aliyuncs.com/Supporting_Data_Portability_in_the_Cloud_Under_the_GDPR.pdf
Wang H, Yang B (2001) Fixed and sunk costs revisited. J Econ Educ 32:178–185
Whish R (2001) Competition law. Butterworths, London
Wisniewski CH (2019) Violação de dados pessoais pode ser um desafio antitruste? http://pincade.cade.gov.br/images/Caio-Henrique%2D%2D-Artigo.pdf
Yoo C (2012) When antitrust met Facebook. Geo Mason Law Rev 19(5):1147–1162
Yosifon D (2012) Consumer lock-in and the theory of the firm. Seattle Univ Law Rev 35:1429–1467

Chapter 6
Data as Market Power

6.1 Competition Law in the Data Economy

In the context of the digital economy, data has become the essential input for innovation and the development of new business models. However, the transition to a truly data-driven economy faces significant structural challenges, notably the fragmentation of ecosystems and regulatory frictions that hinder the legitimate and secure flow of information. Against this backdrop, this chapter examines how the competition law framework, in dialogue with sectoral regulation, can serve as a driver for optimizing data reuse or, conversely, how its obstruction through anticompetitive practices can exacerbate market inefficiency.

The starting point for reducing fragmentation lies in understanding the residual and transversal nature of competition law enforcement. This residual nature stems from the fact that, in the absence of specific sectoral legislation that expressly excludes the application of competition rules, these rules must apply fully to any acts that have the potential to produce harmful effects on the economic order.

This application of competition law, in general, constitutes a sound institutional practice widely recognized by international organizations.[1] Based on this premise of universality, the rule is established that competition rules must be applied across all sectors of the economy and to all economic agents, without ad hoc exceptions that could undermine the integrity of the market.

This guideline is primarily based on the principle of competitive neutrality, which holds that antitrust legal provisions must ensure strictly equal treatment for both private companies and public entities engaged in economic activities.[2] From this perspective, state intervention in the prevention and repression of anticompetitive conduct does not allow for distinctions based on the legal nature or

[1] UNCTAD (2002), p. 2.

[2] UNCTAD (2002), p. 2.

D. Copetti Cravo, *Law and the Digital Economy*,
https://doi.org/10.1007/978-3-032-36672-6_6

ownership of the agent, ensuring that the regime of free competition prevails over any attempt to distort market structures, regardless of the origin of capital or the public nature of the activity performed.

It should be noted, however, that competition is only one of the possible forms of state intervention and thus constitutes a specific type thereof. Although there is no doctrinal consensus regarding the terms and types of state intervention,[3] for Eros Grau[4] state action is a generic expression that encompasses the state's activities in public services as well as in areas under private sector ownership (economic activities). The term intervention, on the other hand, refers exclusively to state action in economic activities.

This intervention, according to the classification of Eros Grau,[5] takes two forms: the first, also known as intervention in the economic domain, is when the state acts as an economic agent. This can occur through absorption, when the state fully assumes the means of production and operates under a monopoly regime; or through participation, when the state takes on part of the means of production and competes "with private companies that continue to operate in the same sector."

The second is intervention in the economic domain, in which the state acts as a regulator of economic activity. This intervention may take the form of direction, where the state exerts pressure on the economy through compulsory, binding, and imperative rules aimed at the subjects of economic activity in the strict sense, or induction, in which the state manipulates intervention instruments in accordance with the laws governing the markets but always in a dispositive manner. Such induction may be implemented either positively or negatively.[6] From this classification by Eros Grau,[7] it can be inferred that regulation and competition fall within intervention in the economic domain, more specifically within intervention by direction.

Diogo de Figueiredo Moreira Neto[8] classifies state interventions into four types: regulatory, competitive, monopolistic, and sanctioning. Furthermore, José dos Santos Carvalho Filho[9] states that the state acts in the economic order in two ways, namely, as regulator and as executor. In its regulatory capacity, the state may engage in regulation, repression of economic power abuse, supply control, and price fixing.

In any case, since regulation and competition are both forms of regulation in the broad sense[10] or of state intervention in the economic domain (without delving into

---

[3] Aragão (2013), p. 1833.

[4] Grau (2006), pp. 148–151.

[5] Grau (2006), pp. 148–151.

[6] Grau (2006), pp. 148–151.

[7] Grau (2006), pp. 148–151.

[8] Moreira Neto (2003), p. 129.

[9] Carvalho Filho (2013), p. 915.

[10] It should be considered that, broadly speaking, every market is regulated. Furthermore, not all regulation is essentially focused on sensitive economic issues, such as criteria for setting tariffs and capital remuneration; it may also concern the technical regulation of standards and targets to be observed by economic agents. Oliveira and Rodas (2013), p. 137.

terminological disputes), it is necessary to examine how these two will interact, in order to determine whether they can coexist or if one will exclude the other.

These possibilities pertain to different institutional arrangements, as elucidated by Gesner de Oliveira and João Grandino Rodas[11] in the following manner: (1) antitrust exemption: sectoral regulations take precedence over competition rules, so that it is the responsibility of regulatory authorities to weigh competition issues; (2) concurrent jurisdiction: a situation in which competition law is enforced by both regulatory authorities and competition authorities; (3) complementary competencies: in this case, regulatory authorities focus solely on technical and economic regulation, while competition authorities complement this by applying competition rules; (4) antitrust regulation: the competition authority is responsible for enforcing both antitrust legislation and regulatory rules, with the former prevailing; (5) deregulation: only competition law is applied.

Comparing these possible arrangements with our legal system, it becomes evident that the Constitution did not choose one over the other; instead, it placed the defense of competition (Article 173, §4) and regulation (Article 174, *caput*) side by side within the economic order. This contrasts with what occurred in the European Union, where the Treaty on the Functioning of the European Union provides for the possibility of antitrust exemptions.

Accordingly, in Brazil, the prevailing model is one of complementary jurisdictions, according to the classification by Gesner de Oliveira and João Grandino Rodas.[12] In this regard, former CADE Commissioner Ricardo Villas Bôas Cueva argued in his concurring opinion in Administrative Proceeding No. 08012.007443/99-17[13] that there should be no question of the predominance of either regulatory or antitrust legislation, since there is, in fact, an undeniable relationship of complementarity between them.

There are situations, however, in which this complementarity may appear as an apparent antinomy of norms, thus becoming a *hard case.* These are cases in which the regulatory norm permits conduct that, from an antitrust perspective, would be considered unlawful.

Precisely to resolve such a conflict, the *State Action Doctrine* was developed in American law. This doctrine emerged with the case of Parker v. Brown[14] in 1943 and sought to establish that the act of the regulator, a public act in the strict sense, would be covered by an antitrust exemption, in order to enable the sovereign adoption and implementation of public policies.[15] Furthermore, the doctrine was conceived to ensure respect for federalism, especially considering situations in which regulatory acts were carried out by state entities.

---

[11] Oliveira and Rodas (2013), p. 149.

[12] Oliveira and Rodas (2013), p. 149.

[13] Brazil. Administrative Council for Economic Defense. Case No. 08012.007443/99-17.

[14] Inman (1996), p. 1251.

[15] Taufick (2010).

This theory was recently applied by the Superior Court of Justice (STJ),[16] when it overturned a decision by the Federal Regional Court of the 4th Region, which had convicted gas distribution companies in Porto Alegre and Canoas for cartel formation due to price fixing and rotation in sales. Considering that this price fixing was imposed by the Public Authority and the rotation was authorized by the National Department of Fuels, the STJ found that the requirements of the *State Action Doctrine* were met, for the following reasons: (1) there was regulation; (2) the state required the companies to comply with the regulation, supervising them; and (3) the regulation served a public purpose.

Thus, it should be understood that, as a rule and in light of the above, Brazil establishes the simultaneous application of regulatory and competition rules. This means that the existence of regulation does not automatically grant competitive immunity to the economic agent.

Exceptionally, regulatory norms may exclude antitrust analysis.[17,18] However, this will only apply to specific cases that meet the following criteria summarized in CADE Case No. 08012.005422/2003-03:[19] (1) the regulation must be clearly embedded in a public policy that opts for the substitution of competition, and (2) there must be effective supervision and oversight of the regulatory obligations imposed on private entities.

Having addressed this necessary preliminary issue, we proceed to analyze the operationalization of data access and sharing through competition law provisions, in order to assess (1) whether a refusal to grant access to or share data may constitute a violation of economic order; (2) under which category such conduct would fall; (3) what the requirements for such a finding are; (4) whether additional regulatory measures are necessary; and (5) whether data portability or another data-sharing mechanism may be applied as an antitrust remedy.

Well, the emergence of antitrust law was triggered by the rise, in the United States, of trusts and large conglomerates in the fields of steel, transportation, and

---

[16] Brazil. Superior Court of Justice. *Special Appeal No. 1,390,875*. Justice Napoleão Nunes Maia Filho. Judged on June 9, 2015.

[17] International organizations and specific studies that have examined the legal systems of various countries around the world recommend that competition rules should only be set aside in exceptional circumstances, as follows: (1) Exemptions should be granted for a limited period, with a "sunset" clause and provisions for periodic review. (2) The review of exemptions should include an analysis of their impact on economic efficiency and consumer welfare, and, within a cost-benefit framework, the "winners" and "losers" should be identified, as well as whether there are primary benefits to consumers or to broader economic interests. (3) Exemptions should be granted only after public hearings with the participation of interested and affected parties. (4) Exemptions should be as minimally restrictive as possible. (5) Exemptions should be generic in nature, relating to types of activities or economic arrangements. UNCTAD (2002), p. 2.

[18] Calixto Salomão Filho argues that the replacement of the competitive system by regulation can even occur implicitly, when such extensive powers are granted to the regulatory authority that it is required to take competitive aspects into account in its decisions. Salomão Filho (2003), p. 278.

[19] Brazil. Administrative Council for Economic Defense. *Administrative Proceeding No. 08012.005422/2003-03*. Reporting Commissioner Gilvandro Vasconcelos Coelho de Araujo.

electricity. The symbol of the era was John D. Rockefeller, of the Standard Oil Trust, depicted in the popular press as a menacing octopus with far-reaching tentacles encircling American territory.[20] All of this culminated in the policy of the trust-busters[21] and the Sherman Act of 1890, legislation that inspired numerous laws around the world.

It seems that history is repeating itself: now, in the digital market. As previously highlighted, the current economy is based on major winners, characterized by players who hold, on average, 80–90% of the market.[22] For comparison, Brazilian competition law presumes a dominant position when at least 20% of the relevant market is controlled (Article 36, §2, of Law 12,529/2011).[23] In other words, controlling 80–90% of the market is extremely concerning.

Alongside the emergence of large corporations, significant competition concerns arise, given that their ability to impact the market is far greater than that of small or medium-sized enterprises in a fragmented market. This concern was evident, for example, in the acquisition of Whole Foods by Amazon,[24] which demonstrated the possibility of a single digital company dominating multiple sectors of the economy.

As a result of the significant power accumulated by corporations, concerns regarding the impact of this power on democracy have resurfaced. It is worth noting that the origins of antitrust law were conceived in light of this very issue, as highlighted in the judgment of the United States v. Columbia Steel Co.:[25] the curse of being large poses a threat to democracy and to social, industrial, and political structures.

---

[20] Peritz (1996), p. 9.

[21] Soon after the Sherman Act came into force, major cases were prosecuted, which attracted enormous public interest. As a result, groups supporting antitrust enforcement became known as the Trust Busters. Among them was Theodore Roosevelt, who was launching his campaign for the US presidency in 1904. This effort was continued by Roosevelt's presidential successor, William Howard Taft. Rogers (2013), p. 13.

[22] Van Alstyne (2016), p. 3.

[23] It should be noted, however, that this presumption is relative. Brazilian antitrust legislation has not adopted only the criterion of *market share* but also that of *market power*. Paula Forgioni explains that a high market share by a company does not always indicate the existence of a dominant position. Likewise, a small market share does not, in itself, mean the absence of power. Forgioni (2008), p. 333.

[24] FTC (2007).

[25] The United States, pursuant to § 4 of the Sherman Act, brought an action against the acquisition by United States Steel Corporation of the assets of Consolidated Steel Corporation, the largest independent steel manufacturer on the West Coast, alleging a violation of §§ 1 and 2 of the Act. The essence of the complaint was (1) that the acquisition would restrain trade, because all manufacturers other than United States Steel would be excluded from supplying Consolidated's requirements for rolled steel products and because the existing competition between Consolidated and United in the sale of fabricated structural products and pipes would be eliminated, and (2) that the proposed acquisition, in light of United States Steel's previous acquisitions, constituted an attempt to monopolize the production and sale of fabricated steel products in the United States, a consolidated market area. United States of America. Supreme Court. *United States v. Columbia Steel Co.* 334 U.S. 495. Decided in June 1948.

It should be noted that the purpose of antitrust has never been to directly address political issues at the macro level.[26] However, it can indeed contribute to this objective by fulfilling its role of reducing or preventing the concentration of power.

Currently, the issue has resurfaced, albeit in a new guise. In October 2017, legal representatives from Facebook, Google, and Twitter participated in discussions in the United States Congress regarding possible Russian interference in the 2016 United States presidential election.[27] Some argue that the business model of these companies, particularly due to their algorithms, has facilitated, even if unintentionally, the spread of false news, resulting in disproportionate impacts on the elections.[28]

Although the concerns remain the same—market power concentration and abuses—the business model is different. There has undoubtedly been a transformation of both the economy and society. Whereas previously there were predatory prices, today there are free services. In other words, competition is no longer about prices but rather about data and algorithms.[29]

As previously analyzed, data is one of the primary inputs of the digital economy. Indeed, various new forms of market advantage are being implemented, such as the manipulation of consumers through information held about them by their counterparts (whether state or private entities), as noted by Fabiano Menke.[30]

Note that, in this case, the holder of the information invariably assumes a privileged position, taking shortcuts. Thus, the power of manipulation and steering arises, since the relationship does not develop "from scratch," as it would in a chance encounter.

Although data are generally "free," nonexclusive, and non-rivalrous, access to them remains difficult. This is because the infrastructure for data collection, storage, and distribution is typically embedded with technological barriers; in addition, there are legal and behavioral barriers to access.[31]

In light of competition law studies,[32] it is observed that companies which have experienced significant turnovers in the market typically base their business models on the use of data, generally personal data, obtained through the large number of users in their respective sectors. The most prominent examples of this are Google Search and Facebook.[33]

Furthermore, it is acknowledged that companies make significant investments to collect and store more data and seek to prevent third parties from accessing them,[34]

---

[26] Shapiro (2017).

[27] Hendrickson and Galston (2017).

[28] Illing (2017).

[29] Conway (2015), p. 257.

[30] Menke (2014), p. 211.

[31] Lundqvist (2018).

[32] Autorité de la Concurrence and Bundeskartellamt (2016).

[33] Autorité de la Concurrence and Bundeskartellamt (2016).

[34] Stucke and Grunes (2016).

which may create obstacles to the development[35] of horizontal or complementary services. The creation of barriers to data access may be related to refusal to deal and may be considered an abuse of dominant position.[36,37]

The occurrence of data-driven mergers was also observed. These transactions may have enabled companies to acquire personal data for the development of products and services aimed at the targeted online advertising market or to enter other markets.[38] Such situations are concerning due to network effects, which make it difficult to challenge the dominant position of agents with large-scale access to data. When a company is successful in the market, attracting new customers becomes almost automatic, contributing to the "winner takes all" phenomenon.[39]

Therefore, the current priority is to ensure that competition in these markets functions effectively.[40] Since the collection, processing, and use of user data for commercial purposes ultimately constitute a competitive advantage, fairer competition may be achievable through data portability, especially if this is combined with other tools such as interoperability.

In this context, large companies may end up adopting measures to prevent or hinder such data migration between providers.[41] Consequently, can these practices be subject to antitrust scrutiny?

---

35 As an example, reference is made to the FCT investigation involving Google AdWords.

36 Such behaviors may also be related to interoperability limitations through the creation of obstacles to data transfer between platforms and restrictions on the use of APIs. In this regard, reference is made to the lawsuit filed by the FTC against Facebook in 2020.

37 However, it is not clear whether the refusal to provide data to competitors would constitute a refusal to contract/negotiate within the context of competition law, particularly given the requirement to demonstrate indispensability (OECD 2021). In Brazil, CADE decided to initiate administrative proceedings to investigate a possible abuse of dominant position by Bradesco in the financial market (GuiaBolso/Bradesco Case). The authority found that, although the conduct did not amount to an explicit refusal (there was a requirement for two-factor authentication to access banking information), there were indications of a possible abuse of dominant position. During the investigation, in 2020, the bank agreed to cease the conduct and signed a Term of Commitment, undertaking to implement an interoperability mechanism to allow GuiaBolso to access its Internet banking system, until the Central Bank of Brazil's open banking regulation comes into effect. OECD (2021).

38 Motta (2021).

39 CADE (2021).

40 Indeed, it is possible for anticompetitive practices to be employed in order to acquire a dominant position, which would ensure greater access to data, as well as the abuse of any existing market position. Such abuse may occur through the leveraging of complementary services or by creating obstacles to the development of competing, substitute, or complementary services. In this regard, reference is made to the European Commission case concerning Google Shopping: European Commission. *39740 Google Search (Shopping)*. In this case, the Commission identified clear evidence of an attempt to leverage Google Shopping, which is systematically positioned and prominently displayed on the Google Search results page. Unlike its competitors, Google Shopping (1) does not follow the organic ranking system, (2) appears above both sponsored and organic results, and (3) receives an additional advantage, namely, visual appeal through photographs, which is not subject to negotiation. In Brazil, a similar case was dismissed by CADE. Brazil. Administrative Council for Economic Defense. Case No. 08700.009083/2013-03.

41 Geradin and Kuschewsky (2013).

According to Peter Swire and Yianni Lagos,[42] the competitive implications of a refusal to grant access to or share data can be viewed in three ways: as a refusal to deal (which would pertain to the refusal to proceed with portability, sharing, access, or interoperability), denial of access to an essential facility (the essential facilities doctrine), and tying (considering that an entity would be conditioning its offer on a non-interoperable software module).

The refusal to deal, as the term itself suggests, refers to the refusal or denial to supply a product or service to a prospective buyer, who is generally a retailer or wholesaler. Typically, this practice is implemented as a mechanism to compel a reseller to adhere to a resale price or as a means of fulfilling an exclusivity agreement with a third party. Such an exclusivity agreement may be limited to a specific class of customers or a particular geographic region.[43]

These two examples (enforcing resale price maintenance and compliance with an exclusivity clause) can be classified as means-based refusal. In contrast, ends-based refusal does not form part of a broader context of restrictions and is aimed at eliminating current and future competitors.[44]

In this context, refusal to contract may be implemented as either a horizontal or vertical restriction. In the first form, competitors within the same market exclude another competitor or prevent their entry. This generally occurs through boycotts organized by professional, commercial, or producers' associations. In the second form, the practice takes place in the relationship between supplier and purchaser.[45] Furthermore, refusal to contract may occur within the context of an agreement (cartel[46]) or through abuse of dominant position.

Regardless of the form adopted, for these behaviors to be considered an antitrust violation rather than a mere ordinary commercial practice, it is necessary that they be implemented through an abuse that excludes competitors from the market,[47] which requires market power. According to Priscila Gonçalves,[48] although it is not a sufficient requirement in itself, the existence of economic power is indispensable.

A famous case involving refusal to deal was Aspen Skiing.[49] The city of Aspen is a renowned tourist destination with a ski resort. The resort comprises four mountains, three of which were owned by the defendant, Aspen Skiing, while the fourth belonged to the plaintiff, Aspen Highlands. For many years, the two companies offered a joint, multi-day ticket valid throughout the entire area. Suddenly, Aspen

42 Swire and Lagos (2013), p. 335.

43 OECD (1993).

44 Gonçalves (2008), p. 119.

45 Gonçalves (2008), p. 114.

46 A cartel can be understood as a collusion or agreement aimed at raising prices for buyers or minimizing prices for input suppliers. Domingues and Gaban (2016), p. 207.

47 OECD (2007).

48 Gonçalves (2008), p. 116.

49 United States. Supreme Court. *Aspen Skiing Co. v. Aspen Highlands Skiing Corp.*, 472 U.S. 585 (1985).

Skiing began to demand a larger share of the ticket sales revenue and subsequently terminated the joint ticketing agreement.[50]

Although the plaintiff, Aspen Highlands, made several attempts to recreate the joint ticket, Aspen Skiing refused. As a result, the Court held that Aspen Skiing's refusal was an attempt to exclude competitors for reasons other than the promotion of efficiency.[51]

In Brazil, the conduct of refusal to contract is codified in Law 12,529/2011, Article 36, §3, item XI. This item establishes that refusing to sell goods or provide services under normal payment conditions according to commercial practices constitutes a violation of economic order.

At times, the refusal to contract may concern access to a public utility good[52] or to a "*bottleneck facility*."[53] In such cases, the refusal is interpreted in light of the essential facilities doctrine, which will also be addressed in our analysis.

The *essential facilities doctrine* concerns situations in which an entity has access to a facility or infrastructure whose duplication by competitors is impossible or extremely difficult due to physical, geographical, legal, or economic constraints, as is the case with a national electricity grid used for distributing energy to end consumers. Consequently, other competitors require access to this facility or infrastructure because it is essential. An unreasonable denial of access may be considered an abuse of dominant position and constitute a violation of economic order.[54]

The central issue in identifying anticompetitive unlawfulness lies in the problem of essential access, which arises when the supply of certain products or services cannot occur without access to an essential input;[55] in other words, competition will not exist at all.[56] Thus, if the market in such cases is unable to provide effective solutions to the problem, antitrust intervention will be necessary.

It is important to emphasize that the concept of what is considered essential for the purposes of applying the essential facility doctrine is flexible and variable, depending on time, place, and technological development,[57] since what was once essential may no longer be so, and what is considered essential now may not have even existed previously due to advancements in development. Priscila Gonçalves[58] argues, moreover, that the meaning of essential facility has been broadened to also encompass situations involving economies of scale and networks, whether physical or virtual, natural or artificial.

[50] Candeub (2005), p. 828.
[51] Candeub (2005), p. 828.
[52] Gonçalves (2008), p. 205.
[53] Candeub (2005), p. 828.
[54] OECD (1993), p. 178.
[55] Gonçalves (2008), p. 205.
[56] Geradin and Kuschewsky (2013).
[57] Gonçalves (2008), p. 207.
[58] Gonçalves (2008), p. 207.

In the United States, the doctrine of essential facility is grounded in the idea that refusal to deal in situations involving an essential good or input constitutes an attempt to monopolize the market and is therefore subject to Section 2 of the Sherman Act. This doctrine originated in the case the United States v. Terminal Railroad Ass'n of St. Louis,[59] which concerned the use of a bridge over the Mississippi River considered essential by operators who were not part of the association known as the "Robber Baron."[60]

Currently, the essential facilities doctrine, as established in the case MCI Communications Corp. v. AT&T,[61] will only be applied if the following four-pronged test is satisfied: (1) the essential facility must be controlled by the monopolist; (2) the competitor must be unable to practically or reasonably duplicate the essential facility; (3) the monopolist must have denied the competitor access to the facility; and (4) it must be feasible for the monopolist to provide access to the facility.[62]

Despite the development of the doctrine and its recognition by the courts, there have been subsequent cases that contradicted this requirements test and even the necessity for a monopolist to contract with its competitors so that they may have access to an essential facility. This was particularly evident in the case of *Verizon Communications v. Trinko*,[63,64] which was widely criticized[65] and, above all, did not prevent the continued application of the essential facilities doctrine in subsequent cases.[66]

Due to these divergences, Priscila Gonçalves[67] acknowledges that the issue is much more settled in the European Union. In the 2007 decision of Microsoft v. Commission,[68] the conditions required to recognize a refusal to deal involving essential facilities were systematized. These are as follows: first, the refusal must concern a product or service that is indispensable for the exercise of another activity; second, the refusal must eliminate all effective competition; and finally, third, the refusal must prevent the emergence of a new product for which there is potential consumer demand.[69]

Another highly praised aspect there concerns the conditions of access, so that the courts not only determine access to an essential facility but also how this access will

---

59 United States of America. Supreme Court. *United States v. Terminal Railroad Ass'n of St. Louis*. Decided in 1912.

60 Candeub (2005), p. 828.

61 United States of America. Supreme Court. *MCI Communications Corp. v. AT&T*. Decided in 1994.

62 Candeub (2005), p. 828.

63 United States of America. Supreme Court. *Verizon Communications v. Trinko*. Decided in 2004.

64 Candeub (2005), p. 828.

65 Candeub (2005), p. 828.

66 Candeub (2005), p. 828.

67 Gonçalves (2008), p. 207.

68 European Union. Court of Justice. *Microsoft v. Commission*. Decided in 2007.

69 Swire and Lagos (2013), p. 361.

occur, in order to ensure that it is reasonable and nondiscriminatory (including in the sense that an excessive price is not charged for access).[70]

In Brazil, the doctrine of essential facilities can find support in our legal system through the application of Article 36, §3, items III, IV, and V of Law 12,529/2011. These items establish that the following practices constitute violations of economic order, respectively: limiting or preventing the entry of new companies into the market; creating difficulties for the establishment, operation, or development of a competing company or of a supplier, purchaser, or financier of goods or services; and preventing competitors from accessing sources of inputs, raw materials, equipment or technology, as well as distribution channels. Furthermore, if a particular situation does not fit precisely within these scenarios, it may still be characterized as abuse of dominant position, which is a broader and more flexible conduct.

Despite the stringent requirements necessary for the application of the essential facilities doctrine, it can be asserted, following the reasoning of Aysem Diker Vanberg and Mehmet Ünver,[71] that the doctrine may be applied in technology markets and network industries when a company controls data. Consequently, if the data held by a company are crucial to facilitating market access for other competitors in a specific market, such as social networks or search engines, the application of the doctrine may be indispensable.

According to Aysem Diker Vanberg and Mehmet Ünver,[72] the Court of Justice of the European Union, in the cases of *Magill*,[73] *IMS Health*,[74] and *Microsoft*,[75] concluded that in order to grant mandatory access to data, the applicant must demonstrate that the data are essential for offering a new product and that there is no other way to obtain them or to develop the product or service without such access.

In the United States, Aysem Diker Vanberg and Mehmet Ünver[76] report two cases involving access to and extraction of data. The first is the case of *Facebook v. Power Ventures Inc.*[77] Power Ventures[78] sought to extract data from social network users

---

[70] Candeub (2005), p. 221.

[71] Diker Vanberg and Ünver (2017).

[72] Diker Vanberg and Ünver (2017).

[73] European Union. Court of Justice of the European Union. *Radio Telefis Eireann (RTE) and Independent Television Publications Ltd (ITP) v Commission of the European Communities.* Judgment of April 6, 1995.

[74] European Union. Court of Justice of the European Union. *IMS Health GmbH & Co. OHG v NDC Health GmbH & Co. KG.* Judgment of April 29, 2004.

[75] European Union. Court of Justice of the European Union. *Microsoft v. Commission.* Decided in 2007.

[76] Diker Vanberg and Ünver (2017).

[77] United States of America. District Court for the Northern District of California. *Facebook, Inc. v. Power Ventures, Inc.* Decided on May 11, 2009.

[78] It should be added that Power Ventures offers a website called Power.com, which is designed to allow end users to integrate all their social network contacts into a single site. To this end, Power.com uses Facebook login information provided by its users to scrape information and display it on Power.com. In this way, Power.com could represent precisely the type of adaptation that dissipates market power arising from network effects. In addition to this factor, Power Ventures alleged that

and make it available on its own platform. As a preventive measure, Facebook sued *Power Ventures Inc.* for violation of its terms of service.

In response, *Power Ventures Inc.* filed a counterclaim, alleging exclusionary conduct by Facebook, which, by denying access to data, was allegedly preventing its participation in the market. This argument was not accepted by the Court, which held that Facebook had the *"right to control access to and use of its site"*.[79]

The second case, in turn, was *PeopleBrowsr v. Twitter*,[80] which concerned PeopleBrowsr's request for Twitter to grant it access to its data in order to develop analytical services. After Twitter denied the request, PeopleBrowsr filed a lawsuit alleging anticompetitive practices.

Such an allegation led to the granting of a precautionary measure, allowing PeopleBrowsr to access the data. Nevertheless, the case was ultimately closed through a settlement. As a result, unfortunately, no precedent was established regarding the legality or illegality of Twitter's conduct under competition law.[81]

Another important point is that the refusal to provide data can often be concealed under the argument that such refusal is necessary for compliance with data protection regulations. According to a study by the European Data Protection Supervisor (EDPS),[82] this may serve as an opportunistic excuse, since a company with dominant market power may already have violated data protection regulations in various other ways, notably by using personal data in a manner incompatible with the original consent for collection. In this context, cooperation between data protection authorities and competition authorities becomes imperative.

Thus, the conclusion that can be drawn at this point, although nothing is yet firmly established, is that if data are understood as an essential facility, there may be an obligation to share databases when these are the only means to enable competition. Such a measure has the potential to significantly alter market dynamics.[83]

A further antitrust concern arises when data portability and interoperability are not completely denied but are offered only under conditions that reinforce the ecosystem of the incumbent firm. In these situations, the restriction does not operate through a refusal to share data but rather through mechanisms that induce or compel users to consume complementary products or services. Such conduct may be examined under the framework of tying and bundling arrangements.

Facebook engaged in discrimination by allowing Gmail, AOL, and Yahoo to collect information from Facebook, since these services could be accessed through Facebook login. This defense was not accepted by the district court on the grounds that the fact that other sites access Facebook does not create a duty for Facebook to provide third-party sites with unrestricted access. Furthermore, for the Court, the introduction of a product that is not interoperable with competing products would not violate antitrust laws (Yoo 2012, p. 1155).

[79] Diker Vanberg and Ünver (2017).

[80] United States of America. District Court for the Northern District of California. *PeopleBrowsr v. Twitter.*

[81] Diker Vanberg and Ünver (2017).

[82] EDPS (2014).

[83] Mattiuzzo (2014), p. 56.

Tying arrangements constitute a category that comprises two types. The first type is known as *tying*, which occurs when a supplier sells a product (the *tying product*) on the condition that the buyer also purchases a different product, referred to as the *tied product*, either from the same supplier or from a third party designated by the supplier.[84]

When this requirement is imposed immediately, at the very moment of attempting to purchase the desired product, the situation is referred to as a *tie-in*. When the requirement is imposed at a later stage, through complementary services, for example, the tying arrangement is referred to as a *tie-out*.[85]

It is clear that tying sales are only characterized when there is no reasonable justification for the joint sale; otherwise, even the sale of a carton of eggs would be considered a tying sale. Another illustrative example is the sale of a pair of shoes,[86] which occurs as such because selling them separately would be counterproductive, given the necessity for both shoes to be identical. Products that are normally sold together, such as a pack of yogurts or a set of cookware, are also not considered tying sales.[87]

The second type of tying arrangement refers to bundling, which is simply the sale of a package containing two or more products, with the individual sale of the package components not being permitted.[88] This type of arrangement can sometimes occur in a subtle manner, as seen in the technology market, where there is an integration of products that would originally be sold separately.

Tied selling may be motivated by the following effects: (1) gaining market share in the tied product market through leveraging; (2) closing or increasing barriers in the tied product market, which hinders the entry of new players; (3) price discrimination; (4) exploitation of consumers or buyers; and (5) circumventing price regulation in regulated markets.[89]

In domestic legislation, in addition to the provisions of consumer law, tying arrangements are addressed in Article 36, § 3, item XVIII, of Law 12,529/2011, which defines as an infraction against economic order the conduct of "conditioning the sale of a good on the acquisition of another or on the use of a service, or conditioning the provision of a service on the use of another or on the acquisition of a good."

In light of competitive logic, the mere practice of this conduct does not in itself constitute illegality. For this to occur, there must be harm to free competition or to free enterprise.

However, for these effects to occur, the agent engaging in the conduct must meet two requirements: (1) possess market power and (2) abuse that power. These

---

[84] European Union (2005).

[85] U.S. Department of Justice (2009).

[86] Pfeiffer (2010), pp. 131–151.

[87] Raymond (2004).

[88] U.S. Department of Justice (2009).

[89] Sullivan and Grimes (2000).

requirements are justified by the need for the consumer to feel compelled to purchase the products or services together; otherwise, such a practice will have no impact on market structures.[90]

In this regard, it should be noted that, in the European Union, an agent engaging in tying practices is subject to Article 102 of the Treaty on the Functioning of the European Union,[91] provided that the following elements are present: (1) possession of market power in the tying product market; (2) the tying involves products from distinct markets; (3) the existence of coercion; (4) an attempt to foreclose the market; (5) the practice is not objectively justified; and (6) the efficiencies generated do not justify the conduct.[92] Similarly, the United States recognizes the lawfulness of tying arrangements when they provide benefits or efficiencies to the market and consumers, which is why such conduct is not considered a per se violation.[93]

Some paradigmatic antitrust cases have involved tying arrangements. Among these are the Kodak[94] and Microsoft[95] cases in the United States, as well as the Xerox[96] case in Brazil, all of which have been previously discussed. There are also some noteworthy cases adjudicated in Brazil by the Superior Court of Justice (STJ) that address tying arrangements in light of the Consumer Defense Code (CDC).

Minister Herman Benjamin, in Special Appeal No. 384,284,[97] for example, addresses the practice of conditioning the installment payment for the purchase of the product sought by the consumer—namely, gasoline—on the acquisition of another product not desired by the consumer: a soft drink. The reporting judge held that this would constitute an unequivocal abusive practice, specifically in the form of tied selling.[98]

In the judgment of Special Appeal No. 744,602,[99] known as the Cinemas case, the reporting Justice, Minister Luiz Fux, found that the abusive practice was evident, considering that the cinema company allows the entry of products purchased on its premises while prohibiting those acquired elsewhere.[100]

---

[90] Forgioni (2008), p. 373.

[91] European Union (2005).

[92] European Union (2005).

[93] U.S. Department of Justice (2009).

[94] United States of America. *Eastman Kodak Co. v. Image Technical Servs. Inc.*, 504 U.S. 451, 458 (1992).

[95] United States of America. *United States District Court for the District of Columbia*. United States v. Microsoft Corporation, Decided in 2002.

[96] Brazil. Administrative Council for Economic Defense. *Case No*. 23/91. Decided in 1993.

[97] Brazil. Superior Court of Justice. Special Appeal No. 384,284-RS. Rapporteur: Justice Herman Benjamin. Judged on December 15, 2009.

[98] Brazil. Superior Court of Justice. Special Appeal No. 384,284-RS. Rapporteur: Justice Herman Benjamin. Judged on December 15, 2009.

[99] Brazil. Superior Court of Justice. Special Appeal No. 744,602. Rapporteur: Justice Luiz Fux, adjudicated on March 23, 2003.

[100] Brazil. Superior Court of Justice. Special Appeal No. 744,602. Rapporteur: Justice Luiz Fux, adjudicated on March 23, 2003.

Still within the theme of cinema, the Allegation of Breach of Fundamental Precept (ADPF) 398[101] addressed the possibility of prohibiting food and beverages from other commercial establishments in movie theaters. The purpose of this ADPF was to "improperly" challenge Special Appeal No. 744,602[102] mentioned above, which classified the practice as tying. In 2022, the ADPF was dismissed, and the decision has become res judicata.

Furthermore, the Supreme Federal Court, when analyzing a municipal law that requires the hiring of an employee to perform a specific task in a business establishment, held that the obligation to provide packaging services together with the sale of retail goods constitutes a violation of the constitutional guarantee of consumer protection (Art. 5, XXXII). This is because it amounts to a form of tying arrangement, a practice prohibited by Art. 39, I, of the Consumer Protection Code, resulting in increased prices for all consumers, even those who do not need the service or cannot afford it.[103]

Another paradigmatic case concerns the joint sale by fast food chains of meals accompanied by children's toys. Considering this practice to be abusive, the Public Prosecutor's Office of the State of São Paulo filed a public civil action against the Bob's restaurant chain.

On the same grounds, the Federal Public Prosecutor's Office filed a public civil action against McDonald's and Burger King. Upon the raising of a jurisdictional conflict between the São Paulo state court and the federal court, the Superior Court of Justice (STJ) ruled that the 15th Civil Court of the Federal Judicial Section of São Paulo had jurisdiction to hear the case.

Another interesting case is that of Pandurata Alimentos, owner of the Bauducco brand, which had launched the promotional campaign "It's Shrek Time," offering a watch featuring the character Shrek, conditional upon the purchase of five packages from the "Gulosos" product line and an additional payment of R$ 5.00. The São Paulo Public Prosecutor's Office (MPSP) filed a public civil action (ACP) against the campaign, arguing that it constituted tied selling.

The São Paulo Court of Justice (TJSP) upheld the public civil action, considering the practice to constitute tied selling. The decision was subsequently affirmed by the Second Panel of the Superior Court of Justice (STJ), which set an important precedent by deeming advertising directed at children to be abusive and reinforcing that the practice of tied selling is illegal.[104]

[101] Brazil. Federal Supreme Court. Allegation of Breach of Fundamental Precept No. 398. Reporting Justice Edson Fachin.

[102] Brazil. Superior Court of Justice. Special Appeal No. 744,602. Rapporteur: Justice Luiz Fux, adjudicated on March 23, 2003.

[103] Brazil. Federal Supreme Court. RE 839950, Rapporteur: Luiz Fux, Full Bench, judged on 10-24-2018, Electronic Proceedings General Repercussion—Merit DJe-081 Disclosed 04-01-2020 Published 04-02-2020.

[104] Brazil. Superior Court of Justice. Special Appeal No. 1,558,086/SP, rapporteur Minister Humberto Martins, Second Panel, judged on 03/10/2016, Electronic Justice Gazette of 04/15/2016.

It can thus be concluded that the denial of access to or sharing of data may constitute a practice analogous to tying, insofar as the provider conditions the granting of portability on the use of a product or service that it offers itself or that is supplied by a commercial partner. If portability is requested for access to a competitor's product or service, it is denied.[105]

Another example of tying arrangements would be, for instance, when a social network is linked to specific software that controls the export of data to other services. As can be seen, this analogy is not very precise. Furthermore, in general, there may not be a separate product for data export.[106]

Ultimately, the possible classifications discussed above, although some are characterized by strict requirements, demonstrate the possibility that conduct involving the refusal to grant access to or share data may be considered an infringement of economic order. Thus, the partial conclusion is that there is a potential application of competition rules to the situation at hand, with the precise legal classification being of lesser importance.

As a result, the prevailing view is that antitrust enforcement (ex post regulation) requires abuse in the broad sense (*lato sensu*). This abuse and its consequences will be addressed in the following chapter.

6.2 Abuse of Dominant Position in Data-Driven Markets

As previously discussed, regardless of the specific category related to the type of infraction against economic order, it is evident that the modalities analyzed above share a common denominator, namely, that they constitute a form of abuse of dominant position. Before analyzing the characteristics of this abuse, it is important to emphasize that, for the purposes of antitrust liability, the classification and categorization of the conduct are not essential.

In fact, the classification of conduct serves primarily didactic and organizational purposes, since the list of practices in Law 12,529/2011 is merely illustrative. Indeed, the Brazilian competition system adopts an open[107] and exemplary typification, subject to the possibility of excluding unlawfulness if certain efficiencies or specific benefits to society or the market are achieved.

According to Francisco Mendes,[108] this open-ended classification is necessary because the creation of an exhaustive list of specific and precise hypotheses of violations against the economic order could, at times, result in the unjust acquittal of conduct harmful to the market—such as new practices in a dynamic market that

[105] Swire and Lagos (2013), p. 363.

[106] Swire and Lagos (2013), p. 335.

[107] Francisco Mendes states that the spectrum of repression of violations against economic order is so broad that, for this reason, it is not easy to sustain typification in competition law. Mendes (2013), p. 73.

[108] Mendes (2013), p. 73.

would not be covered by a legal list—and the condemnation of practices that could potentially be pro-competitive. Thus, an essentially closed normative framework would not "in any way contribute to the construction of a more precise and legitimate repressive system."[109]

It is evident, therefore, that this open-ended typification (which, according to some studies, dispenses with the requirement of culpability for the offender in order to establish unlawfulness[110,111]) distances the attribution of liability for antitrust violations from the traditional tenets of the theory of liability. What is concerning, however, is that there has not yet been a substantial reflection on "the specificities of defining unlawful conduct in the field of competition law,"[112] despite the significant expansion of antitrust enforcement in our country.

The vagueness of competition rules is not a mere coincidence. It actually stems from the very nature of their protection, which is the proper functioning of the market. Since the essence of competition law lies in economic facts, it is inevitable that this branch of law is influenced by economic science. In fact, there is a genuine need to seek support in economics to clarify several indeterminate legal concepts introduced by competition law.

That said, it is necessary to examine what constitutes abuse of dominant position, as one of the effects capable of rendering conduct unlawful, regardless of the manner in which this effect is pursued, given the open-ended typification mentioned above. First, it is important to analyze what is meant by dominant position and, subsequently, to determine what would constitute its abuse. In the words of Modesto Carvalhosa,[113] a dominant position is the situation in which an economic entity holds significant influence over price determination.

Preliminarily, it should be noted that dominant position is not to be confused with economic power, although they are related and may even serve to define similar situations.[114] Thus, dominant position refers to the share that a given company holds in a particular market[115] or its capacity to exert influence within that market. Economic power, on the other hand, refers to the intervention of a company—even

---

[109] Mendes (2013), p. 73.

[110] In this regard, Francisco Mendes argues that Brazilian antitrust law has adopted strict liability, making it unnecessary to analyze intent or fault on the part of economic agents in the conduct of their business activities. Mendes (2013), p. 77.

[111] Regarding culpability, it is important to mention Direct Action of Unconstitutionality No. 1094, filed by the National Confederation of Industry (CNI), which, among other challenges, contested the constitutionality of the expression "regardless of fault" as provided in Law No. 8884/94. This action was ultimately dismissed in 2020 due to the subsequent repeal of the challenged normative provisions. Brazil. Federal Supreme Court. Direct Action of Unconstitutionality No. 1094. Justice Celso de Mello. Virtual Session from 09/25/2020 to 10/02/2020.

[112] Mendes (2013), p. 11.

[113] Carvalhosa (1967), p. 8.

[114] Bagnoli (2005), p. 148.

[115] Bagnoli (2005), p. 148.

one with a small market share or segment[116]—that generates effects and has the ability to exert influence by belonging to an economic group or by holding dominance in another market, which provides it with resources to invest and the leverage to undertake business activities.

In this regard, there are companies that become highly successful in a given market and, from there, venture into new enterprises, sometimes in markets that are very different from their original ones. With the experience and capital gained from previous activities, they can enter another market with effective strategies, thereby competing directly with other players or even drastically influencing this new market. Furthermore, it is possible for them to finance anticompetitive practices, such as engaging in predatory pricing.

Dominant position is generally associated with a high percentage of market share. This is the quantitative criterion established by law, set at a minimum of 20% of the relevant market (Article 36, §2, of Law 12,529/2011). However, this percentage must always be assessed in comparison with the market shares held by other competitors.[117]

In addition to the quantitative criterion, dominant position may also be identified through a qualitative criterion, namely, *market power*. This refers to the ability of an agent to unilaterally or coordinately alter market conditions.[118]

Thus, dominant position may result from market share or market power. The mere presence of one or both of these criteria is not sufficient to establish an unlawful act. In this regard, Miguel Reale[119] warns that what is unlawful is not power itself, as a normal or natural instrument for the production and circulation of wealth in society, but rather its abuse or misuse.

Illegality only arises if non-legitimate means are employed to achieve a dominant position or, when a dominant position is established based on business success resulting from the superior efficiency of a particular company in the sector,[120] the agent subsequently uses this legitimately obtained position for anticompetitive purposes.

This guidance can be derived from the normative text. Law 12,529/11, in Article 36, §1 º, states that "market share gained as a result of a natural process based on greater efficiency does not constitute the offense set forth in item II of the caput of this article." The offense described in item II is that of dominating a relevant market for goods or services, whose legal interest is the free functioning of the market, encouraging competitive advantages achieved through efficiency and suppressing those obtained fraudulently, that is, all those not based solely on the agent's superiority.[121]

---

[116] Bagnoli (2005), p. 149.

[117] Forgioni (2008), p. 333.

[118] Bagnoli (2005), p. 148.

[119] Reale (1985), p. 520.

[120] Nassif (2011), p. 531.

[121] Forgioni (2008), p. 322.

Item IV of the same article provides for the abusive exercise of a dominant position. Indeed, it can be stated that unlawfulness lies in the unlawful attempt to achieve a dominant position in the market or in the abuse of a dominant position, even when such a position has been attained naturally.

This last form, abuse of dominant position, represents one of the greatest interpretative challenges in antitrust law. This difficulty arises from the approach adopted by the law, which expressly defines the abuse of dominant position but does not specify its content. The law provides only a few examples of conduct that fall within the concept of abuse of dominant position.

Such a situation creates legal instability and uncertainty (due to the lack of reliability, calculability, and cognoscibility[122]). In practice, this makes antitrust analysis necessarily case specific, with no methodology that can be considered unique and inflexible.[123]

Thus, competition law comes to serve as the best example of the burial of traditional positivism.[124] The specificity of antitrust lies in the absence of a ready-made, single answer, as if it were a "recipe book."

Indeed, Mario Luiz Possas[125] asserts that it is essential to establish objective criteria for identifying abusive conduct. Thus, even though the concept of economic power is indeterminate and complex, we must develop parameters that "delineate with the necessary precision the application of the law."[126]

An OECD study[127] proposes that the analysis of abuse of dominant position should be conducted in two stages. The first concerns the verification of the condition or *status* of the agent in relation to the market. This *status* refers to the *market share* or *market power* of a given company or a group of companies, since they may be acting jointly, either through an agreement or through *joint dominance*.

The second stage concerns the assessment of the conduct being employed by the company or companies (in the case of an agreement or joint dominance). The evaluation of the conduct, in order to characterize abuse, takes into account the adverse effects produced, determining whether these harm or do not harm free competition.[128]

In conclusion, the OECD[129] asserts that the definition of what constitutes abusive or at least illegal conduct depends on the objective of each law. Indeed, given the broad normative scope of competition law, which is based on principles (thus ensuring a certain degree of flexibility), only conduct that runs counter to the state of

---

122 Ávila (2011), p. 682.

123 Frazão (2015), p. 190.

124 Forgioni (2015), pp. 9–12.

125 Possas (1996), p. 93.

126 Possas (1996), p. 93.

127 OECD (1996), p. 7.

128 OECD (1996), p. 7.

129 OECD (1996), p. 7.

affairs sought by the law—supported by the economic definition of competition—will be considered unlawful.[130,131]

It is worth reflecting briefly on how principles are fundamental to antitrust doctrine. Drawing inspiration from foreign doctrines, especially the North American tradition, which advocated that judges should interpret the applicable legislation solely with a view to maximizing some measure of economic welfare,[132] a consequentialist normative theory[133] of antitrust was developed in Brazil, in which the definition of unlawful conduct is constructed based on objectives.

Thus, the definition of abuse of dominant position, as well as other violations of the economic order, will be based on the objectives.[134] The next step is to determine what these objectives are, which unfortunately is not an easy task due to the ongoing controversy surrounding this issue.

Not even in the United States, a country where antitrust law has been codified since 1890, has it been possible to consolidate this subject, either in case law or in legal doctrine. In fact, it is reported that there has always been a certain flexibility regarding the objectives of competition protection there. And it could not be otherwise, since competition, as Vinicius Marques de Carvalho affirms,[135] "is not a uniform or ahistorical phenomenon," with its intensity depending on a range of cultural, economic, political, and social factors.

In the American political cycle, there has been an attempt to narrow antitrust to a more specific and targeted objective, according to Maurice E. Stucke.[136] In this case, the chosen objective was consumer welfare.

---

130 Houssiaux (1960), p. 37.

131 Jacques Houssiaux explains that competition has two concepts: one legal and one economic. In the legal sense, competition is the characteristic of an exchange system in which the economic agent enjoys complete freedom of choice and negotiation, not merely the freedom to buy or not to buy, to sell or not to sell. This definition of legal competition is complemented in the long term by an additional condition: competition is an exchange system that guarantees all economic agents total freedom to undertake and to establish themselves. The economic definition, as described by Jacques Houssiaux, defines competition and specifies its nature according to the objectives of the competitive regime. In the short term, competition is the system of exchanges that balances supply and demand in each market so as to satisfy the greatest number of participants in the exchanges, without any of them being able, by their presence, to interfere with the outcome achieved. In the long term, competition generally leads to maximizing the growth rate of production. These two perspectives, economic and legal, are presented as complementary aspects of competition. The legal definition is a definition of means, while the economic definition is a definition of results. In this regard, the idea to be retained is that policy serves to demonstrate the teleology of competition rules, assisting in the definition of conduct that infringes the economic order. Houssiaux (1960), p. 37.

132 Schuartz (2009).

133 As a point of interest, it is worth noting that the term consequentialism originates from moral philosophy and was coined by Elisabeth Ascombe. Carvalho (2011), pp. XIII–XIX, p. XIII.

134 OECD (1996), p. 7.

135 Carvalho (2015), p. 19.

136 Stucke (2012), p. 568.

While on the one hand this may be welcomed with applause, on the other, the issue should be approached with caution. This is because, as Maurice E. Stucke warns,[137] there is no clear concept regarding the scope and meaning of well-being, and as a result of this indeterminacy, there is even a certain abuse of the term, both in 1987 and today. In this regard, Charles-Etienne Gudin[138] rhetorically asks whether the expression well-being is not, for the jurist, a utopia.

The fundamental point of the reasoning outlined here is what Guilhermo Cuevas postulates:[139] none of the major systems of competition regulation originated exclusively from consumer protection. In this regard, the author states, for example, that competition law in the European Union has an additional specificity, which is to ensure the effective establishment of a common market and the free movement of goods within it, without prejudice to consumer protection.[140,141]

Thus, it can be stated, with support from Valentine Korah,[142] that the objective of competition for the European Union is, and has always been, to promote integration within the common market, now referred to as the internal market. In fact, this purpose is considered even more important than mere efficiency.

In this regard, Richard Whish[143] states that if the sole function of competition were the maximization of consumer welfare through the efficient allocation of resources and the greatest possible cost reduction, then the formulation of legal rules and their enforcement would be relatively straightforward. In this sense, a single or unified objective would bring advantages, particularly by reducing the challenges faced by lawyers when stepping outside the boundaries of the legal discipline.

In practice, many objectives have been attributed to competition policy, some of which are not even aligned with consumer welfare. As a result, the policy may come to be implemented in an inconsistent and contradictory manner.

The question arises at this point as to what objectives are pursued by developing countries such as Brazil. Eduardo Gaban,[144] in addressing this question, observes that these countries are always the most affected by distortions of competition,[145] given their rather peculiar characteristics, such as statism, corruption, artificial barriers, privileges granted by the state, an informal economy, poor or underdeveloped infrastructure, a weak financial market, and deficient corporate governance.

---

137 Stucke (2012), p. 568.

138 Gudin (1998), p. 223.

139 Cabanellas de las Cuevas (2005), p. 45.

140 Cabanellas de las Cuevas (2005), p. 45.

141 Andressa Schneider states that the current concept of competition in the European Union tends toward the pursuit of effective competition, which is based on concerns of economic efficiency and welfare, within limits of atomicity established *a priori*. Schneider (2016).

142 Korah (2004), p. 12.

143 Whish (2001), p. 15.

144 Gaban (2012), p. 29.

145 Godfrey (2008).

The protection of competition in markets at this stage becomes a *sine qua non* condition for achieving development. According to Nick Godfrey,[146] competitive markets are a necessary tool for a nation's resources to be used in the most efficient manner, generating better technologies and innovation, which in turn foster productivity and competitiveness, including integration into the international market and poverty reduction.

Hassan Qaqaya and George Lipimile[147] report that experiences from developing countries demonstrate that prudent competition policies and their enforcement can help key sectors accommodate or include new entrants. Furthermore, it has been observed that economies with competitive domestic markets generally tend to have higher rates of per capita income growth.[148]

Thus, it can be stated that competition law in developing countries, particularly in Brazil, has development as one of its objectives, alongside consumer welfare. In this regard, Article 1 of Law 12,529/2011 establishes that the prevention and repression of violations against the economic order shall be guided by the constitutional principles of freedom of enterprise, free competition, the social function of property, consumer protection, and the repression of the abuse of economic power.

Well then, returning to the topic of abuse of dominant position, conduct will only be capable of constituting this offense if it has the potential to affect consumer welfare and the country's economic development, thereby harming the market and efficiency. As Jorge Fagundes reports,[149] more recent decisions by CADE have identified consumer welfare as the basis for the repression of abuse of dominant position.

In comparative law, there is a greater systematization of the abuse of dominant position, which can complement the analysis of this conduct in Brazil. In the United States, the abuse of dominant position falls under Section 2 of the *Sherman Act* and is therefore understood as monopolization or attempted monopolization. Thus, abuse is characterized by conduct with exclusionary or predatory purposes, whether to acquire a dominant position in the market or to maintain an already existing position.[150]

Just as Brazilian legislation sought to establish exceptions, the mere possession of market power or share is not considered illegal under the US system, provided it is not accompanied by abusive conduct.[151] This understanding can be drawn from the famous case the *United States v. Aluminum Co. of America,*[152] in which the US Supreme Court had the opportunity to state that the mere size of a company in the

---

[146] Godfrey (2008).

[147] Qaqaya and Lipimile (2008), p. 12.

[148] Qaqaya and Lipimile (2008), p. 10.

[149] Fagundes (2005).

[150] U.S. Department of Justice (2009).

[151] Candeub (2005), p. 828.

[152] United States of America. Supreme Court. *United States v. Aluminum Co. of America, 1964.*

market does not give rise to liability, since a dominant position may be consistent with the spirit of antitrust laws.

Another development can be drawn from the Microsoft case,[153] which involved abuse of dominant position and the technology market. In this case, in the words of Christopher Yoo,[154] it was established that a monopolist does not violate antitrust laws simply by developing a product that is incompatible with those of its rivals. Thus, incompatibility is only problematic if accompanied by an exclusivity agreement or an unjustifiable technical design.[155]

Ultimately, in the United States, for the purposes of determining unlawfulness, economic rationality and the impacts on the competitive process and consumer welfare are taken into account, rather than the interests of specific competitors. Furthermore, there is no intention to suppress market dominance that is lawfully established on the basis of a competitor's greater efficiency.

In turn, within the European Union, the abuse of a dominant position is set forth in Article 102 of the Treaty on the Functioning of the European Union. This article states that it is incompatible with the internal market for one or more undertakings to exploit their dominant position in an abusive manner. Additionally, the article provides examples of conduct that constitute abuse, including the following: imposing prices, limiting production or distribution, and applying dissimilar conditions to trading partners.

In the European Union, as previously observed with respect to Brazil and the United States, a dominant position is a necessary but not sufficient condition for the establishment of an infringement.[156] Indeed, in addition to market dominance, there must also be abuse, which falls into two categories: exploitative abuse, where the dominant firm derives excessive advantages from its market power, and exclusionary abuse, which aims to hinder or restrict effective competition, whether from current or potential competitors.[157]

One of the cases that best exemplifies this European perspective is Hoffmann-La Roche Co. AG v. Commission of the European Communities,[158] which concerned the conclusion of exclusivity agreements between La Roche and vitamin purchasers, who were incentivized through loyalty discounts. In this case, the Court of Justice defined a dominant position as a situation that grants a company the power to prevent effective competition in the market and to act independently of its competitors, customers, and consumers.

Another important case was the so-called Banana Chiquita case, which involved the companies United Brands Company/United Brands Continental BV and the

---

153 United States of America. *United States District Court for the District of Columbia.* United States v. Microsoft Corporation, Decided in 2002.

154 Yoo (2012), p. 1155.

155 Yoo (2012), p. 1155.

156 Lescop (2008), p. 7.

157 Lescop (2008), p. 7.

158 European Union. Court of Justice of the European Communities. *Hoffmann-La Roche & Co. AG v. Commission of the European Communities.* Judgment delivered on February 13, 1979.

Commission of the European Communities,[159] decided by the then Court of Justice of the European Community in 1978. Upon reviewing the Commission's decision, the Court found that United Brands had abused its dominant position through discriminatory pricing, restrictive resale clauses, and refusal to continue supplying. According to the Court, these practices caused a significant distortion of competition in the relevant banana market, allowing only companies dependent on United Brands to remain in business.

It should be added that there are certain peculiarities that distinguish the European system from the North American one, which has led to the former being referred to as the *gentlemen* approach and the latter as the *cowboy* approach. This is because, in the European Union, there is oversight of the conduct of dominant firms, whereas in the United States, the focus is on preventing the creation or maintenance of monopolies.[160]

Indeed, it is said that the application of Section 2 of the Sherman Act does not suppress aggressive competitive conduct, as it is precisely this type of competition that advances consumer interests, which the law seeks to promote. In contrast, within the European context, large companies do not possess the right to such unfettered freedom and must therefore always be mindful of maintaining their rivals. These are the reasons behind the terms *cowboys* and *gentleman competitors.*[161]

That said, in comparison with the North American and European experiences, it can be stated that Brazil adopts a hybrid system. In this regard, there is repression both of practices aimed at market domination (in line with the North American system) and of abusive practices (in this respect, resembling the European system).

Advancing in the research subject, now that the requirements for abuse of dominant position have been outlined, it becomes necessary, therefore, to define the relevant market and the power held within it when analyzing a given conduct, such as that implemented through a refusal of portability, which is the central issue of this work. In antitrust practice, this definition is considered a *sine qua non* condition for the characterization of an infringement, in order to avoid the prosecution of impossible violations (by analogy to "impossible" crimes).[162]

However, defining the market power of a data operator can be a very difficult task and even a challenge. The relevant market, for example, of a provider of free

---

159 European Union. Court of Justice of the European Communities. *United Brands Company/ United Brands Continental BV v. Commission of the European Communities*. Judgment of February 14, 1978.

160 McDonald (2005).

161 McDonald (2005).

162 It is argued that such analysis is always necessary, even in cases involving per se violations, as expressed by the United States Supreme Court. Thus, there would not be a clear line separating the per se analysis from the rule of reason, since in both cases an investigation into market conditions is required. United States of America. Supreme Court. *California Dental Assn v. FTC*, Decided in 1999.

services on the Internet cannot be simplistically calculated solely based on the volume of data accumulated through regular transactions.[163]

Carol Conway[164] argues that the dynamism of e-markets, which are strongly driven by innovation, challenges the recognition of market dominance as established by classical antitrust theory. Therefore, it will be necessary to employ additional complementary analyses, given that the market structure can change constantly and rapidly.

In fact, as Ana de Oliveira Frazão[165] points out, competition analyses tend to pay little attention to the issue of technology, precisely due to the inherent difficulties in measuring the innovation factor. For this reason, Bernardo Gouthier Macedo, Silvia Fagá de Almeida, and Carolina Policarpo Garcia[166] argue that antitrust enforcement should be more cautious, so that society can benefit from the gains brought about by the dynamism of the digital market.

Thus, it is necessary to develop techniques for defining the relevant market that take into account even technological convergence, which can transform products that were once complementary into substitutes, as in the case of handheld devices that can now compete directly with notebooks and desktop computers—something unimaginable 10 years ago. As for the definition of the geographic market, this may not exist for certain services in the digital market, such as search engines, email, or document sharing, which are not confined to a particular area or country but are instead uniformly available in the global online market.[167]

However, it is argued that interaction between competition authorities, consumer protection agencies, and data protection authorities would be necessary so that, together, they could identify scenarios and develop standards for measuring market power in matters related to data. Once a standard is established, it could then be adopted by all three areas in the performance of their respective duties.

Marcela Mattiuzzo[168] also addresses the issue of defining the market and the corresponding market power in the analysis of online advertising. In her view, it would be preferable to define the relevant market as the retail of personal data rather than as a two-sided platform market. Based on this, there is room for the application of the essential facilities doctrine in matters concerning personal data.

Additionally, Damien Geradin and Monika Kuschewsky[169] point out potential controversies regarding the recognition of an infringement of economic order, given the difficulty in establishing the existence of a "data" market. This challenge in

---

163 EDPS (2014).

164 Conway (2015), p. 257.

165 Frazão (2015), p. 198.

166 Macedo et al. (2015), p. 108.

167 EDPS (2014).

168 Mattiuzzo (2014), p. 70.

169 Geradin and Kuschewsky (2013).

defining the market would persist even if the precedent set in the Bronner case[170] were adopted, in which the Court of Justice of the European Union held that the existence of a potential or hypothetical market was sufficient.[171]

In any case, once this initial difficulty regarding the definition of the data market is overcome—which will occur over time and through cooperation among different regulatory authorities—it must be acknowledged that competition rules, such as Article 102 of the Treaty on the Functioning of the European Union and Article 36, item IV, of Law 12,529/2011, may allow for data portability by facilitating mandatory access to specific data.

A case involving dominant abuse and data-related issues is that of Google AdWords, which is accused of imposing contractual restrictions on software developers, preventing them from offering tools that enable the continuous transfer of search advertising campaigns between the dominant Google AdWords platform and other search advertising platforms. Through this practice, advertisers are prevented from exporting data to other Google platforms or to those of its competitors.[172]

As a result, the FTC investigated Google's conduct, and the company committed to promoting data portability between different search platforms, allowing advertisers to produce "one-size-fits-all" advertisements. However, these commitments were criticized, particularly because the FTC did not consult the parties affected by Google's practices. Furthermore, there are doubts as to whether the commitments offered by Google will be sufficient to ensure the transfer of data between advertising platforms.[173,174,175]

At this point, it is important to consider that portability does not refer solely to personal data but may also involve data belonging to market agents. Furthermore, the question arises regarding data ownership: do these data belong to the advertisers or to Google? If they belong to the advertisers, they would have the right to remove and export them to another system.[176]

Ultimately, from an antitrust perspective, the refusal to grant access to data should not be considered a per se violation nor should it be treated as an all-or-nothing matter,[177] since such an approach could reduce consumer welfare by penalizing conduct that is more efficient and arises from the natural dynamics of the

---

[170] European Union. Court of Justice of the European Union. *Oscar Bronner GmbH & Co. KG v Mediaprint Zeitungs*. Judgment of November 26, 1998.

[171] Geradin and Kuschewsky (2013).

[172] Geradin and Kuschewsky (2013).

[173] Geradin and Kuschewsky (2013).

[174] Marcela Mattiuzzo notes that the closure of the FTC investigation occurred without a satisfactory response to data portability issues that had arisen over the years, which led to criticism from several companies, including Microsoft. This is a relevant topic that should be on the agenda of competition authorities. Mattiuzzo (2014), p. 54.

[175] As previously mentioned, the same issue is currently under review in Brazil by CADE, in Administrative Proceeding No. 08700.005694/2013-19.

[176] Mattiuzzo (2014), p. 54.

[177] Diker Vanberg and Ünver (2017).

market.[178] However, it may be regarded as an infringement of economic order[179], and, consequently, the sharing of databases may be required when this is the only way to enable competition, either because it is impossible to access the data or because it is impossible to replicate them.

Furthermore, it is suggested that a competitive analysis, both in merger control[180] and in conduct investigations, should take into account the following factors: (1) the impact of the concentration considering a "data" market; (2) whether the transaction or conduct results in market dominance and a tendency to reduce product quality, including with respect to privacy policies;[181] (3) whether the acquired data help the company to gain or maintain market power; (4) whether the concentration increases barriers and hinders the entry of new players; and (5) whether there is abuse of dominant position through refusal to share data.[182]

If the potential or actual harm to the market is identified, whether in the analysis of a merger or in antitrust enforcement, the application of drastic and highly interventionist remedies—such as the prohibition of mergers or the breakup/divestiture of a company—should be avoided. This consideration is even more critical when dealing with technological markets, which are in constant transformation, in order to prevent (1) higher costs for consumers, as occurred with Microsoft in the European Union, and (2) the ineffectiveness of the measure, since companies found liable may already have profited sufficiently from a given anticompetitive practice.

The question, however, is which remedy to apply. An antitrust remedy that emerges in this new digital reality is the requirement to share databases with a

178 Swire and Lagos (2013), p. 350.

179 In July 2022, the Italian Competition Authority announced the initiation of an investigation against Google for a possible abuse of dominant position, in violation of Article 102 of the Treaty on the Functioning of the European Union. According to the Authority, Google hindered the sharing of data on its platform with others, such as the Weople app, which could restrict the right to personal data portability established by Article 20 of the GDPR, as well as the economic benefits that consumers may derive from their data. This alleged abuse could also harm competition by limiting the ability of alternative operators to develop innovative data-driven services. To close the investigation, Google committed to implementing three measures to facilitate data portability and improve interoperability with other platforms. These measures include supplementary solutions to the Takeout service for data export and the development of a new solution for direct service-to-service data portability. The Authority considered these commitments adequate to address competition concerns, allowing users and third-party operators to utilize the new mechanisms for data portability and interoperability.

180 As analyzed in the article coauthored with Lucas Griebeler da Motta, CADE, when it does not ignore the issue of data access in merger control proceedings, tends to conduct only a superficial analysis regarding database sharing, especially with respect to personal data. Cravo and Motta (2023).

181 Wisniewski (2019).

182 According to Aysem Diker Vanberg and Mehmet Ünver, the Court of Justice of the European Union, in the *Magil*, *IMS Health*, and *Microsoft* cases, concluded that, in order to grant mandatory access to data, the applicant must prove that the data are essential for offering a new product and that there is no other way to obtain them or to develop the product or service without such access. In cases where there is a refusal to share or the creation of obstacles, the application of the *essential facilities* doctrine to data-related matters is possible. Diker Vanberg and Ünver (2017).

specific competitor or with several competitors, through portability.[183] This mechanism, in addition to serving as a specific measure imposed by the competition authority or the judiciary, can also be exercised individually, when a user asserts their right to transfer data to another platform or application.

However, when the antitrust remedy adopted by the competition authority involves the sharing of databases that include personal data, certain safeguards must be implemented in light of the data minimization principle.[184]

This principle establishes that only personal information strictly necessary for the fulfillment of a specific measure should be shared, which, in the context under discussion, would be to enable competition. Thus, competition authorities should require data sharing only as a last resort and solely with respect to information essential to the intended purpose.[185]

Where possible, the antitrust authority should seek to implement alternative measures to halt the effects of anticompetitive conduct involving refusal of access or abuse of dominant position. These alternatives may be developed with the support of agencies specialized in data protection,[186] through legitimate cooperative activity.

The European Data Protection Supervisor[187] suggests some alternative remedies to competition authorities, which are as follows: (1) require the agent to offer paid services that minimize the collection and retention of personal information; (2) impose a proportional data retention limit; and (3) provide consumers with the opportunity to voluntarily implement portability, enabling them to extract their data and transfer it to other services.

Data portability can serve as a remedy in cases of both abuse and concentration acts.[188] However, its application depends on the specific circumstances of each case.

In the Facebook/WhatsApp Case, the European Commission, for example, "found no evidence suggesting that data portability issues would constitute a significant barrier for consumers switching between communication apps." Given that communication via apps tends to consist largely of short, spontaneous chats—which do not necessarily hold long-term value for consumers—that contact lists can be ported, and that message histories remain accessible on a user's smartphone, the Commission concluded that even if the acquired entity were to control and restrict

[183] It is noteworthy that, in other areas, the Administrative Council for Economic Defense (CADE) has already applied portability as a competition remedy. As an example, reference can be made to the approval of the merger involving the acquisition of HSBC by Bradesco, adjudicated in June 2016 by CADE's Tribunal (Brazil. Administrative Council for Economic Defense. *Merger Case No. 08700.010790/2015-41*. Adjudicated on June 8, 2016.)

[184] EDPS (2014).

[185] EDPS (2014).

[186] Cooperation between competition authorities and data protection agencies is of utmost importance. In Brazil, a Technical Cooperation Agreement was signed between CADE and ANPD in 2021.

[187] EDPS (2014).

[188] OECD (2021).

data portability (such as message history), this would be unlikely to result in user *lock-in*.[189]

On the other hand, in the Ticketmaster/Live Nation case, it was established that if any customer of the defendants' primary ticketing services chooses not to renew a contract for primary ticketing services with the defendants for some or all of their venues, after the termination of that contract and upon the customer's written request, the defendants must, within 45 days, provide the customer with a complete copy of all customer ticketing data and all ticket purchaser data historically maintained by the defendants in the ordinary course of business, in a format that is reusable by the customer.[190]

It should be noted, however, that the supervision and implementation of data portability as an antitrust remedy can be challenging.[191] In the Ticketmaster/Live Nation case, the amendment introduced in 2020 also sought to ensure more effective compliance with the imposed remedies, establishing, for example, the appointment of an independent monitoring trustee.[192]

Furthermore, there are risks associated with collusion due to the transparency of competitively sensitive data and intellectual property, which will need to be assessed.[193] Additionally, data protection issues cannot be disregarded when data portability is applied as a remedy, as previously mentioned.

One way to balance the interests of data protection and competition would be, whenever possible, to prioritize voluntary portability by data subjects, which can be facilitated through intermediary services such as PIMSs—*Personal Information Management Services*.[194] Another approach would be through the principles of necessity and minimization, ensuring that data sharing is limited strictly to the data necessary for the intended purpose[195] and, whenever possible, anonymized.

It is also worth noting that there are numerous new developments and proposed legislative changes in various countries aimed at addressing issues in the digital market.[196] In Germany, the range of prohibited practices under the new provision of the German Competition Act includes "hindering competition by impeding interoperability or data portability." Such prohibitions may be imposed by the

[189] European Commission. *C(2014) 7239 final*.

[190] United States District Court for the District of Columbia. *Amended Final Judgment Case 1:10-cv-00139-RMC*, 2020.

[191] OECD (2021).

[192] OECD (2021).

[193] OECD (2021).

[194] Competition and Markets Authority (2020).

[195] EDPS (2014).

[196] In the United States, during Joe Biden's administration, there was a continuation of antitrust initiatives targeting major digital platforms, including allegations related to the restriction of interoperability and data portability. Additionally, during that period, the possibility of adopting specific regulations aimed at promoting these mechanisms was also discussed. Langenfeld et al. (2021).

Bundeskartellamt on companies recognized as having *paramount cross-market significance.*[197]

The British government is also seeking solutions to address the challenges of the digital market, and a dedicated Digital Markets Unit will be established to introduce and enforce a new code governing the conduct of platforms that currently dominate the market.[198] In the European Union, the regulation on contestability and fairness of markets in the digital sector (Digital Markets Regulation) imposes an obligation on the *gatekeeper* to provide effective portability of data generated in the course of activities by a business or end user.[199]

Despite these developments involving data portability, it is important to emphasize that this measure alone may not be sufficient to promote or protect competition in the market.[200] In some cases, this remedy may only be effective if combined with other measures.[201]

Therefore, it is concluded that, alongside the protection of competition, regulation is also necessary; that is, both ex ante and ex post regulation must exist. Firstly, because competition will only address issues involving abuse and, even then, only in exceptional situations where the impossibility of competition is evident, as indicated by precedents to date.

Second, due to the initial difficulty in dealing with technological issues that add complexity to the work of the antitrust authority, such as the very definition of the relevant market. Third, because the data protected under competition law may differ from those covered by regulation, which may encompass only personal data (as is the case with the regulatory model for data protection).[202,203] Fourth, because ex post regulation may not be sufficient or even effective in identifying the costs resulting from the elimination of competition. Fifth, because in the context of competition, data portability may be granted to a specific provider or to several providers, whereas under regulation, data portability is requested by the individual data subject. Sixth,

---

[197] Bundeskartellamt (2020).

[198] UK Government. *Press release: New competition regime for tech giants to give consumers more choice and control over their data, and ensure businesses are fairly treated.*

[199] European Commission. Proposal for a Regulation of the European Parliament and of the Council on contestable and fair markets in the digital sector (Digital Markets Act).

[200] The lesson learned at the FTC Workshop in 2020 was that data portability is not a cure-all for every anticompetitive problem. Langenfeld et al. (2021).

[201] OECD (2021).

[202] Data portability has already been used for the transfer of nonpersonal data. This is the case with Article 6 of European Regulation No. 2018/1807, which establishes the framework for the free flow of nonpersonal data within the European Union. Thus, in the European Union, in addition to the portability of personal data provided for in the GDPR, there is also encouragement for the adoption of portability for nonpersonal data. To support this objective, there is an obligation to develop a code of conduct to ensure exchange and mobility.

[203] It is important to note, however, that although in theory the distinction between personal and nonpersonal data may seem straightforward, in practice this is not always the case. For example, large datasets in which personal and nonpersonal data are mixed (known as mixed datasets) make it difficult to determine the applicable legal regime. Zufall and Zingg (2021), pp. 215–234.

and most importantly, because data portability is an individual right and promotes informational self-determination.

The research conducted throughout this chapter demonstrates that the transition to a genuinely data-driven economy requires a sophisticated reinterpretation of the antitrust framework, moving away from rigid dogmas to adopt a functional and technologically informed approach. It has become evident that, although competition law possesses well-established tools—such as the essential facilities doctrine, the analysis of refusal to deal, and the scrutiny of tying practices—the application of these concepts to digital markets demands overcoming structural challenges, notably the definition of the relevant market and the measurement of market power in ecosystems characterized by network effects and the apparent gratuity of services.

The potential of data as a source of market power is undeniable, but the response to this phenomenon should not result in excessive interventionism that undermines the very dynamism of innovation. It follows that the use of data portability and interoperability as antitrust remedies must be guided by caution and applied only in exceptional circumstances (*ultima ratio*), preserving investment incentives and fully respecting data protection principles, especially the principle of minimization. Harmonizing entrepreneurial freedom with the need for market contestability is the balance point that will enable the unlocking of data value in a safe and efficient manner.

To mitigate regulatory fragmentation and reduce the frictions that hinder the legitimate flow of information, the solution does not lie in the isolated primacy of competition enforcement nor in the rigidity of sector-specific regulations. As an essential guideline for unlocking the value of data, a governance model based on institutional synergy is proposed. Complementary action among competition authorities, data protection agencies, and sectoral regulatory bodies is the path to creating an environment where legal certainty and market fluidity can coexist.

Ultimately, the law must evolve from an ex post reactive stance to an institutional framework that promotes portability and interoperability as mechanisms of informational self-determination and levers of economic efficiency. Only through this integrated approach will it be possible to overcome artificial barriers to data circulation, ensuring that the value generated by the digital economy is fully harnessed by society without compromising the integrity of the economic order or the sovereignty of data subjects. The future of competition in digital markets therefore depends on our ability to build an ecosystem where access to data is not an insurmountable barrier but rather a dynamic input for continuous innovation.

References

Aragão AS (2013) Artigo 174. In: Canotilho JJG, Mendes GF, Sarlet I, Streck L (coords) Comentários à Constituição do Brasil. Saraiva, São Paulo, pp 1833–1836

Autorité de la Concurrence, Bundeskartellamt (2016) Competition law and data. http://www.autoritedelaconcurrence.fr/doc/reportcompetitionlawanddatafinal.pdf

Ávila H (2011) Segurança jurídica: entre permanência, mudança e realização no Direito Tributário. Malheiros, São Paulo
Bagnoli V (2005) Introdução ao direito da concorrência. Singular, São Paulo
Bundeskartellamt (2020). Abuse of Dominance in Digital Markets: Contribution from Germany.
Cabanellas de las Cuevas G (2005) Derecho antimonopólico y de defensa de la competencia. Heliasta, Buenos Aires
CADE (2021). Digital platform markets.
Candeub A (2005) Trinko and re-grounding the refusal to deal doctrine. Univ Pittsburgh Law Rev 66:821–870
Carvalho PB (2011) Prefacio. In: Piscitelli TS (ed) Argumentando pelas consequências no direito tributário. Noeses, São Paulo, pp XIII–XIX
Carvalho VM (2015) A política de defesa da concorrência quatro anos depois: ainda em busca de melhores práticas? In: Carvalho VM (ed) A Lei 12.529/2011 e a nova política de defesa da concorrência. Singular, São Paulo, pp 13–29
Carvalho Filho JS (2013) Manual de direito administrativo. Atlas, São Paulo
Carvalhosa MSB (1967) Poder econômico: a fenomenologia seu disciplinamento jurídico. RT, São Paulo
Competition and Markets Authority. (2020). Online platforms and digital advertising: Market study final report.
Conway CE (2015) Concorrência: a Lei 12.529/2011 e os e-mercados. In: Carvalho VM (ed) A Lei 12.529/2011 e a nova política de defesa da concorrência. Singular, São Paulo, pp 255–268
Cravo DC, Motta LG (2023) Oportunidades perdidas de análise: acesso a dados pessoais em atos de concentração: reflexões sobre Magalu Pagamentos/Hub Prepaid e Lojas Americanas/Hortigil Hortifruti? In: Dados, mercados digitais e concorrência, 1st edn. Letramento, pp 17–35
Diker Vanberg A, Ünver M (2017) The right to data portability in the GDPR and EU competition law: odd couple or dynamic duo? Eur J Law Technol 8(1)
Domingues JO, Gaban EM (2016) Direito antitruste, 4th edn. Saraiva, São Paulo
European Data Protection Supervisor (2014) Privacy and competitiveness in the age of big data. EDPS, Brussels
European Union. (2025). DG Competition discussion paper on the application of Article 82 of the Treaty to exclusionary abuses.
Fagundes J (2005) Abuso de posição dominante (APD): abordagem e questões econômicas. IBRAC XI Seminário Internacional de Defesa da Concorrência, Campos do Jordão
Forgioni PA (2008) Os fundamentos do antitruste. Revista dos Tribunais, São Paulo
Frazão A (2015) A análise de eficiências em atos de concentração sob o enfoque do princípio retributivo. In: Carvalho VM (ed) A Lei 12.529/2011 e a nova política de defesa da concorrência. Singular, São Paulo, pp 181–200
FTC (2007) Federal Trade Commission closes Google/DoubleClick investigation.
Gaban EM (2012) Regulação do setor postal. Saraiva, São Paulo
Geradin D, Kuschewsky M (2013) Competition law and personal data: preliminary thoughts on a complex issue. https://papers.ssrn.com/sol3/papers.cfm?abstract_id=2216088
Godfrey N (2008) Why is competition important for growth and poverty reduction? http://www.oecd.org/investment/globalforum/40315399.pdf
Gonçalves PB (2008) A obrigatoriedade de contratar como sanção fundada no direito concorrencial. Dissertation, Universidade de São Paulo
Grau ER (2006) A ordem econômica na Constituição de 1988, 11th edn. Malheiros Editores, São Paulo
Gudin C-E (1998) Qu'est devenu le consommateur em droit communautaire e de la concurrence? Revue des Affaires Européennes 8(3):221–233
Hendrickson C, Galston W (2017) Big technology firms challenge traditional assumptions about antitrust enforcement. https://www.brookings.edu/blog/techtank/2017/12/06/big-technology-firms-challenge-traditional-assumptions-about-antitrust-enforcement/
Houssiaux J (1960) Concurrence et marché commun. Éditions Génin, Paris

Illing S (2017) Why fake news is an antitrust problem. Vox. https://www.vox.com/technology/2017/9/22/16330008/facebook-google-amazon-monopoly-antitrust-regulation

Inman R (1996) Making sense of the antitrust state-action doctrine: balancing political participation and economic efficiency in regulatory federalism. Tex Law Rev 75:1203–1297

Korah V (2004) An introductory guide to EC competition law and practice. Hart Publishing, Oxford

Langenfeld J, Ring C, Clark S (2021) Regulating digital platforms: interoperability and data portability. Concurrences 1-2021

Lescop D (2008) Régulation des comportements individuels. Université Paris I, Paris

Lundqvist B (2018) Portability in datasets under intellectual property, competition law, and blockchain. Stockholm University Research Paper No. 62

Macedo BG, Almeida SF, Garcia CP (2015) In: Carvalho VM (ed) A Lei 12.529/2011 e a nova política de defesa da concorrência. Singular, São Paulo, pp 97–114

Mattiuzzo M (2014) Propaganda online e privacidade: o varejo de dados pessoais na perspectiva antitruste. Prêmio SEAE, Brasília

McDonald JB (2005) Cowboys and gentlemen. College of Europe, Global Competition Law Centre, Brussels

Mendes FS (2013) O controle de condutas no direito concorrencial brasileiro: características e especificidades. Dissertation, Universidade de Brasília

Menke F (2014) A proteção de dados e novo direito fundamental à garantia da confidencialidade e da integridade dos sistemas técnico-informacionais no direito alemão. In: Mendes G, Sarlet I, Coelho A (orgs) Direito, inovação e tecnologia. Saraiva, São Paulo, pp 205–230

Moreira Neto DF (2003) Direito regulatório. Renovar, Rio de Janeiro

Motta LG (2021) Análise multijurisdicional de aquisições centradas em dados: diagnóstico atual e propostas de política pública para o Brasil. Associação Data Privacy Brasil de Pesquisa, São Paulo

Nassif EVS (2011) Efeitos das práticas restritivas sobre economia brasileira, e a repressão às condutas anticoncorrenciais. In: Secretaria de Acompanhamento Econômico do Ministério da Fazenda (org) V Prêmio SEAE 2010: concurso de monografias sobre os temas: defesa da concorrência e regulação econômica/Ministério da Fazenda. Edições Valentim, Brasília

OECD (1993) Glossary of Industrial Organisation Economics and Competition Law. Organisation for Economic Co-operation and Development, Paris.

OECD (1996) Abuse of dominance and monopolisation. OECD, Paris

OECD (2007) Roundtable on Refusals to Deal. Organisation for Economic Co-operation and Development, Paris.

OECD. (2021). Data portability, interoperability and digital platform competition (OECD Competition Committee Discussion Paper).

Oliveira G, Rodas JG (2013) Direito e economia da concorrência. Revista dos Tribunais, São Paulo

Peritz RJR (1996) Competition policy in America - 1888-1992. Oxford University Press, New York

Pfeiffer RAC (2010) Proteção do consumidor e defesa da concorrência: paralelo entre práticas abusivas e infrações contra a ordem econômica. Rev Direito Consumidor 19(76):131–151

Possas ML (1996) Os conceitos de mercado relevante e de poder de mercado no âmbito da defesa da concorrência. Rev IBRAC 3(5):93

Qaqaya H, Lipimile G (2008) The effects of anti-competitive business practices on developing countries and their development prospects. http://unctad.org/en/Docs/ditcclp20082_en.pdf

Raymond G (2004) Incidences de la loi MURCEF sur le marketing des établissements de crédit. Pulim, Limoges

Reale M (1985) Abuso do poder econômico e garantias individuais. In: Franceschini JIG, Franceschini JLV (eds) Poder econômico: exercício e abuso. Revista dos Tribunais, São Paulo, pp 520–525

Rogers CP (2013) A concise history of corporate mergers and the antitrust laws in the United States. Natl Law Sch India Rev 24(2):10–31

Salomão Filho C (2003) Direito concorrencial: as condutas. Malheiros, São Paulo

Schneider A (2016) Do direito da concorrência ao direito à concorrência: o reconhecimento do direito fundamental à concorrência a partir do direito fundamental à defesa do consumidor. Dissertation, Universidade Federal do Rio Grande do Sul
Schuartz LF (2009) A desconstitucionalização do direito de defesa da concorrência. Revista de Direito Administrativo 250:117–142. http://academico.direito-rio.fgv.br/ccmw/images/e/e0/Schuartz_-_Desconstitucionaliza%C3%A7%C3%A3o.pdf
Shapiro C (2017) Antitrust in a time of populism. https://faculty.haas.berkeley.edu/shapiro/antitrustpopulism.pdf
Stucke ME (2012) Reconsidering antitrust's goals. Boston Coll Law Rev 53:551–629
Stucke ME, Grunes AP (2016) Big data and competition policy. Oxford University Press, Oxford
Sullivan LA, Grimes WS (2000) The law of antitrust: an integrated handbook. West Group, St. Paul
Swire P, Lagos Y (2013) Why the right to data portability likely reduces consumer welfare: antitrust and privacy critique. Maryland Law Rev 335:335–380
Taufick R (2010) Imunidade Parker v. Brown: releitura das doutrinas state action e pervasive power no ordenamento jurídico brasileiro. Revista ANTT 2(2)
UNCTAD (2002) Application of competition law: exemptions and exceptions. United Nations, New York
U.S. Department of Justice. (2009). Competition and monopoly: Single-firm conduct under Section 2 of the Sherman Act. Washington, DC: U.S. Department of Justice.
Van Alstyne M (2016) A platform strategy: creating new forms of value in the digital age. Capgemini Consulting
Whish R (2001) Competition law. Butterworths, London
Wisniewski CH (2019) Violação de dados pessoais pode ser um desafio antitruste? http://pincade.cade.gov.br/images/Caio-Henrique%2D%2D-Artigo.pdf
Yoo C (2012) When antitrust met Facebook. Geo Mason Law Rev 19(5):1147–1162
Zufall F, Zingg R (2021) Data portability in a data-driven world. In: Peng S, Lin C-F, Streinz T (eds) Artificial intelligence and international economic law: disruption, regulation, and reconfiguration. Cambridge University Press, Cambridge, pp 215–234

Chapter 7
Foundations of the Right to Portability: Self-Determination and the Intersection of Protections

7.1 The Electronic Body and Informational Self-Determination

The widespread and intensive use of data in the digital economy requires government action on multiple fronts, as any isolated and self-contained policy, in addition to being ineffective, may even be detrimental to the desired state of affairs.[1] In this context, it is evident that the issue of data protection, in certain areas, intersects with consumer protection and competition law.

As previously discussed, data protection laws seek—among other objectives—to empower[2,3] individuals whose data are processed by numerous services in the digital market, which are, in most cases, provided by monopolistic or near-monopolistic companies holding a significant market share. To illustrate, at the outset of the research for this book, Google held over 91% of the search engine market in Europe; Android accounted for 80% of the mobile operating system market; Microsoft controlled more than 90% of the desktop operating system market; Facebook had 1.6 billion users on its platform; and Alibaba concentrated 80% of all e-commerce transactions.[4]

It is of little use to grant individuals numerous rights without providing them with effective mechanisms and tools to seek out services that respect their rights or have policies that better suit their preferences. It is essential to allow data subjects

[1] As an example, reference can be made to the joint action in Brazil by CADE, ANPD, SENACON, and the Federal Public Prosecutor's Office (MPF) through a Recommendation to WhatsApp, which aimed to protect the rights of data subjects and consumers and to mitigate potential effects on competition arising from the new policy to be implemented by the company.

[2] Article 29 Data Protection Working Party (2016), p. 3.

[3] Janal (2017), p. 1.

[4] Van Alstyne (2016), p. 3.

D. Copetti Cravo, *Law and the Digital Economy*,
https://doi.org/10.1007/978-3-032-36672-6_7

to migrate to services or products that prioritize privacy and data protection, which may lead these aspects to become a competitive advantage.[5]

In this context, the right to data portability arises[6] as an extension of the data subject's ability to control their personal data[7] and exercise their right of choice,[8] also serving as an incentive for the market to adopt standards desired by society.

Therefore, it cannot be denied, in essence, that the rationale behind the right to data portability is to reinforce the implementation of human rights related to privacy, data protection, and the free development of human personality. On a broader scale, it also enables individuals to exercise their right to informational self-determination.[9,10,11]

As Rodotà explains,[12] information technologies construct an electronic body, which is the set of personal information stored in countless databases and exists alongside the physical body. The individual, immersed in the flow of electronic communication, comes to be characterized by a dual body: the physical and the electronic.

The latter, the electronic body, is unknowable, partial, and mobile and can circulate independently of the physical body.[13] This situation creates the need for control mechanisms by the individual, precisely to prevent harm to their personality resulting from the improper circulation of their information and, consequently, of their electronic body.

In this context, informational self-determination emerges as the right of each individual to control their own information and to determine how they wish to construct their private sphere. One of the ways to promote the exercise of private

---

[5] Bioni (2015), p. 56.

[6] In 2007, the Declaration of Rights of Social Web Users was issued, which included data portability. Subsequently, the Data Portability Project was launched, with the participation of Google, Facebook, Microsoft, and LinkedIn, among others (Bozdag 2018).

[7] Bioni (2015), p. 56.

[8] Article 29 Data Protection Working Party (2016), p. 3.

[9] Zanfir (2012), p. 4.

[10] According to Gabriela Zanfir, the concept of informational self-determination represents the essence of data protection and was adopted by the German Constitutional Court in 1983 in its famous *Census decision*. The Court in Karlsruhe ruled that anyone who could not, with sufficient assurance, ascertain information relating to themselves, known in certain areas of their social environment, and who was not in a position to assess, more or less, the knowledge of potential communication partners, could be fundamentally hindered in their freedom to make plans or decisions based on their own self-determination. With this understanding, the Court explicitly emphasized the right to informational self-determination, interpreting the broader notion of personality rights. Zanfir (2012), p. 4.

[11] Fabiano Menke adds that informational self-determination grants the individual the power to decide regarding the disclosure or use of their personal data. This is encompassed within the right to self-presentation, which is one of the three categories of the general right of personality. Its core concerns the prohibition of using information about the individual that is false, unauthorized, or secret. Menke (2014), pp. 210–211.

[12] Rodotà (2005), pp. 25–29.

[13] Rodotà (2005), pp. 25–29.

autonomy in this new reality of human expression—namely, the electronic body—is through data portability.[14]

The association of data portability with the free development of personality arises from the concept of "digital identity," since personal data and their combinations can be understood as an extension of personality in the digital environment.[15] Accordingly, data subjects must have the right to manage their data, determining when and with whom such data should be shared, without prejudice to the data subject's own enjoyment of this ecosystem in their domestic activities.

Therefore, data portability is a user-centered tool that enables the data subject to play an active role in the data ecosystem.[16,17] For example, it can assist the data subject in assessing the impact of their consumption patterns or in adopting more sustainable habits. Among other possibilities, this includes transferring shopping lists to a nutritional advice application or using our transportation and energy consumption data to create an individual carbon index.

Regarding the development of the Internet of Things, data portability will be essential to promote the indispensable transfer of data necessary for the operation of this technology.[18] In this context, portability may allow the data subject to transfer their data between different applications and services, thereby enhancing their right of choice.[19]

Furthermore, data portability is a fundamental element for the development *of Personal Information Management Systems* (PIMS). PIMS provide the data subject with a *dashboard* for monitoring the use of their data, allowing the data subject to directly transfer their data to external controllers.[20,21]

Such systems enable individuals to manage and control their own online identities. This fosters a human-centered approach, protecting them against illegal tracking techniques and profiling practices that seek to circumvent key data protection principles.[22]

The subject of portability is also advancing in other areas, with portability being identified as an instrument to allow for the assignment of a destination to the data of a deceased individual (postmortem protection of personality rights).[23] This concerns the posthumous right to portability, which, however, requires further discussion and

---

14 Negri and Korkmaz (2021), pp. 660–674.

15 Negri and Korkmaz (2021), pp. 660–674.

16 Article 29 Data Protection Working Party (2016), p. 4.

17 Portability can also be understood as a right of a new generation (Monteleone 2017, p. 202).

18 Graef et al. (2019).

19 As an example, a consumer may wish to port their data and migrate to another smart food supply service, different from the one that came with their new Amazon refrigerator. Stigler Committee (2019).

20 CERRE (2020).

21 The development of technical solutions to promote PIMS is highlighted in the document prepared by the Helsinki EU Office. Helsinki EU Office (2020).

22 EDPS (2014).

23 Colombo and Goulart (2020), pp. 90–109.

reflection, although it can already be found in Italy, where it is provided for in legislation that establishes certain requirements.[24]

In this context, the portability of data related to health and genetic information is also of particular relevance for succession planning.[25] Given the exponential growth in diagnostics and prognostics for health promotion and the development of preventive treatments, posthumous portability of such data may be significant.

The portability of health data, moreover, represents a direct link between the physical body and the electronic body. It should be noted that medical records, when properly organized and updated, "are essential for individuals to exercise their right to health and, ultimately, their right to life.[26]"

Nevertheless, portability may be used by the data subject for altruistic purposes.[27] Citizens may request their data in order to make them available in the future through a public data call, conducted within the context of a public policy or scientific mission.[28]

Therefore, data portability embodies the progress of the new generation of data protection laws, taking a step beyond the traditional rights of access, rectification, erasure, and objection.[29] These highly significant rights are ultimately complemented by data portability.

Thus, it is undeniable that data portability, in addition to its potential effects on the market[30] and consumer welfare,[31] constitutes an individual right, not only enabling greater management and control of data by the data subject but also allowing the individual to benefit from the data ecosystem.

Thus, new possibilities arise from the establishment of data portability, which can be considered a novelty. It should be noted that data portability differs from other types of portability, such as mobile number portability, although some of the resulting effects may be similar.

In this regard, an OECD study reports that the introduction of mobile number portability has served to reduce the costs involved for consumers when switching service providers. However, it did not entirely eliminate the burdens on consumers, such as potential delays between the request for portability and its actual implementation.[32]

---

[24] Negri et al. (2021).

[25] Negri and Korkmaz (2021), pp. 660–674.

[26] Negri et al. (2021).

[27] Data portability can also contribute to the use of data for the public good, for example, through data calls to promote research, in a form of data altruism. European Commission (2020).

[28] Villani (2018).

[29] In the current context, the traditional access, rectification, erasure, and objection (ARCO) rights would no longer be sufficient to ensure adequate protection. Kessler and Dresch (2020), p. 23.

[30] To this end, digital entrepreneurs and small service providers should be advised and educated about the growth and innovation opportunities that a well-implemented data portability infrastructure and legislation can offer them. With greater awareness, they will be encouraged to implement more user-friendly data import options for data subjects. Syrmoudis (2021), pp. 351–372.

[31] Geradin and Kuschewsky (2013).

[32] OECD (2018).

On the other hand, several indirect benefits to consumers were observed, not directly related to the switching of providers by consumers. An example of this includes discounts, offers, and incentives that began to be offered to consumers to prevent them from changing operators. Additionally, loyalty programs were strengthened, new devices emerged, as well as new services,[33] resulting in a more dynamic and competitive market.

In relation to Brazil, on March 19, 2007, the General Portability Regulation (RGP) was approved through ANATEL Resolution No. 460, with the aim of establishing the conditions for the implementation of access code portability by telecommunications service providers of public interest.

In addition to portability in telecommunications, other forms of the concept are already in place or under discussion, such as portability in the context of contract termination, in roaming service communications, and consumer access to cross-border services.[34] Credit portability between financial institutions is another example, which can be defined as the possibility of transferring credit operations (loans and financing) and leasing agreements from one financial institution to another, at the initiative of the consumer, whether an individual or a legal entity, through the early settlement of the operation with the original institution.

This type of credit portability was implemented in Brazil through Resolution No. 4292, of December 20, 2013.[35] Its functionality is as follows: the consumer will negotiate the terms of the new transaction with the institution granting the new credit, which will be responsible for settling the previous transaction with the original institution.

As a result, there has been an increase in competition among financial institutions, given the enhanced decision-making power granted to consumers. Consumers will be able to choose among economic agents that offer lower interest rates or other incentives arising from the new negotiation process.

It should be noted, however, that data portability is different from the other types of portability mentioned above, such as telephone number portability and credit portability (portability of the contract or legal relationship). This is because, as will be discussed in due course, data portability as a right of the data subject provided for in the General Data Protection Regulation (GDPR) or the General Data Protection Law (LGPD) does not necessarily imply the termination of the relationship[36] but

[33] OECD (2018).

[34] Article 29 Data Protection Working Party (2016), p. 4.

[35] Central Bank of Brazil. Resolution No. 3401, of September 6, 2006.

[36] As a rule, the processing of data is not terminated simply by exercising the right to data portability, except when the data subject intends to end the relationship (strict sense portability) and requests the deletion of the data or if any of the grounds for termination of data processing are present (Article 15 of the LGPD).

rather access to a copy of the data for reuse[37] either in a domestic context or with another controller.[38]

In the United States, there are already some examples of data portability. The *Health Insurance Portability and Accountability Act* (HIPAA) led to the creation of the HIPAA Privacy Rule in 2003, which specified that patients have the right to obtain a copy of their personal health information. This requirement was expanded by *the Health Information Technology for Economic and Clinical Health Act* (HITECH), which established the right to receive this information in electronic format and to transmit it to a third party.[39]

In 2016, the United States Congress passed the 21st Century Cures Act, which established additional requirements for data portability, including data exchange standards and secure application programming interfaces (APIs) for the transfer of health information, as well as stronger rules to prevent data blocking. In parallel, there was also the development of the voluntary "Blue Button" initiative, which reflected an effort to streamline patient access to their personal health data.[40]

Also in the United States, but in the financial sector, Section 1033 of the Dodd-Frank Wall Street Reform and Consumer Protection Act of 2010 grants consumers the right to access their financial information in electronic format. Recently, the Consumer Financial Protection Bureau (CFPB) initiated a regulatory process for the aforementioned section, whose significance was highlighted by President Biden in 2021.

Globally, the debate on portability began with the recognition of the need for users of digital services or products to migrate their list of friends and contacts, email addresses, and other data—which they spent hours adding—to other services or websites. Data portability is, at its core, a means of promoting the sharing of social information.[41]

By allowing the data subject to receive back their personal data provided to a controller in a structured, commonly used, and machine-readable format, so that they may then transmit it to another controller[42] of their choosing, the right to data portability has come to be regarded as a new tool under data protection legislation.[43] The subject of data portability extends beyond names and email addresses,

[37] It is important to highlight that data portability will play a crucial role in Web 3.0 (*Semantic Web technologies integrated into, or powering, large-scale Web applications*), which can be understood as the phenomenon in which individuals cease to be mere users and become part of the applications themselves, acting as both producers and beneficiaries of dig data. Bouchagiar (2018).

[38] This concerns the possibility for the data subject to establish a "second digital home." In this regard, Vitor Fidalgo notes that, under the GDPR, there is no data portability in cases of data erasure (Article 17 of the GDPR). Fidalgo (2019).

[39] Castro (2021).

[40] Castro (2021).

[41] Zanfir (2012).

[42] Article 29 Data Protection Working Party (2016), p. 3.

[43] Graef (2016), p. 2.

acquiring new dimensions and scope in light of the extensive collection of a wide variety of individual data, as previously discussed.

It is argued that the right to portability concerns data regulation rather than competition regulation, since the new European Union Regulation does not limit the right to those who intend to switch providers.[44,45] Similarly, Damien Geradin and Monika Kuschewsky[46] argue that data portability is an individual right and is not related to the right of other providers or competitors to access the same data.

It is agreed that data portability should exist regardless of whether it is used for switching between providers, and its recognition as an individual right is important. In addition, portability also has technical implications[47] in other areas.[48]

The transition to the normative protection model outlined here, centered on the recognition of portability as an active tool for managing digital identity and the electronic body, necessitates overcoming compartmentalized views within the legal system. The effectiveness of this prerogative, however, cannot be understood in isolation, as it fundamentally depends on the integration between the spheres that protect data subjects and those that regulate market relations. For this reason, it is imperative to investigate how personal data protection and consumer protection coexist in the digital environment, moving beyond the notion of normative compartmentalization in favor of a harmonious system. On this premise, the next section is dedicated to exploring the coexistence of these protections and the transformative potential of the dialogue between legal sources as a mechanism for legal certainty and the promotion of competitiveness.

7.2 The Dialogue of Sources: Data Protection and Consumer Defense

Before the emergence of consumer law, it was argued that competition was capable of placing the consumer in the position of king,[49] making him responsible for ordering the market. Thus, the initial protection of the consumer was developed by

[44] Article 29 Data Protection Working Party (2016), p. 3.

[45] This emphasis has been criticized by data protection experts, who argue that competition is an element of the right to data portability and should be included in the work carried out by the task force. Boardman et al. (2017).

[46] Geradin and Kuschewsky (2013).

[47] Zanfir (2012), p. 1.

[48] Portability can enable the creation of datasets and access to data, an important element for the development of new technologies and artificial intelligence. Access to data in the development and deployment of artificial intelligence is fundamental (European Commission 2018). In particular, mention is made of the indispensable need for the transfer and exchange of data between businesses and sectors for the purpose of developing the Internet of Things (Graef et al. 2019, p. 23).

[49] This assertion is based on the so-called theory of value, which holds that in the capitalist system the consumer is sovereign, being free to spend their money as they see fit. As a result, production

commercial and economic law,[50] more specifically within the framework of competition law.[51] Over time, and as a result of the ills of unrestrained capitalism, it became evident that this was not sufficient, particularly due to the failures present in supplier–consumer relationships that distort or prevent the consumer from making an effective choice.[52]

A historic milestone demonstrating the desire for change occurred in the 1960s, when the need for direct consumer protection was recognized. In this regard, as a precursor, reference is made to the statement by US President John Kennedy to Congress on March 15, 1962, declaring that we are all consumers.

In Brazil, the consumer movement emerged only in the 1980s but with enough momentum to place the issue on the political agenda at the same time as the country was undergoing redemocratization. The movement was so successful that consumer protection was enshrined in the 1988 Federal Constitution as a fundamental right and as a principle of the economic order.[53]

With such constitutional provisions, the system underwent a renewal, centered on the attempt to equalize legal relationships whose main feature is inequality, which may manifest in various forms (economic, access related, informational, etc.). Bruno Miragem[54] explains that the individualistic paradigm gives way to new interests equally recognized by the state, such as intervention on behalf of the vulnerable to restore legal equality.

The Constitution also mandated the important creation of a code for consumer protection. In compliance with this constitutional directive, the Consumer Protection Code (Código de Defesa do Consumidor—CDC) was enacted in 1990, which came to embody the trend toward new rights and responsibilities centered on consumer relations.[55]

Although consumers now enjoy direct protection, complementary and indirect protection of competition cannot be disregarded, as it is essential for the realization

---

must respond to the voluntary choices of consumers, which, in theory, would make them "kings" in the market. Ghodke (1985). Claudia Lima Marques, drawing on a socioeconomic perspective, rejects this view of the consumer as the "king" of the market, who would make sovereign decisions regarding the purchase or refusal to purchase a product. According to the author, such a perspective ignores structural elements of the market, such as the effects of advertising and fashion, as well as aggressive and emotional marketing and contracting techniques. Benjamin et al. (2013), p. 45.

[50] Comparato (2011), pp. 167–186.

[51] Benjamin (1994), p. 20.

[52] Ricardo Lorenzetti refutes the classical view that competition could grant the consumer a bargaining position. Lorenzetti (2001), p. 223.

[53] Benjamin et al. (2013), p. 33.

[54] Miragem (2016), p. 45.

[55] Sarney (2012).

of the consumer's right of choice.[56] Thus, not only in Brazil but also in most countries, there is complementarity between consumer protection and competition law.[57]

This supplementation of consumer protection by competition represents the crystallization of the legal reality established by so-called social law, as elucidated by Cristiano Heineck Schmitt.[58] In this context, although the economy is based on free enterprise, it is structured according to criteria of social justice.

In addition to the application of consumer protection regulations alongside competition rules, it is important to emphasize that consumer protection is one of the guiding principles of economic activity, as established in Article 170, item V, of the Federal Constitution. As a result, consumer protection applies to the entire economic order, as highlighted in Extraordinary Appeal 351.750/RJ.[59]

This means that protective regulations for vulnerable parties in the market will apply to economic activities in general, whether these are conducted under a competitive regime or are regulated. Thus, although free enterprise is one of the foundations of the Republic, the inclusion of consumer protection as one of the principles of the economic order, alongside other values, demonstrates that it is not unlimited. In this regard, Marcelo Schenk Duque clarifies[60] that all freedoms proclaimed by the Constitution must be exercised harmoniously, in observance of the limits defined by the constitutional order itself.

Thus, consumer protection regulations, enacted on constitutional grounds, will have broad applicability, as clearly established by Article 3, §2 of the Consumer Defense Code (CDC), which defines a service as any activity offered in the consumer market. An example of this is the application of such regulations to the financial market, even though, given its importance to the country's stability and development, it is regulated by supplementary law and supervised by the Central Bank of Brazil, as duly noted in ADI 2591.[61]

It is necessary to consider the application of consumer protection regulations even in the case of state monopolies (or privileges, when it comes to public

[56] Carpena (2005).

[57] This trend of complementarity also took place in the European Union through the following stages: first, regulation based on competition (Articles 85 and 86 of the Treaty of Rome); subsequently, the authorization to harmonize national legislation on consumer law (new Article 100 of the Treaty of Rome). Then, the transfer of competence to harmonize consumer law, adopted in 1992 in the Maastricht Treaty, and, finally, the recognition that consumer protection is one of the fundamental objectives of the Union (Article 153, Treaty of Amsterdam).

[58] Schmitt (2009), pp. 10–31.

[59] Brazil. Federal Supreme Court. *Extraordinary Appeal No. 351,750*. Reporting Justice for the judgment: Justice Carlos Britto, adjudicated on March 17, 2009.

[60] Duque (2014).

[61] Brazil. Federal Supreme Court. *Direct Action of Unconstitutionality No. 2591*. Reporting Justice for the Judgment: Justice Eros Grau. Decided on June 7, 2006.

services[62]), such as the postal service,[63] as well as public services in general, when these involve specific remuneration for the provision of the service and are part of the consumer market in a divisible and individually measurable manner.[64]

In this context, it can be stated that compliance with consumer rights, in matters of public services that meet the above requirements, will be the same whether the public services are provided by companies under state shareholding control or by private concessionaires (Art. 22, Law No. 8078/90). The establishment of regulatory agencies as a result of the privatization of public services does not eliminate the obligations set forth by the Consumer Defense Code (CDC), since regulation has a different mission, although it must also ensure consumer protection. In this regard, regulatory agencies seek to reconcile the public interest, the obligations inherent to the concession of the service, and consumer protection with the freedom necessary for the profitable management of the business, a characteristic of private companies.[65]

However, despite the existence of regulatory agencies, providers of regulated services still frequently appear on official lists of the largest recipients of consumer complaints. This may suggest challenges related to the effectiveness of oversight mechanisms and the timeliness of sanctioning procedures.[66]

A significant part of this problem originated in the very conception of the Brazilian regulatory model, which did not take into account how regulation would specifically protect consumers. In practice, economic aspects may end up being prioritized, while consumers receive comparatively less attention.[67]

With regard to data, it is argued that even if personal data is regulated in Brazil, consumer protection laws would still apply to all suppliers, including those already subject to general data regulation, provided that the requirements characterizing a consumer relationship are met.

---

[62] This terminological distinction was made by Eros Grau in the context of ADPF No. 46, emphasizing the need to differentiate between the regime of privilege, related to the provision of public services, and the regime of monopoly, in which the state engages in the exploitation of economic activity in the strict sense. Brazil. Supreme Federal Court. *Allegation of Breach of Fundamental Precept No. 46*. Justice Eros Grau, Reporting Justice for the Judgment. Decided on August 5, 2009.

[63] The case law of the Superior Court of Justice recognizes the application of consumer protection regulations to public services provided by the Postal Service. In the judgment of the Divergence Embargoes in Special Appeal No. 1,097,266, the Court affirmed that public companies providing public services are subject to the strict liability regime, as established in Article 37, § 6, of the Federal Constitution, as well as in Articles 14 and 22 of the Consumer Protection Code.

[64] It cannot be denied that there are numerous disagreements regarding the types of public services subject to the rules of the Consumer Defense Code (CDC). The controversies concern whether the activity must be directly remunerated, through fees, tariffs, or public prices or whether it could be remunerated indirectly and remotely, as occurs with taxes. For the purposes of this work, the position adopted is that a specific remuneration for the service is required and that it must be provided within the context of the consumer market. Benjamin et al. (2013), p. 226.

[65] Farena (2013), p. 2.

[66] Farena (2013), p. 13.

[67] Brazilian Institute for Consumer Protection (2010), p. 25.

This defense is based on the characterization of consumer protection as a fundamental right (and, therefore, a constitutional guarantee) and as a principle of the economic order.[68] Thus, it would not be a case of a (mere) conflict of norms, which would seek resolution through the classical methods established in the Law of Introduction to the Rules of Brazilian Law, but rather an interpretation grounded in the Constitution, in order to preserve values of utmost importance, such as consumer protection and the safeguarding of personal data.[69]

Given the special protection focused on the individual (emphasizing vulnerability) rather than the subject matter, consumer protection rules should not be disregarded, even in the presence of general data protection regulation. Both are specific, and neither prevails over the other.

In this regard, it is important to note that the LGPD itself contains mechanisms that reinforce the complementarity and harmonization of these protections. Firstly, Article 2 of the LGPD establishes that consumer protection is one of the foundations of personal data protection.

According to paragraph 8 of Article 18 of the LGPD, the right to file petitions may also be exercised before consumer protection agencies. Third, Article 64 of the LGPD establishes that "the rights and principles set forth in this Law do not exclude others provided for in the national legal system relating to the subject matter or in international treaties to which the Federative Republic of Brazil is a party."

Finally, to promote legal certainty and ensure the consistent application of data protection rules, Article 55-K provides that the authority to impose sanctions under the LGPD rests exclusively with the National Data Protection Authority (ANPD). The provision further establishes that, in matters concerning the protection of personal data, the ANPD's decisions and regulatory authority shall prevail over the related competences of other public administrative bodies and entities.

In addition, Article 55-K requires the ANPD to coordinate its activities with other regulatory and enforcement authorities whose mandates relate to personal data protection. The provision also designates the ANPD as the central authority responsible for interpreting the LGPD and for issuing the rules and guidelines necessary for its implementation.

Indeed, there is a mutual reinforcement between the regimes: while one form of protection focuses on the subject, the other is directed at the regulated matter. Within consumer law, the rules seek to ensure protection for the individual qualified as the final recipient in the consumer market (Article 2).[70] It should be noted, however, that

---

[68] Brazil. Federal Supreme Court. *Extraordinary Appeal No. 351,750*. Reporting Justice for the judgment: Justice Carlos Britto, adjudicated on March 17, 2009.

[69] Miragem (2012), pp. 67–111.

[70] In the words of Minister Cezar Peluso in his concurring opinion in Extraordinary Appeal 351.750-3, the Consumer Protection Code is not intended to regulate a specific subject matter but rather to protect a certain category of individuals, even if they are also protected by other legal regimes (Art. 7). Hence its highly specialized nature. Brazil. Federal Supreme Court. *Extraordinary Appeal No. 351.750*. Reporting Justice for the judgment: Minister Carlos Britto, decided on March 17, 2009.

defining who may be considered the final recipient is not a simple task, especially given the lack of explicit clarification in the legislation, a circumstance that has given rise to intense doctrinal debate.[71]

Two schools of thought have addressed this challenge: the maximalist approach, which considers only the factual criterion for characterizing the final recipient, requiring merely that the consumer objectively terminates the production chain in which the product or service is inserted; and the finalist approach, which takes into account the subjective criterion, restricting the concept of consumer to those who acquire (or use) a product for their own use or for their family. The consumer, in this sense, would be the nonprofessional.[72]

Although the finalistic theory is the one that best addresses the state of affairs targeted by the special protection afforded to consumers, there are cases in which it may lead to injustices by excluding from protection individuals who are in a position of disadvantage in the consumer market. As a result, the finalistic theory has been further developed to also recognize as consumers small businesses or vulnerable professionals who purchase a product or contract a service outside their field of expertise.

The mitigated finalism has been embraced by case law and has, to date, been applied by Brazilian courts.[73] Indeed, the focus for legitimizing consumer protection is the vulnerability of the party, whether a natural person or a legal entity.

Vulnerability, according to Antônio Herman Benjamin,[74] is a trait common to all consumers, whether rich or poor, educated or uneducated, shrewd or credulous. It is a condition that creates an imbalance in relationships established within the consumer market, which can be observed from different perspectives.

With regard to these, three types of vulnerability can be identified: technical, legal, and factual.[75] In summary, technical vulnerability refers to the lack of specific knowledge about the object of purchase. Legal or scientific vulnerability concerns the absence of specific legal knowledge, as well as knowledge of accounting or economics.[76] This type of vulnerability is exacerbated by the frequent use by

---

[71] Benjamin et al. (2013), p. 92.

[72] Benjamin et al. (2013), p. 94.

[73] In this context, the case law of the Superior Court of Justice has consolidated the understanding that, as a rule, the definition of consumer status must follow the finalistic theory, according to which only those who are the actual and economic end recipients of a good or service, thereby permanently removing it from the consumer market, are considered consumers. From this perspective, the so-called intermediate consumption—when the product or service is incorporated into the production chain to form part of the cost of another good or service—does not fall under the protection afforded by consumer legislation. Nevertheless, the case law has allowed for a mitigated application of this theory with respect to legal entities, recognizing their equivalence to consumers when a situation of vulnerability in relation to the supplier is demonstrated, an approach that legal scholarship has termed "deepened finalism" (Brazil. Superior Court of Justice. Special Appeal No. 1,195,642, Rapporteur: Justice Nancy Andrighi, adjudicated on November 13, 2012).

[74] Benjamin et al. (1998), p. 300.

[75] Marques et al. (2016), p. 262.

[76] Benjamin et al. (2013), p. 101.

suppliers of legal mechanisms that harm consumers or prevent the contractual instrument from being adapted to their needs, as is the case with standard form contracts.

Finally, the factual or economic vulnerability refers to the power held by the supplier, which enables them to adopt unilateral and independent actions that are often detrimental to consumers. In addition to these three types, there is also informational vulnerability, which concerns the insufficiency of data available to the consumer for decision-making.[77] Despite the identification of these types of vulnerability, the Superior Court of Justice (STJ) has already indicated that other forms of vulnerability may be recognized in specific cases, demonstrating that these are merely illustrative.[78]

Unlike the scope of application of the Consumer Defense Code (CDC), which focuses on the vulnerable party, a general data protection law will focus on regulating the use of data, especially in response to the challenges posed by the automation of collection mechanisms and the development of a market in which data is the main asset. In the general protection of personal data, individuals will be protected regardless of whether or not they are classified as consumers and, therefore, as end recipients.

The proposal for a general and unified law for data protection aims to provide a uniform level of protection for personal data, regardless of the sector in which it is being used. This serves to reduce uncertainty for citizens, who would otherwise be subject to varying levels of protection depending on the sector in which their data is processed, considering the common transfer of data across different markets, as explained by Danilo Doneda and Laura Mendes.[79]

Experience from the European Union demonstrates that, even with the existence of a general law, there is the possibility for the general provision to coexist with other specific regulations.[80] This was already present in Directive 95/46/EC and is now expressly provided for in the GDPR, as can be inferred from Recital 10.

This general law does not exclude or dispense with the special treatment afforded to consumers by consumer protection regulations, which may also play a role in the protection of personal data, as they have done up to now. Such involvement is particularly relevant given the tradition and consolidation of the consumer protection system in Brazil, with state, municipal, and federal agencies (PROCONs and SENACON), demonstrating its extensive reach, as well as the significant role played by the judiciary in consumer law matters, which deals with these issues on a daily basis.

---

[77] Benjamin et al. (2013), p. 99.

[78] Brazil. Superior Court of Justice. *Special Appeal No. 1358.23*. Rapporteur: Justice Nancy Andrighi. Judged on June 17, 2013.

[79] Doneda and Mendes (2017), p. 47.

[80] Mendes (2014), p. 49.

In this regard, there have already been practical cases in the consumer protection sphere related to the issue of personal data protection.[81] In this context, several cases involving SENACON's actions in Brazil can be cited, such as investigation of the security incident involving the TIM Negocia service, investigation into data processing by Rappi, notification to the Zoom application for clarification regarding the processing of personal data, imposition of a fine of R$ 6.6 million on Facebook Inc. and Facebook Serviços Online do Brasil Ltda for the improper sharing of user data, and the conviction of Decolar.com to pay a fine of R$ 7,500,000.00 (seven million five hundred thousand reais) for price differentiation of accommodations and denial of available offers based on the consumer's geographic location, through techniques known as *geo pricing* and *geo blocking*.

This joint and/or complementary action by consumer authorities and data protection authorities is evidenced in Brazil by the Technical Cooperation Agreement signed between SENACON and ANPD in 2021. Through this agreement, SENACON will begin to share information collected regarding consumer complaints related to personal data protection with ANPD, which, in turn, will establish the necessary interpretations for the application of the General Data Protection Law (LGPD).

Accordingly, it is argued that, alongside a right to data portability established in a general regulation on the protection of personal data, there should also be data protection within the scope of consumer protection, which may include the right to data portability.

In this regard, the Consumer Defense Code (CDC) and the General Data Protection Law (LGPD) must coexist, applying in a complementary manner through the dialogue of sources.[82] Through this dialogue, as explained by Claudia Lima Marques,[83] a new order of sources emerges, so that one law no longer repeals the other; instead, the norms interact with each other, allowing for a joint and harmonious application guided by constitutional values and human rights.

Through this new model, laws are no longer understood as isolated fortresses, as exclusive domains of a single law. Thus, in the postmodern era, there is a shift from monologue to the coexistence of norms.[84]

Marcelo Schenk Duque[85] further emphasizes the need for fruitful communication among normative sources. Thus, the dialogue of sources is employed to ensure the coherent application of legal norms, which should prioritize the functionality of a plural and complex system that characterizes contemporary law as a whole.

---

[81] On this topic, see: Cravo and Joelsons (2020).

[82] Bruno Miragem clarifies that the dialogue of sources is not merely a method of interpretation. It is also a method of application, serving as a means to overcome the classical criteria for resolving conflicts, which at times sacrifice constitutional values of utmost relevance, such as those pertaining to fundamental rights. Miragem (2012), pp. 67–111.

[83] Marques (2012), p. 27.

[84] Marques (2012), pp. 17–66.

[85] Duque (2012), pp. 125–157.

Indeed, the dialogue of sources can serve as a basis for the possible coexistence of the two special laws: the LGPD and the CDC.[86] Through this dialogue, it will be possible to achieve a simultaneous, coherent, and coordinated application of these regulations.

Given this interaction between data protection and consumer rights, how might we envision the right to data portability within consumer protection regulations? In Australia, the Consumer Data Right (CDR) was introduced in 2017 with the aim of granting consumers greater access to and control over their data. The CDR establishes consumer rights to access and transfer their data in the Australian banking, energy, and telecommunications sectors through the implementation of mandatory APIs.[87]

In the United States, some state laws already recognize consumers' right to data portability. The California Consumer Privacy Act (CCPA), for example, establishes that when a consumer requests access to their personal information, the company must provide it free of charge and in a timely manner, either in physical or electronic form. When provided electronically, the data must be presented in a portable format and, whenever technically feasible, in an easily usable format, allowing the data subject to transmit it to another entity without hindrance. The legislation also stipulates that companies are not required·to comply with such requests more than twice within a 12-month period (Cal. Civ. Code § 1798.100(d)).

Similarly, the legislation of the State of Colorado also guarantees consumers the right to data portability. The Colorado Privacy Act provides that data subjects may obtain their personal data in a portable format and, whenever technically feasible, in a readily usable format that allows its transmission to another entity without hindrance. The regulation further establishes that this right may be exercised up to twice per calendar year. Unlike California legislation, however, Colorado law explicitly states that the exercise of this right may not result in the disclosure of the data controller's trade secrets (Colo. Rev. Stat. § 6-1-1306(1)(e)).

Similarly, the Virginia Consumer Data Protection Act also provides for the right to data portability, ensuring that consumers have the ability to obtain a copy of the personal data they have previously provided to the controller. This data must be made available in a portable format and, whenever technically feasible, in a readily usable format that allows its transmission to another controller without hindrance, especially when processing is carried out by automated means (§ 59.1-573(4)).

Ultimately, data portability is essential for the development of a healthy and dynamic market. With it, consumers will be able to effectively make their choices and favor reputable providers who are committed to delivering higher-quality services and products that comply with current regulations.

---

[86] Marques (2012), pp. 17–66.

[87] Marques (2012), pp. 17–66.

With regard to the digital market, this right serves as a remedy against new monopolies that rely on network effects. In addition, mechanisms are created to reduce barriers to entry.

The right to data portability should not be safeguarded solely by a specific policy. Considering that this right involves data protection, competition law, and consumer protection, it is essential that these three areas work together, for all the reasons previously outlined.[88]

As previously argued, the protection of personal data is a fundamental right, intrinsically linked to personality and not merely a property right.[89] Data portability reinforces this core protection of personal data, thus serving as a guarantee of the effectiveness of this right. Furthermore, portability can be seen as the realization of consumer protection, a fundamental right established in Article 5, item XXXII, of the Federal Constitution.

Therefore, the situation brought about by data portability cannot remain confined to the discretionary sphere of public authorities, understood here in their broadest sense—legislative, executive, or judiciary. On the contrary, there is a binding obligation (a duty), in view of the objective dimension of the fundamental right at issue.

Clèmerson Merlin Clève[90] explains that the objective dimension of fundamental rights encompasses the commitment of the constituted powers to fundamental rights, in the sense of providing the necessary public services, exercising police powers, and legislating in order to give effect to constitutional normative commands. This dimension also extends to the judiciary, which will carry out constitutional filtering, that is, the reinterpretation of infraconstitutional law in light of constitutional precepts.[91]

This filtering is based on the radiating effectiveness of fundamental rights, which also imposes on the state the duty to act. This duty concerns the establishment and implementation of public policies, which also include institutional adaptation.[92]

In this regard, data portability, incorporated within a regulatory context as an extension of objective effectiveness, serves to establish a plurality of choices, thereby ensuring the institutional guarantee of competition,[93] which could be compromised by untimely *ex post* regulation. Thus, as previously demonstrated, the protection of competition may not be sufficient to safeguard access to markets where there are utilities deemed essential and controlled by companies with excessive market power.

---

[88] A recent OECD report highlights a growing need for cooperation and regulatory coordination among agencies, especially in areas where data portability is cross-sectoral. According to the report, in most cases, data portability involves personal data and may be driven by privacy, consumer protection, and competition considerations. This requires multidisciplinary enforcement collaboration, particularly when other sector-specific regulators are involved. OECD (2021).

[89] Mendes (2014), p. 124.

[90] Clève (2006), p. 31.

[91] Clève (2006), p. 54.

[92] Martel (2010), p. 71.

[93] Salomão Filho (2003).

Furthermore, as previously discussed, data portability allows the data subject to determine how their data will circulate, which will be subject to their request and the exercise of their will. This is clearly the affirmation of informational self-determination, which is essential for the protection of the electronic body.

From this conclusion arises the need for an *ex ante* provision, without prejudice to a complementary role for competition in matters of portability. This competitive role, more than merely complementary, will in certain cases be exclusive, as it may encompass data not covered by regulation.

A combined approach utilizing both *ex ante* and *ex post* mechanisms[94] offers several additional advantages that deserve to be highlighted. First, regulatory agencies possess a higher degree of specialization than competition authorities. Second, precisely because the competition authority is not as specialized or as closely connected to economic agents, it is better positioned to avoid partiality and the risk of regulatory capture,[95] which is a potential concern in regulation.

By differentiating the roles of each of these spheres of state intervention, it is possible to observe that regulation deals with an enormous and continuous flow of information, whereas competition intervention relies on more case-specific information, generally obtained from interested parties such as competitors, suppliers, and consumers. Regulatory agencies tend to favor behavioral remedies, while competition authorities are more inclined toward structural solutions.[96]

An important point to highlight is that although regulation is an interventionist approach in the economy, it does not address only strictly economic issues, such as price and supply. Regulation may also concern technical matters, such as standards or targets to be observed by economic agents,[97] as will be the case with the regulation of personal data, which should encompass standards for the preservation of privacy and rights of data subjects, such as the right to data portability.

Ultimately, data portability is synthesized as an indispensable pillar for enabling informational self-determination and promoting efficiency in the digital economy, overcoming, through the dialogue of sources, any potential fragmentation between personal data protection and consumer protection. The analysis was based on the premise that personal data constitute an extension of personality, or a true electronic body, whose active management by the data subject is a *sine qua non* condition for private autonomy in the digital environment.

---

[94] Gesner de Oliveira and João Grandino Rodas emphasize that the interaction between regulatory agencies and competition authorities is indispensable for the process of economic modernization. Oliveira and Rodas (2013), p. 149.

[95] The capture theory was developed by George Stigler, who argues that regulatory agencies are subject to "capture" by the companies they regulate, thereby adopting measures and policies that benefit these companies while neglecting other interests at stake. As a result, regulated companies, instead of using their resources to improve their products or services, end up investing capital to exert pressure on regulators in order to achieve their desired outcomes. Stigler (1971), pp. 3–21.

[96] Sampaio (2013), p. 88.

[97] Oliveira and Rodas (2013), p. 137.

In examining the intersection between the LGPD and the Consumer Defense Code (CDC), it has been demonstrated that the right to data portability transcends its nature as an individual prerogative, establishing itself as a strategic mechanism for enhancing competitive leverage that mitigates the phenomenon of technological lock-in and reduces the informational asymmetry inherent in market relations. In doing so, it promotes the much-needed consumer right of choice.

The contribution of this chapter to the central objective of the work—which examines how legal and institutional frameworks can be designed to reduce fragmentation, minimize regulatory frictions, and provide legal certainty for the safe and legitimate reuse of data—is substantial. Firstly, by arguing that portability should not be treated as an isolated legal niche but rather as the point of convergence between the protection of personality rights and the promotion of the right to choose, an integrated normative foundation is established that avoids conflicting interpretations and reduces systemic fragmentation. This cohesive approach enables the legal system, instead of operating through isolated silos, to foster a functional and coordinated normative coexistence.

With regard to reducing regulatory frictions, the text indicates that recognizing the dialogue of sources as a methodology for interpretation and implementation is the necessary path to ensure a smooth flow of data. By understanding that regulation should be designed with a focus on interoperability and user empowerment, the set of technical and contractual barriers that currently operate as unjustified obstacles to data reuse is eliminated. Consequently, it can be inferred that legal certainty for such legitimate reuse arises from clarity regarding the fundamental nature of the right to portability. When the institutional framework recognizes this prerogative from the perspective of the objective dimension of fundamental rights, data reuse ceases to be an activity shrouded in uncertainty and becomes a structured, protected, and encouraged practice.

In conclusion, it is evident that the legal framework required for the contemporary data ecosystem cannot be established through mere normative layering but rather through the strategic orchestration of competencies among regulatory authorities and consumer protection bodies. The transition from a fragmented model to a governance system aligned with the demands of a human-centered digital market is, therefore, the essential foundation for data reuse to become a sustainable driver of economic development and social progress, ultimately ensuring the stability and predictability demanded by economic agents and civil society.

Thus, having examined the foundations of this right and demonstrated that it may also be protected through other means, such as consumer and competition law, it becomes necessary to analyze in greater detail how the right to data portability is specifically structured within personal data protection regulations. It is precisely from these regulations that the more precise legal contours of the right to portability are defined, as well as the limits and conditions for its exercise.

References

Article 29 Data Protection Working Party (2016) Guidelines on the right to data portability. European Commission, Brussels

Benjamin AH (1994) Consumer protection and patents: the case of medicines [Proteção do consumidor e patentes: o caso dos medicamentos]. Rev Direito Consumidor 10:21–26

Benjamin AH, Grinover AP, Fink DR et al (1998) Brazilian consumer protection code: commented by the authors of the draft bill [Código brasileiro de defesa do consumidor: comentado pelos autores do anteprojeto], 5th edn. Forense Universitária, Rio de Janeiro

Benjamin AH, Marques CL, Bessa LR (2013) Manual of consumer law [Manual de direito do consumidor], 5th edn. Revista dos Tribunais, São Paulo

Bioni B (2015) Checkmate: the tripod of personal data protection in the chess game of legislative initiatives in Brazil [Xeque-mate: o tripé da proteção de dados pessoais no jogo de xadrez das iniciativas legislativas no Brasil]. GPoPAI/USP, São Paulo

Boardman R, Mullock J, Mole A (2017) Guide to the General Data Protection Regulation. Bird & Bird, London

Bouchagiar G (2018) Privacy and Web 3.0: implementing trust and learning from social networks. Rev Eur Stud 10(4):89–102

Bozdag E (2018) Data portability under GDPR: technical challenges. https://ssrn.com/abstract=3111866

Brazilian Institute for Consumer Protection (2010) Series thinking about law: regulatory agencies and consumer protection. Secretariat of Legislative Affairs of the Ministry of Justice (SAL/MJ), National School of Consumer Defense, Brasília

Carpena H (2005) Consumer in competition law [Consumidor no direito da concorrência]. Renovar, Rio de Janeiro

Castro D (2021) Improving consumer welfare with data portability. Center for Data Innovation, Washington

Centre on Regulation in Europe (CERRE) (2020) Making data portability more effective for the digital economy. CERRE, Brussels

Clève CM (2006) The effectiveness of fundamental social rights [A eficácia dos direitos fundamentais sociais]. Rev Direito Const Int 54:28–36

Colombo C, Goulart G (2020) Posthumous right to personal data portability in cyberspace in light of Brazilian law [Direito póstumo à portabilidade de dados pessoais no ciberespaço à luz do direito brasileiro]. In: Flores AJDM (org) Perspectives of legal discourse: digital revolution and globalized society [Perspectivas do discurso jurídico: revolução digital e sociedade globalizada], vol 1. Editora da FURG, Rio Grande, pp 90–109

Comparato FK (2011) Consumer protection: an important chapter of economic law [A proteção do consumidor: importante capítulo de direito econômico]. In: Marques CL, Miragem B (orgs) Consumer law: essential doctrines [Direito do consumidor: doutrinas essenciais], vol 1. Revista dos Tribunais, São Paulo, pp 167–186

Cravo DC, Joelsons M (2020) The importance of the CDC in the treatment of personal data of consumers in the context of pandemic and vacatio legis of the LGPD [A importância do CDC no tratamento de dados pessoais de consumidores no contexto de pandemia e de vacatio legis da LGPD]. Rev Direito Consumidor 28:185–202

Doneda D, Mendes LSF (2017) Legislative initiatives on personal data protection in Brazil [Iniciativas legislativas sobre proteção de dados pessoais no Brasil]. Revista Uruguaya de Protección de Datos Personales 2:44–52

Duque MS (2012) The transport of the theory of the dialogue of sources to the theory of the constitution [O transporte da teoria do diálogo das fontes para a teoria da constituição]. In: Marques CL (coord) Dialogue of sources: from conflict to coordination of norms in Brazilian law [Diálogo das fontes: do conflito à coordenação de normas do direito brasileiro]. Revista dos Tribunais, São Paulo, pp 125–157

Duque MS (2014) Fundamental rights: theory and practice [Direitos fundamentais: teoria e prática]. Revista dos Tribunais, São Paulo

European Commission (2018) GDPR data portability and core vocabularies. European Commission, Brussels

European Commission (2020) A European strategy for data. European Commission, Brussels

European Data Protection Supervisor (EDPS) (2014) Privacy and competitiveness in the age of big data: the interplay between data protection, competition law and consumer protection in the digital economy. EDPS, Brussels

Farena DVM (2013) Regulatory agencies: inspection of public services and consumer protection [Agências reguladoras: fiscalização dos serviços públicos e defesa do consumidor]. Custos Legis Rev Eletrônica Minist Público Federal 2013:1–14

Fidalgo VP (2019) The right to personal data portability [O direito à portabilidade de dados pessoais]. Rev Direito Tecnol 1(1):123–145

Geradin D, Kuschewsky M (2013) Competition law and personal data: preliminary thoughts on a complex issue. https://papers.ssrn.com/sol3/papers.cfm?abstract_id=2216088

Ghodke NB (1985) Encyclopaedic dictionary of economics. Mittal, Delhi

Graef I (2016) Data portability at the crossroads of data protection and competition policy. Autorità Garante della Concorrenza e del Mercato, Rome

Graef I, Husovec M, van den Boom J (2019) Spill-overs in data governance: the relationship between the GDPR's right to data portability and EU sector-specific data access regimes. TILEC Discussion Paper No. DP 2019-005

Helsinki EU Office (2020) Data agile economy: from reactive to proactive approach for the benefit of the citizens. Helsinki EU Office, Helsinki

Janal R (2017) Data portability: a tale of two concepts. JIPITEC 8(1):59–69

Kessler DS, Dresch RFV (2020) Right to data portability in the Brazilian and European context [Direito à portabilidade de dados no contexto brasileiro e europeu]. In: Cravo DC, Kessler DS, Dresch RFV (orgs) Data portability in the General Data Protection Law [Portabilidade de dados na Lei Geral de Proteção de Dados]. Foco, Indaiatuba

Lorenzetti R (2001) Electronic commerce [Comercio electrónico]. Abeledo-Perrot, Buenos Aires

Marques CL (2012) The dialogue of sources as a method of the new general theory of law: a tribute to Erik Jayme [O diálogo das fontes como método da nova teoria geral do direito: um tributo a Erik Jayme]. In: Marques CL (coord) Dialogue of sources: from conflict to coordination of norms in Brazilian law [Diálogo das fontes: do conflito à coordenação de normas do direito brasileiro]. Revista dos Tribunais, São Paulo, pp 17–66

Marques CL, Benjamin AH, Miragem B (2016) Comments on the Consumer Protection Code [Comentários ao Código de Defesa do Consumidor]. Editora Revista dos Tribunais, São Paulo

Martel LCV (2010) Fundamental rights: analysis of their effectiveness in the private sphere [Direitos fundamentais: análise da sua eficácia na esfera privada]. Livraria do Advogado, Porto Alegre

Mendes LS (2014) Privacy, data protection and consumer defense: general lines of a new fundamental right [Privacidade, proteção de dados e defesa do consumidor: linhas gerais de um novo direito fundamental]. Saraiva, São Paulo

Menke F (2014) Data protection and the new fundamental right to the guarantee of confidentiality and integrity of technical-informational systems in German law [A proteção de dados e novo direito fundamental à garantia da confidencialidade e da integridade dos sistemas técnico-informacionais no direito alemão]. In: Mendes G, Sarlet I, Coelho A (orgs) Law, innovation and technology [Direito, inovação e tecnologia]. Saraiva, São Paulo, pp 205–230

Miragem B (2012) Eppur si muove: dialogue of sources as a method of systematic interpretation in Brazilian law [Eppur si muove: diálogo das fontes como método de interpretação sistemática no direito brasileiro]. In: Marques CL (coord) Dialogue of sources: from conflict to coordination of norms in Brazilian law [Diálogo das fontes: do conflito à coordenação de normas do direito brasileiro]. Revista dos Tribunais, São Paulo, pp 67–111

Miragem B (2016) Course of consumer law [Curso de direito do consumidor], 6th edn. Revista dos Tribunais, São Paulo
Monteleone AG (2017) The right to data portability: between personal rights and market rights [Il direito alla portabilità dei dados: tra direitos da pessoa e direitos do mercado]. LUISS Law Rev 2:189–205
Negri S, Korkmaz MR (2021) Private autonomy, data portability, and estate planning [Autonomia privada, portabilidade de dados e planejamento sucessório]. In: Teixeira DC (org) Architecture of estate planning [Arquitetura do planejamento sucessório], vol 2. Fórum, Belo Horizonte, pp 660–674
Negri S, Korkmaz MR, Fernandes E (2021) Portability and personal data protection: tensions between person and market [Portabilidade e proteção de dados pessoais: tensões entre pessoa e mercado]. Civilistica.com 10(1)
OECD (2018) Personal data portability: translation of a user-centric right into a competition tool. OECD Publishing, Paris
OECD (2021) Data portability, interoperability and digital platform competition. OECD Competition Committee Discussion Paper, Paris
Oliveira G, Rodas JG (2013) Law and economics of competition [Direito e economia da concorrência]. Revista dos Tribunais, São Paulo
Rodotà S (2005) Person, freedom, technology. Notes for a discussion [Persona, libertà, tecnologia. Note per uma discussione]. Diritto & Questioni Pubbliche 5:25–29
Salomão Filho C (2003) Competition law: conducts [Direito concorrencial: as condutas]. Malheiros, São Paulo
Sampaio PRP (2013) Regulation and competition [Regulação e concorrência]. Saraiva, São Paulo
Sarney J (2012) Speech on the occasion of the inauguration of the Commission for the Update of the Consumer Protection Code [Discurso por ocasião da posse da Comissão de Atualização do Código de Defesa do Consumidor]. Senate Portal, Brasília
Schmitt CH (2009) The protection of consumer interest through the guarantee of freedom of competition [A proteção do interesse do consumidor por meio da garantia à liberdade de concorrência]. Rev Tribunais: Doutrina Civil 98:10–31
Stigler G (1971) The theory of economic regulation. Bell J Econ Manag Sci 2(1):3–21
Stigler Committee on Digital Platforms (2019) Final report. Stigler Center at the University of Chicago Booth School of Business, Chicago
Syrmoudis E, Mager S, Kuebler-Wachendorff S et al (2021) Data portability between online services: an empirical analysis on the effectiveness of GDPR Art. 20. Proc Privacy Enhancing Technol 2021(3):351–372
Van Alstyne M (2016) A platform strategy: creating new forms of value in the digital age. Capgemini Consulting
Villani C (2018) For a meaningful artificial intelligence: towards a French and European strategy. Mission Villani Report, Paris
Zanfir G (2012) The right to data portability in the context of the EU data protection reform. Int Data Privacy Law 2(3):149–162

Chapter 8
Data Portability in Personal Data Protection Regulations

8.1 General Aspects of Personal Data Portability

The portability of personal data is one of the most innovative instruments in the field of data protection, particularly as it enables greater control by data subjects over their information and fosters more dynamic competitive environments. In this context, this chapter examines the right to data portability as outlined in the European General Data Protection Regulation (GDPR)[1] and the Brazilian General Data Protection Law (LGPD).[2,3]

[1] The right to data portability is regulated by Article 20 of the GDPR, which establishes that the data subject may obtain the personal data concerning them, which they have provided to a data controller, in a structured, commonly used, and machine-readable format, as well as transmit those data to another controller without undue interference from the original controller. This prerogative applies when the processing is based on consent or on the performance of a contract and is carried out by automated means. The provision also ensures, whenever technically feasible, the direct transmission of data between controllers. Furthermore, the exercise of this right does not preclude the application of other safeguards provided for in the regulation nor does it apply to processing necessary for the performance of tasks carried out in the public interest or in the exercise of official authority. Finally, it is noted that portability must be exercised in accordance with the protection of the rights and freedoms of third parties.

[2] In the General Data Protection Law, the right to data portability is provided for in Article 18, item V, ensuring the data subject the possibility of requesting the transfer of their data to another service or product provider, upon express request, in accordance with the guidelines to be established by the national authority, as well as the protection of trade secrets. Additionally, Article 19, §3, of the LGPD expands on this principle by establishing that, in cases where processing is based on the data subject's consent or on a contract, the data subject may request a complete electronic copy of their personal data, in a format that enables its subsequent use, including in other processing operations, while also respecting trade and industrial secrets and the regulations of the competent authority.

[3] According to Paula Ponce, in the text of the first stage of the public consultation for the creation of the draft bill on Personal Data Protection, promoted by the Ministry of Justice and concluded in

D. Copetti Cravo, *Law and the Digital Economy*,
https://doi.org/10.1007/978-3-032-36672-6_8

In addition to these statutes, it is observed that several other jurisdictions have incorporated provisions regarding the portability of personal data into their regulatory frameworks. Although with varying levels of regulatory detail and scopes of application, countries such as China, Thailand, Zambia, Panama, and Benin[4,5] already include, to some extent, this right in their legislation, highlighting a global trend toward strengthening data subjects' prerogatives in the digital ecosystem.

Data portability is a new right,[6] not provided for in the former European Directive No. 95/46/EC. It is an extremely modern right, introduced by the General Data Protection Regulation (GDPR).

Although the right to data portability is closely related to the right of access, as both promote the data subject's control over their data, these rights are distinct and complementary. During the legislative discussions of the GDPR, the possibility of including data portability within the right of access was considered. However, data portability was ultimately established as an autonomous right, separate from the right of access.[7]

Portability, therefore, can be seen as a step forward, an evolution beyond the right of access, since the data format would no longer be limited to that chosen by the controller, in addition to enabling the reuse of data[8] by the data subject themselves or by another controller.

Another difference between the right of access and the right to data portability within the European framework lies in the limits and applicability of each. Portability will only cover data provided by the data subject and when processing is automated and based on consent or the performance of a contract.[9] Such restrictions and limitations, however, do not apply to the right of access under the GDPR, so that the right of access and the right to data portability end up complementing each other.[10]

In Brazil, there has not been a clear distinction between portability and the right of access, as occurred in the European context. Some aspects that are included under the right to portability in the GDPR have been incorporated into the right of access in the LGPD, as can be seen in paragraph 3 of Article 19 of the LGPD.

April 2011, there was no mention of the right to data portability. This right was only included in 2015 (Ponce 2020, p. 151).

[4] OneTrust (2022).

[5] In India, the Digital Personal Data Protection Act (DPDP), inspired by the EU GDPR, represents a significant step forward but excludes the Right to Data Portability (RtDP) that was present in earlier drafts of the same legislation. However, the law introduces a limited form of data portability through consent managers, who act as intermediaries between users and platforms. These managers, registered with the Data Protection Board, facilitate the provision, management, review, and withdrawal of consent, suggesting an attempt to support some form of data portability. Vrabec et al. (2023).

[6] Prior to its adoption by the GDPR, data portability options were offered only on a voluntary basis in the European Union (EU), as no provision in EU legislation prescribed such a practice (Nebbiai 2022).

[7] Fidalgo (2019), p. 91.

[8] Duarte and Guseinov (2019), p. 110.

[9] Graef et al. (2017), p. 1367.

[10] Stiftung Datenschutz (2017).

It is worth reflecting on whether this choice made by the Brazilian legislator was appropriate, given that there appears to be a certain mismatch and lack of harmony between the provision in item V of Article 18, which does not limit portability to processing based on consent or a contract, and the provision in §3 of Article 19 of the LGPD. Furthermore, in the Brazilian context, the data subject is given the option to choose the means by which the right of access is provided, whether electronically or in printed form (Art. 19, §2, of the LGPD).

With regard to the data covered by data portability, both under the LGPD (§ 7 of Article 18) and the GDPR (Recital 26), anonymous data are not subject to portability. However, it is argued that whenever it is possible to identify the data subject through the provision of additional information, such data should be included within the scope of portability, as has been advocated in the European context, based on Article 11 of the Regulation.[11] Thus, pseudonymized data would be covered by the right to data portability.

With regard to the types of data covered (provided, observed, and inferred), the LGPD does not offer a specific definition. Under the GDPR, since the drafting of the Regulation, there have been controversies concerning the scope of data portability.

As noted by Lucio Scudiero,[12] although there was a campaign for a broad scope of the right to data portability, a scope limited to "provided" personal data was ultimately adopted, which represents a significant change in the final text compared to the initial draft.[13]

Even after defining the type of data, the discussion regarding its scope remains unsettled. This is because the term "provided" receives different interpretations—one restrictive and the other extensive—according to Paul Hert *et al.*[14] According to the restrictive interpretation, provided data would be only those explicitly supplied in writing or through another active means, such as filling out a form or answering specific questions.

In the case of extensive interpretation, provided data refers to any data that controllers have collected through consent or in the legitimate interests of executing a contract, such as GPS data, cookies, user preferences, etc.[15] In this sense, provided data would include data observed by the controller (e.g., location), as long as these data are not the result of any activity by the controller, whether intellectual, economic, or scientific (such as outcomes generated by algorithms).

To address these uncertainties, the Article 29 Working Party (WP29)[16] proposes that the right in question, within the scope of the European Regulation, should encompass both data directly provided by the data subject through an active process, such as filling out a form, and "raw" observed data, obtained without any action or use of technological tools by the controller.

---

[11] Wang and Shah (2017).

[12] Scudiero (2017), pp. 119–127.

[13] The initial project was quite broad, encompassing within the scope of data portability any "data in processing." Hert et al. (2017).

[14] Hert et al. (2017).

[15] Hert et al. (2017).

[16] Article 29 Data Protection Working Party (2016), p. 3.

In other words, an extensive interpretation should be adopted, as advocated by the WP29,[17] so that the right to data portability encompasses both the category of data actively provided by the data subject (such as email address, username, age, among others) and observed data (e.g., "raw" data processed by a smart meter or other types of connected devices, activity logs, website usage history or search activities, location and traffic data, as well as heart rate data).[18]

On the other hand, according to WP29,[19] data created by the controller would not be included within the right to data portability, even if such data were generated using observed or directly provided data as input, as is the case with profiles, statistics, or analyses. This is because these categories of data result from a processing activity, even though their basis is personal data.

Notwithstanding the WP29's conclusion,[20] it should be considered that this interpretation is based on the legal text of the GDPR, which expressly limited the scope of data portability to data provided by the data subject. Therefore, the exclusion of inferred data is justifiable.

Note, therefore, that discussions within the scope of the GDPR revolve around what is encompassed by the term "data provided." In our legal system, there was no such restriction imposed by law, which allows and requires us to discuss whether inferred data will be subject to data portability.

It is understood that further reflection is required regarding the lack of a specific definition in item V of Article 18 of the LGPD. There remains controversy as to whether this absence can be considered an intentional silence on the part of the legislator, intended to encompass all "processed data" (i.e., provided, observed, and inferred),[21] or whether such a definition was reserved for future regulation.

In Singapore,[22] the Personal Data Protection Commission launched a public consultation to define the implementation of data portability. One of the issues addressed in the consultation was the types of data covered by portability.

In this consultation, the Singapore Commission proposed the application of the right to data in electronic format that are (a) provided by the individual and (b) generated by user activities. After receiving feedback, the Commission expressed its

[17] Article 29 Data Protection Working Party (2016), p. 3.

[18] It is understood that the data provided also include observed data. On the other hand, profile data are not covered by the data portability provision under the GDPR. However, companies may voluntarily offer this type of portability as a sign of compliance and trust (Vrabec 2018). Along these lines, data generated by the provider for statistical and analytical purposes related to online reputation are not included (Diker Vanberg and Ünver 2017).

[19] Article 29 Data Protection Working Party (2016), p. 3.

[20] Article 29 Data Protection Working Party (2016), p. 3.

[21] As reported by Paula Ponce, this issue was debated in Congress during the consideration of Provisional Measure No. 869/2018. Amendment No. 42 was proposed to exclude data derived from portability. However, the amendment was rejected by the Joint Committee, which held that portability would only concern data generated by the data subject themselves and not those generated or supplemented by the controller. Ponce (2020), p. 148.

[22] Singapore. Personal Data Protection Commission. *Response to Feedback on the Public Consultation on Proposed Data Portability and Data Innovation Provisions*.

interest in maintaining this scope but intends to issue a list specifying the standard of data that should be subject to portability, in order to ensure greater clarity and certainty for organizations.

With regard to the legal bases encompassed by data portability, under the GDPR, data portability is limited to processing activities carried out on the basis of consent or when necessary for the performance of a contract (Recital 68 and Article 20(1)(a)). Furthermore, the processing must have been carried out by automated means, that is, digitally, and does not apply to cases where data is processed in physical form, on paper (Article 20(1)(b)).

Under the LGPD, the right to data portability has not been subject to any limitation regarding legal bases (such restriction was only applied to the right of access, in the modality provided for in §3 of Article 19). However, it is understood that an overly broad scope of portability may have side effects, precisely due to the challenges and costs associated with compliance. Therefore, it is worth considering whether this issue might be addressed in future regulations to be issued by the National Data Protection Authority (ANPD).

Regarding the subjective aspect of portability, that is, to whom it applies, a quick and literal reading of Article 18, item V, of the LGPD could lead to the conclusion that data portability would only apply to controllers that fall under the concept of "supplier." To define this concept, it would be necessary to engage in a dialogue with the provisions of the Consumer Protection Code (CDC).[23,24]

At this point, it is understood that the LGPD did not employ the best technique by using the term "supplier" in item V of Article 18, especially since this concept creates legal fragmentation, which runs counter to the objective of a general law: to ensure uniformity and legal certainty. Furthermore, the very heading of Article 18 establishes the controller as the party responsible for upholding data subjects' rights, which should also apply to portability, given that it is topographically included within this article.

Additionally, considering that data portability is an individual right and is not limited to promoting consumer welfare and competition, the LGPD should not have

[23] With regard to the application of data portability in the public sector, a literal interpretation of item V, Article 18, of the LGPD would suggest that the public sector is only required to observe portability in cases where it acts as a supplier, that is, in situations where Article 3 of the Consumer Defense Code (CDC) applies. In general, with the exception of public companies and mixed-capital companies engaged in strictly economic activities, the public sector is considered a supplier when it provides public services that are individualized and remunerated by fees. In this case, data portability would apply in an almost "exceptional" manner within the public sector, since most of its activities do not fall under the characteristics described above.

[24] At the European level, the GDPR in its Recital 68 expressly states that, by its very nature, portability should not be exercised in relation to controllers who process personal data in the pursuit of their public tasks or for the exercise of official authority. In other words, within the public sector, its application will be extremely limited, only occurring when acting on the basis of a contract or consent (which is the exception, as in the case of data collection through a *newsletter*). However, data portability may be adopted as a best practice by the public sector in other cases (European Commission 2018, p. 7).

imposed such a restriction. As previously discussed, data portability is closely linked to informational self-determination, which is why it should apply broadly to data processing and not only to those activities carried out within a consumer relationship. An example of this is employment relationships, where data portability can be important and beneficial to the data subject.

In light of these considerations, it becomes apparent that the legislative choice to use the term "supplier" in item V of Article 18 is questionable, as it introduces a conceptual fragmentation incompatible with the logic of a general data protection law, whose central purpose lies in promoting regulatory uniformity and legal certainty. This inconsistency becomes even more evident when one observes that the main section of the aforementioned article assigns to the controller the responsibility for ensuring the rights of data subjects, which, for the sake of systematic coherence, should likewise encompass the right to data portability.

Furthermore, considering that data portability constitutes an individual right directly linked to informational self-determination, its limitation to the scope of consumer relations is not appropriate. The implicit restriction resulting from the terminology used unduly narrows the scope of the institute, which, as previously discussed, has the potential to be applied in multiple contexts of personal data processing, such as in labor relations, where it can play a significant role in ensuring greater informational control by the data subject.

It is precisely from these normative tensions and interpretative challenges that it becomes necessary to advance toward a more in-depth analysis of the practical and structural aspects of data portability, especially with regard to its implementation and the technical requirements that make it feasible.

8.2 Implementation, Interoperability, and Potential Conflicts with Other Rights

The effectiveness of the right to data portability is not exhausted by its normative provision; it largely depends on technical and operational conditions that enable its implementation. In this context, interoperability plays a central role, as it facilitates the transfer of data between different agents and systems.

Before, however, examining the treatment given to the subject by the legal texts (GDPR and LGPD), in order to investigate what they provide regarding this matter, it is necessary to distinguish between the concepts of "interoperable format" and "interoperability." An interoperable format refers to minimum standards that enable data exchange and reuse.[25] At a minimum, it is expected that the data be in a structured, commonly used, and machine-readable format.[26]

---

[25] European Commission (2018).

[26] Article 29 Data Protection Working Party (2016), p. 17.

An interoperable system, or interoperability, refers to the ability to communicate, execute programs, or transfer data among different functional units without requiring knowledge of the unique characteristics of each unit.[27] The topic of interoperable systems is addressed in ISO/IEC 2382-01.

Thus, data interoperability can be defined as follows: "the ability of technology, information, and communication systems, and the processes they support, to share data and exchange information and knowledge, through mechanisms that ensure compatibility of access and format."[28]

In Brazil, at the federal government level,[29] there are several initiatives aimed at developing interoperability for the implementation of electronic government policies. In the Interoperability Guide, as well as in Decree No. 10,046/2019,[30,31] interoperability is defined as the ability of different systems and organizations to work together.

It should be noted that interoperability is an essential tool for public administration, particularly to ensure the provision of more appropriate and efficient public services. However, such development must be accompanied by effective protection of personal data.[32]

Recently, interoperability in public administration was strengthened by Law 14,129/2021 (Digital Government Law). For the purposes of complying with the provisions related to interoperability in the aforementioned law, the Federal Court of Accounts (TCU), through Decision No. 2279/2021, required federal public bodies to implement effective interoperability mechanisms and system integration measures aimed at enhancing the management of public policies through the use of data, evidence-based approaches, and predictive services.

At the European level, Decision No. 922/2009/EC of the European Parliament and of the Council defines in Article 2(a) interoperability as the ability of disparate and diverse organizations to interact through the exchange of data between their respective ICT systems.

Furthermore, in 2020 the European Commission adopted the Communication "Shaping Europe's Digital Future" (COM (2020) 67) under the title "A Europe Fit for the Digital Age." Among the key actions outlined in the Communication is the

[27] Puccinelli (2017), p. 207.

[28] LAPIN (2021).

[29] Ministry of Planning, Budget, and Management (2012).

[30] It should be considered that despite the objectives pursued by Decree 10,046/2019 regarding efficiency in the management of public services and the fight against fraud, some criticisms have been directed at the Decree, precisely due to the lack of safeguards and mechanisms for citizens to control how their data is being processed and by which agencies (Maranhão and Campos 2019).

[31] It should be noted, however, that the constitutionality of this Decree was challenged in Direct Action of Unconstitutionality (ADI) 6649, currently pending before the Supreme Federal Court and assigned, by prevention, to the same Justice presiding over ADPF 695, which also concerns the same Decree. In its ruling, the Supreme Federal Court (STF), by majority vote, decided that federal public administration bodies and entities may share personal data among themselves, provided that certain criteria are observed.

[32] LAPIN (2021).

development of a "strengthened interoperability strategy for EU governments," aimed at promoting coordination and the adoption of common standards for public services and data flows.[33]

In this context, and with the aim of achieving interoperability, the Commission launched the evaluation of the ISA program and the European Interoperability Framework (EIF, COM (2017) 134), as well as an impact assessment for a future public sector interoperability strategy for the European Union.

It is worth noting, finally, that interoperability represents a significant challenge, which becomes even more complex as systems grow more sophisticated. Therefore, prior harmonization and standardization become an absolute necessity.[34]

The absence of interoperability standards[35] is possibly one of the main obstacles to the effective implementation of portability. According to a study by Janis Wong and Tristan Henderson,[36] the practical application of data portability under the GDPR has proven to be complex. The researchers conducted 230 actual requests and identified difficulties such as identifying data controllers, obtaining standardized responses, and the variety of formats used by controllers, which are not always aligned with legal obligations.

These challenges highlight the need to refine the definitions of "structured, commonly used, and machine-readable formats," as well as to promote closer collaboration among regulators, organizations, and developers to establish guidelines, technical standards, and codes of conduct that enable the exercise of this right.[37]

The LGPD allows, in its Article 40, for the ANPD to establish interoperability standards for the purposes of portability. Thus, at present, there is no requirement for interoperability between services.

Precisely due to the absence of a mandatory requirement for interoperability for the purposes of portability, if technical barriers arise during its execution (notably in the case of the direct transfer of data to a new controller), the controller must explain these barriers to the requesting individual in an intelligible and clear manner, in accordance with paragraph 4 of Article 18 of the law.

Thus, in the context of the GDPR, although interoperability is a desirable outcome,[38] it is not required,[39] as clearly stated in Recital 68. According to this recital,

---

[33] European Commission (2021).

[34] ITS Rio (2021).

[35] Data portability differs from other forms of portability, such as number portability in telecommunications. This is because data portability, as a right of the data subject provided for in the GDPR or the LGPD, does not necessarily entail the termination of the relationship but rather grants access to a copy of the data for reuse in a domestic context or by another controller.

[36] Wong and Henderson (2019).

[37] Wong and Henderson (2019).

[38] Article 29 Data Protection Working Party (2016), p. 17.

[39] Note that in the case of direct data transfer (Article 20, no. 2, of the GDPR), the text itself states that this will only be required when technically feasible.

the right of the data subject to transmit or receive personal data does not entail an obligation for data controllers to adopt systems that are compatible with one another.

Although interoperability is not mandatory, Paul Hert *et al.*[40] suggest that it should be required. According to the authors, the true intention of the Regulation is not merely a direct transfer from one controller to another but rather the development of a robust interconnection between different digital services, thereby fostering a *user-centered* system.[41]

Interoperability can be achieved through complementary markets, which will be encouraged to develop or even emerge originally. To this end, exemptions in the field of intellectual property law could be granted to promote a better experience in terms of interoperability and, consequently, portability.

This encouragement of compatibility and interoperability can be found in precedents from the United States, such as the case of Lotus Development Corp. v. Borland International,[42] cited by Peter Swire and Yianni Lagos.[43] In this case, the Court held that Lotus could not use its copyright protection to prevent competitors from creating programs that enabled interoperability.[44]

In the European Union, there is a provision very similar to the North American precedent. This is the 1991 Directive on Computer Programs, which establishes an exception to copyright, allowing third-party companies to observe, study, and copy a third-party program when necessary to achieve interoperability between programs.

Finally, it has been understood that without interoperability, it is very likely that portability will not achieve all of its potential effects.[45] Maurizio Borghi notes that the pro-competitive effects of portability tend to be more pronounced in markets with common data processing systems than in those lacking interoperable standards.[46]

Although interoperability for portability purposes is not yet mandatory in Brazil, it is argued that, when carrying out data portability, the controller should use interoperable formats to enable data reuse. Note that the LGPD does not specify requirements regarding data formats, but a teleological interpretation of the regulation leads to this conclusion, since it is essential that the data subject is able to reuse the data without significant obstacles.[47]

It is worth noting that the Brazilian legal framework already includes provisions promoting the use of interoperable data formats. Decree No. 8771/2016, which regulates the Brazilian Civil Rights Framework for the Internet, establishes in Article 15 that data must be maintained in an interoperable and structured format to

---

[40] Hert et al. (2017).

[41] Hert et al. (2017).

[42] United States of America. Court of Appeals for the First Circuit. *Lotus Development Corp. v. Borland International*. Decided in 1995.

[43] Swire and Lagos (2013), p. 340.

[44] Swire and Lagos (2013), p. 340.

[45] The recent OECD report "Going Digital in Brazil" highlights the importance of developing interoperability standards for data portability purposes OECD (2020).

[46] Borghi (2019), p. 15.

[47] Colombo and Goulart (2020), p. 94.

facilitate access resulting from a court order or legal requirement. Furthermore, Article 25 of the General Data Protection Law (LGPD) stipulates that data must be kept in an interoperable and structured format for shared use, with the aim of supporting the implementation of public policies, the provision of public services, and access to information by society.

Thus, it is concluded that, in Brazil, there is currently no requirement for interoperability for the purposes of data portability, although such a requirement may be established by the ANPD, pursuant to Article 40 of the LGPD. This conclusion does not eliminate the need to observe an interoperable format, so that the data is, at a minimum, structured, commonly used, and machine readable. In the European context, it is understood that, for the purposes of complying with data portability, the data controller must provide personal data in an interoperable, structured, commonly used, and machine-readable format (Recital 68 of the GDPR).

It is important to note that in the original draft of the GDPR, the Commission was assigned the role of identifying a common transfer format. However, the need to define such a format was ultimately abandoned, precisely due to existing divergences and debates regarding the competitive implications of imposing a format.[48,49]

In this context, the importance of developing application programming interfaces (APIs) is highlighted. APIs are a set of protocols that define how software components communicate with each other. By enabling a company to easily access data generated by another company, the development of interoperability between different agents becomes feasible.[50]

In this regard, the use of APIs for data storage and access emerges as an essential element for the portability and replication of technology models in a wide range of cities and communities, serving as an important guideline for the development of smart cities.[51,52,53,54]

---

48 Monteleone (2017), p. 209.

49 To prevent the frustration of the objectives of portability, and given the absence of a specification for the required electronic format by the competent authority, collaboration among the parties becomes indispensable (Diker Vanberg and Ünver 2017).

50 Borgogno and Colangelo (2018).

51 SynchroniCity (2020).

52 According to the OECD, although the concept of smart cities may vary between countries and international organizations, they are generally defined as those that use digital innovations to enhance competitiveness and the efficiency of urban services. OECD (2023).

53 In the contemporary context, cities are emerging as hubs at the forefront of technological innovation, transforming themselves into genuine "smart cities." Under this paradigm, we are witnessing the exponential proliferation of sensors throughout the urban fabric, eager to collect and integrate data. For example, cameras installed on *billboards* now have the capability not only to capture images but also to interpret viewers' gazes, facial expressions, and body movements in response to the displayed content. When subjected to advanced data analysis through artificial intelligence, this information can reveal much more than users wish or expect to disclose. OECD (2023).

54 The concept of "smart cities" has gained global prominence as an innovative response to contemporary urban challenges. These cities employ advanced technologies to enhance the efficiency of public services, promote sustainability, increase citizen participation, and improve quality of life. In Brazil, the Brazilian Charter for Smart Cities serves as a strategic guide for the digital transformation of cities, integrating sustainable urban development with technological solutions. Ministry of Regional Development (2020).

It should also be noted that the use of standardized APIs can enable seamless portability[55] and access to data regardless of their location.[56] The role of APIs in data reuse was also recognized in European Union Directive 2019/1024, which addresses open data.

Thus, the importance of developing APIs is reaffirmed so that portability can fully achieve its intended effects, such as promoting the right of choice, informational self-determination, and fostering competition. This assertion is supported by the successful experience of open banking,[57] whose implementation is based on APIs.[58]

The promotion of interoperability and the development of APIs can be carried out not only by the ANPD but also by regulatory authorities of sectoral markets. Furthermore, market participants may propose interoperability initiatives based on best practices, pursuant to Article 50 of the LGPD.

The Amsterdam Court had the opportunity to examine two important cases involving data portability and the issue of formats. The lawsuits were filed by ride-hailing drivers against Uber and Ola Cabs, in which the drivers requested access to their data based on Article 20 of the GDPR. They asked for this data to be provided via an API or a CSV file. However, the Court concluded that the requirement in Article 20 for a "machine-readable" format does not oblige controllers to provide the data specifically through an API or a CSV file.

In the context of implementing portability, it is worth noting that other technological approaches are being developed to facilitate the transfer of data between online service providers (OSPs). Dedicated platforms, such as the Data Transfer Project led by major companies like Google, Facebook, and Apple, aim to simplify the export and import of data through OAuth and APIs.[59]

Furthermore, solutions based on open protocols and service portals enable the continuous transfer of real-time data between different platforms. Examples include Matrix bridges, which connect messaging services using various protocols, providing integration, although they may raise concerns regarding privacy and regulatory compliance.[60]

Another emerging approach is the concept of self-hosting and personal data storage, where users control their own data hosted by third parties. This not only promotes user independence and competition based on service quality but also reduces the centralization of data under the exclusive control of online service providers.[61]

---

[55] CERRE (2020).

[56] EDPS (2014).

[57] Open banking can be understood as a sectoral regulatory mandate requiring financial institutions to allow portability and interoperability of their systems while ensuring data protection in these processes. Trindade (2020), p. 1977.

[58] Souto (2020), pp. 13–32.

[59] Kranz et al. (2023), pp. 597–607.

[60] Kranz et al. (2023), pp. 597–607.

[61] Kranz et al. (2023), pp. 597–607.

These innovations not only address technical and implementation challenges but also raise important questions regarding governance, privacy, and regulatory compliance. The evolution of these technologies is shaping the future of data portability, influencing how users can access and control their data in a constantly changing digital ecosystem.[62]

Furthermore, it is possible that the right to data portability may come into conflict with other rights,[63] such as trade secret protection or the safeguarding of intellectual creations.[64] Another issue that may arise concerns the privacy rights of third parties,[65] for instance, when an individual wishes to transfer a photograph in which several people appear.[66]

In such cases, it is possible to invoke the provision set forth in item II of § 4 of Article 18 of the LGPD, based on a legal ground that prevents the adoption of portability. There is also an express exception in item V of Article 18, which establishes that portability shall respect trade secrets.[67]

At the European level, Article 20(4) expressly provides that portability may not adversely affect the rights and freedoms of third parties. In the same vein, Recital 68 warns that, when a particular set of personal data concerns more than one data subject, the exercise of rights by one shall not prejudice the rights and freedoms of the others.

It should be emphasized that the application of these exceptions, whether based on Article 20(4) of the GDPR or item II of §4 of Article 18 of the LGPD, should not occur in any case of potential harm to the rights of others but rather when portability adversely affects those rights, that is, in an unjustified or illegitimate manner. This therefore requires a *case-by-case approach.*[68]

According to the Article 29 Data Protection Working Party (Art. 29 WP), controllers will often process data relating to multiple data subjects. However, this fact should not be used as grounds to deny or restrict data portability. What must be ensured is that the new controller does not process third-party data when such processing could adversely affect those individuals.[69]

---

[62] Kranz et al. (2023), pp. 597–607.

[63] As Indra Spiecker points out, until a standardized right to information is established that provides an appropriate balance between interests, the right to data protection will repeatedly come into conflict with other rights. Spiecker (2018), p. 30.

[64] According to Nebbiai, "under the pretext of protecting trade secrets and intellectual property rights, in order to counteract competitors' reverse engineering techniques, data controllers may increasingly restrict the set of data available for portability." Nebbiai (2022).

[65] This issue is also raised in the White Paper published by Facebook. Facebook (2019).

[66] Swire and Lagos (2013), p. 349.

[67] The LGPD does not specify to what extent or degree this interest should be observed nor does it define what may be considered trade and industrial secrets.

[68] Hert et al. (2017).

[69] Article 29 Data Protection Working Party (2016), pp. 11–12.

Thus, Article 29 WP[70] suggests that, in order to avoid adverse effects on third parties involved, the processing of such personal data by another controller is only permissible to the extent that the data remain under the exclusive control of the requesting data subject and are managed solely for purely personal or domestic needs. In other words, without a legal basis, the new controller may not use third-party data for its own activities, such as profile enrichment, statistical analysis, or targeted marketing.

Another interesting tool proposed by the Article 29 Working Party is that, prior to the execution of data portability, data subjects may select which data they wish to transmit. With this solution, the data subject can already exclude third-party data. It is also possible to encourage the pursuit of consent from these third parties as a way to legitimize the transfer.[71,72]

Among third-party rights, the protection of trade secrets and intellectual property rights is also included. This conclusion can be drawn through an analogous interpretation of Recital 63 of the GDPR. In the Brazilian context, trade secrets (commercial and industrial secrets)[73] are expressly provided for in item V, Article 18, of the LGPD.

Regardless of the choices made regarding the degree of protection afforded to trade secrets, especially when such protection conflicts with the rights of the data subject,[74] it should be considered that if the protection of trade secrets is conditioned upon an act of unfair competition, the mere acquisition of a copy of the data for personal use or the right of access by the data subject cannot, *prima facie*, be denied on the grounds of trade secrecy, since, as a rule, such exercise does not have the potential to cause unfair competitive harm to the company.

Another critical issue involving trade secrets concerns inferences, which are obtained through the processing of raw data, generally carried out using artificial intelligence. These inferences reveal the tastes, preferences, and positions of a given individual. The creation of profiles and rating systems also falls under the category of inferences.

---

[70] Article 29 Data Protection Working Party (2016), pp. 11–12.

[71] Article 29 Data Protection Working Party (2016), pp. 11–12.

[72] To address concerns regarding links with different users, as occurs on social media, certain measures can be adopted, such as using hash identifiers instead of personally identifiable contact information or unique identifiers for individual relationship pairs, in order to enable the other service to reconstruct these connections and relationships if both parties have transferred their data. Castro (2021).

[73] The provisions regarding trade and industrial secrets were introduced by EMP9, received in the Plenary during the consideration of Bill 4060/2012 by the Chamber of Deputies, with Bill 5276/2016 and Bill 6291/16 appended to the main proposal. Despite the legislator's significant concern with the protection of business knowledge within the scope of personal data protection, this remains one of the most neglected and underexplored topics in Brazil (Pela 2018, p. 546).

[74] It should be emphasized that the right to data portability is the right which, among those provided by the LGPD, has the most significant implications for unfair competition, a matter that, in our legal system, governs trade secrets.

Since they are produced by companies through their investments and technologies, could inferences be protected as trade secrets? Answering this question is not an easy task, especially because it would require a thorough investigation into the nature of inferences in order to determine whether they are considered personal data.

In any case, it can be argued that knowledge generated from the use of data that can no longer be associated with the original data, such that the data subject can no longer be identified and *backtrace* is impossible, may be protected as trade secrets. Furthermore, the techniques and algorithms used to obtain information and knowledge may also be covered by trade secret protection.[75]

Ultimately, whenever the exercise of any data subject right, such as portability, infringes upon trade secrets—understood as the technique used or the knowledge itself and not the inferences per se—the controller may justify any denial or limitation of the data subject's rights, provided that this is done transparently and explicitly, specifically demonstrating all internal investments made to protect the trade secret.

In addition, it is necessary for the national authority to take action in order to systematize and clearly regulate the issue of trade secrets, as well as to exercise oversight over possible denials or restrictions of rights provided for in the LGPD on the grounds of trade secret protection.

Regarding the potential conflict between intellectual property and data portability, Vitor Fidalgo[76] argues that this issue is more apparent than real for the following reasons: with respect to raw data, the execution of portability does not constitute an unlawful use of a computer program or a database. In the case of software, the protection granted concerns only its expression, so portability would not, in principle, infringe upon this protected interest. As for databases, these could be decompiled prior to transfer. Finally, regarding the rights of the database manufacturer, portability does not constitute a substantial violation if one considers that only a portion of the database content will be transmitted, which may not even be quantitatively significant.

One of the main concerns of the controller regarding the implementation of data portability is how to ensure data portability securely and without compromising the protection of data subjects.[77] Therefore, to fully realize the benefits of portability, it is essential and urgent that the responsibilities and legal obligations to be observed are established with utmost clarity.[78,79]

The initial stage of a data portability request is highly sensitive, as it is necessary to verify whether the requester is, in fact, the data subject, thereby preventing fraud by malicious individuals. One possibility is the use of two-factor authentication or requiring data subjects to enter their password. Additionally, an email may be sent to the

---

[75] Wachter and Mittelstadt (2019), p. 79.

[76] Fidalgo (2019), p. 125.

[77] Security is one of the main topics addressed at the recent FTC workshop (https://www.ftc.gov/news-events/events-calendar/data-go-ftc-workshop-data-portability).

[78] United Kingdom (2018).

[79] For a more in-depth analysis of liability in portability, see: Cravo et al. (2020), pp. 185–202.

requester's registered address to confirm whether they wish to proceed with the request (and even to block the transfer if the data subject does not recognize the request[80]).

Based on the experience with the GDPR, it has been observed that the speed of response to requests and the verification of the data subject's identity are not always easy to reconcile.[81] For this reason, it is recommended that the controller adopt precautionary measures for authentication purposes.

In the pre-transfer phase, there are still questions as to whether the data controller must ensure that the destination adheres to policies consistent with data protection. Furthermore, should the data controller inform the data subject about potential risks related to the destination of the data?

As noted by Article 29 WP, the data sender is not responsible for the recipient's compliance with data protection legislation, since the sender does not participate in the selection process.[82,83] A possible solution would be the creation of codes of conduct and certifications.[84] With the adoption of such measures, the data controller could carry out data portability with confidence.

Furthermore, during the data transfer phase of portability, measures must be adopted to ensure secure transmission to the correct destination (destination verification measures). In this context, the use of appropriate formats is particularly important, as well as peer-to-peer encryption[85] and new technologies such as blockchain.[86]

It is important to note that data portability is not based on consent but rather on an express request by the data subject. Therefore, the data sender acts more as a mere processor of the activity. However, this does not exempt the data sender from the responsibility of verifying the security of the transfer.[87]

Finally, in the post-transfer phase, the data sender will not be responsible for the processing of data carried out at the destination, even if such processing is abusive.[88] Furthermore, the data sender remains responsible for the data retained in its own systems,[89] which is why it must verify whether there is still a justification (legal basis) for the continued processing.

---

80 Facebook (2020).

81 Huddleston (2020).

82 Article 29 Data Protection Working Party (2016).

83 In this regard, the European Banking Federation issued an opinion stating that it would be necessary to emphasize that the controller transferring the data cannot prevent adverse effects on any third parties involved in the context of data portability. European Banking Federation (2017).

84 Singapore (2020).

85 United Kingdom (2018).

86 European Commission (2020).

87 Viola and Heringer (2020).

88 Viola and Heringer (2020).

89 Article 29 Data Protection Working Party (2016).

The original controller may be held liable for transmitting corrupted data[90] and must ensure that the data have been correctly delivered to the recipient.[91] The new controller, on the other hand, must ensure an appropriate legal basis for data processing.[92]

Ultimately, while portability is one of the greatest innovations introduced by the LGPD, as well as by the GDPR, it also represents one of the major challenges for the market.[93] Concerns regarding the security of data transmission or interoperability are inevitable, as are concerns related to the cost of compliance.[94]

Indeed, there is an undeniable concern that compliance with portability rules may become an excessive burden for small businesses, which could discourage both market entry and continued participation. In the long term, this may lead to market power concentration among large companies, especially if these companies become developers of APIs for implementing portability, thus revealing a potential anticompetitive impact of this tool.

One solution to counterbalance this situation is for the National Data Protection Authority in Brazil to adopt clear and precise guidelines regarding the definition of portability and its scope. In addition to being addressed in the future regulation of the law, such issues may also be included in specific lists, as, for example, proposed in Singapore.

Another possibility for reducing costs is the establishment of certain temporal limitations for the exercise of portability. For example, the California Consumer Privacy Act (CCPA) provides in Section 1798.130(a)(2)(A) that the right only applies to data collected in the last 12 months. Furthermore, the business is not required to provide personal information to a consumer more than twice within a 12-month period (1798.100(d)).

Moreover, it is essential for the ANPD to encourage and promote the adoption of an interoperability standard. However, this responsibility does not need to rest solely with the ANPD; in regulated sectors, such promotion may also be carried out by other regulatory authorities (as is already occurring in the context of Open Finance). Additionally, the market itself can take a leading role in the development

---

[90] Singapore (2020).

[91] Viola and Heringer (2020).

[92] ICO (2023).

[93] As stated in the JRC Digital Economy Working Paper 2020–2005, data portability is not (yet) sufficiently operational. Martens et al. (2020).

[94] Some studies estimate that the expected costs of a federal data portability regime for US companies amount to $340 million out of a total of $510 million—related to the processing of data subject requests. Due to these estimated costs associated with portability, there are regulatory initiatives to exempt certain controllers from complying with portability requirements. CPA Canada (2021). In this regard, reference is made to the recent public consultation on the possibility of exempting small-scale data processing agents from personal data portability obligations in a draft regulation by the National Data Protection Authority (ANPD). However, the final text of the ANPD Resolution did not include such an exemption. Under the CCPA, the portability obligation applies only to businesses that meet certain parameters defined in section 1798.140(d).

of interoperability through best practices, in accordance with Article 50 of the LGPD.[95]

Regardless of the regulatory approach adopted, it is certain that data portability is a right of the data subject, which may be exercised in three distinct ways: the mere transfer of data without terminating the relationship with the controller; obtaining a copy of the data in an automated format; and strict-sense portability, involving the termination of the relationship and the migration of the data subject to another service.

In any case, it is important to emphasize that any mechanism related to data portability must be implemented alongside security policies, especially during the data transfer phase. Finally, it is argued that the right to data portability should be harmonized with other interests and rights.

Whenever the exercise of any data subject right, such as portability, infringes upon trade secrets—understood as the technique employed or anonymized knowledge and not the inferences themselves—the controller may justify any denial or limitation of the data subject's rights, provided that this is done transparently and explicitly, specifically demonstrating all internal investments made to protect the trade secret.

In summary, the analysis of data portability in the context of the LGPD and the GDPR reveals that this mechanism goes beyond a mere individual prerogative, establishing itself as a fundamental component for enabling a dynamic and efficient data reuse ecosystem. In light of the central research question—which seeks to understand how to design legal and institutional frameworks capable of mitigating regulatory fragmentation, reducing regulatory friction, and providing legal certainty for the legitimate reuse of information—this chapter offers essential contributions.

Firstly, when addressing the conceptual disparity between the Brazilian and European legal frameworks, the study demonstrates that overcoming fragmentation requires a harmonized interpretation of the legal bases and the scope of data subject to portability. The proposal to move away from restrictive concepts, such as limiting portability solely to consumer relationships or to data strictly "provided," points to a more cohesive institutional model that recognizes informational self-determination as a foundational principle with cross-sectoral application throughout various areas of the economy.

With regard to the reduction of regulatory frictions, the chapter highlights that portability only achieves its practical purpose when supported by technical interoperability standards. The promotion of standardized APIs and structured data formats emerges as the solution to operational barriers that currently increase the cost of compliance, especially for smaller entities. This technical approach, when integrated with the regulatory governance exercised by the ANPD and other sectoral

[95] It is worth noting that the GDPR provides a certain degree of flexibility in the implementation of portability, allowing for the development of standards and self-regulation. This flexibility does not prevent the European Commission from imposing stricter rules should companies delay or neglect the development of their codes of conduct within a reasonable time frame (Wang and Shah 2017).

authorities, fosters an environment of "minimal friction," where the flow of data between controllers occurs in a smooth and predictable manner.

Finally, legal certainty for safe reuse is addressed through a clear delineation between the right to data portability and the protection of intangible assets, such as trade and industrial secrets. By proposing transparency criteria and the requirement for well-founded justifications for any denial of access, the chapter provides parameters for an institutional framework that balances innovation and competition without undermining companies' technological investments. Thus, data portability is presented not as a burden but as a catalyst for an integrated, secure, and user-centered digital market, essential for the development of public policies and next-generation private services.

References

Article 29 Data Protection Working Party (2016) Guidelines on the right to data portability. European Commission, Brussels

Borghi M (2019) Data portability and regulation of digital markets. CIPPM/Jean Monnet working papers, Bournemouth University

Borgogno O, Colangelo G (2018) Data sharing and interoperability through APIs: insights from European regulatory strategy. Comput Law Secur Rev 34(5):116–128

Castro D (2021) Improving consumer welfare with data portability. Center for Data Innovation, Washington

Centre on Regulation in Europe (CERRE) (2020) Making data portability more effective for the digital economy. CERRE, Brussels

Chartered Professional Accountants of Canada (2021) Implementing data portability: lessons for a made-in-Canada approach. CPA Canada, Toronto

Colombo C, Goulart G (2020) Posthumous right to personal data portability in cyberspace in light of Brazilian law [Direito póstumo à portabilidade de dados pessoais no ciberespaço à luz do direito brasileiro]. In: Flores AJDM (org) Perspectives of legal discourse: digital revolution and globalized society [Perspectivas do discurso jurídico: revolução digital e sociedade globalizada], vol 1. Editora da FURG, Rio Grande, pp 90–109

Cravo DC, Kessler DS, Dresch RFV (2020) Civil liability in data portability [Responsabilidade civil na portabilidade de dados]. In: Rosenvald N, Martins GM (orgs) Civil liability and new technologies [Responsabilidade civil e novas tecnologias], 1st edn Foco, Indaiatuba, pp 185–202

Diker Vanberg A, Ünver M (2017) The right to data portability in the GDPR and EU competition law: odd couple or dynamic duo? Eur J Law Technol 8(1)

Duarte DP, Guseinov A (2019) O direito de portabilidade de dados pessoais [The right to personal data portability]. In: Cordeiro AM, Oliveira AP, Duarte DPD (coords) FinTech II: novos estudos sobre tecnologia financeira [FinTech II: new studies on financial technology]. Almedina, Coimbra, pp 110–135

European Banking Federation (2017) Comments to the working party 29 guidelines on the right to data portability. EBF, Brussels

European Commission (2018) GDPR data portability and core vocabularies. European Commission, Brussels

European Commission (2020) A European strategy for data. European Commission, Brussels

European Commission (2021) Proposal for a Regulation of the European Parliament and of the Council on contestable and fair markets in the digital sector (Digital Markets Act). European Commission, Brussels

European Data Protection Supervisor (EDPS) (2014) Privacy and competitiveness in the age of big data: the interplay between data protection, competition law and consumer protection in the digital economy. EDPS, Brussels
Facebook (2019) Driving innovation in data portability with a new photo transfer tool. Palo Alto
Facebook (2020) Comments to the Federal Trade Commission on data portability. Palo Alto
Fidalgo VP (2019) The right to personal data portability [O direito à portabilidade de dados pessoais]. Rev Direito Tecnol 1(1):123–145
Graef I, Husovec M, Purtova N (2017) Data portability and data control: lessons for an emerging concept in EU law. Ger Law J 19(6):1359–1398
Hert P, Papakonstantinou V, Malgieri G et al (2017) The right to data portability in the GDPR: towards user-centric interoperability of digital services. Comput Law Secur Rev 33(2):193–203
Huddleston J (2020) Comments regarding data to go: an FTC workshop on data portability. Federal Trade Commission, Washington
Information Commissioner's Office (ICO) (2023) Guide to data protection. ICO, London
ITS Rio (Institute for Technology and Society of Rio) (2021) Portabilidade de dados, interoperabilidade e open banking [Data portability, interoperability, and open banking]. ITS Rio, Rio de Janeiro
Kranz J, Kuebler-Wachendorff S, Syrmoudis E et al (2023) Data portability. Bus Inf Syst Eng 65:597–607
LAPIN (Laboratory of Public Policy and Internet) (2021) Technical Note 10: recommendations for data interoperability in the public administration [Nota Técnica 10: Recomendações para a Interoperabilidade de Dados na Administração Pública]. LAPIN, Brasília
Maranhão J, Campos R (2019) A divisão informacional de poderes e o cadastro base do cidadão [The informational division of powers and the citizen's base registry]. Jota
Martens B, Tolan S et al (2020) Data portability is not (yet) sufficiently operational. JRC digital economy working paper 2020-05, European Commission
Ministry of Planning, Budget and Management (2012). Interoperability guide: Manager's manual. Brasília, Brazil: Ministry of Planning, Budget and Management.
Ministry of Regional Development (2020). Brazilian Charter for Smart Cities.
Monteleone AG (2017) The right to data portability: between personal rights and market rights [Il direito alla portabilità dei dados: tra direitos da pessoa e direitos do mercado]. LUISS Law Rev 2:189–205
Nebbiai M (2022) Intermediaries do matter: voluntary standards and the right to data portability. Internet Policy Rev 11(2)
OECD (2020) Going digital in Brazil. OECD Publishing, Paris
OECD (2023) Smart city data governance: challenges and the way forward. OECD Urban Studies, OECD Publishing, Paris
OneTrust (2022) Data subject access rights (DSAR): a comprehensive guide to data portability under GDPR and CCPA. OneTrust Privacy Platform, Atlanta
Pela JK (2018) The Brazilian regulation of trade secrets: a proposal for its review. Gewerblicher Rechtsschutz und Urheberrecht - Internationaler Teil 6:543–552
Ponce PP (2020) Right to data portability: between data protection and competition [Direito à portabilidade de dados: entre a proteção de dados e a concorrência]. Rev Defesa Concorrência 8(1):148–163
Puccinelli OR (2017) El derecho a la portabilidad de los datos personales. Orígenes, sentido y alcances [The right to personal data portability. Origins, meaning, and scope]. Pensam Const 22(22):207–234
Scudiero L (2017) Bringing your data everywhere: a legal reading of the right to portability. Eur Data Prot Law Rev 3(1):119–127
Singapore (2020) Personal Data Protection Commission. Response to feedback on the public consultation on proposed data portability and data innovation provisions. PDPC, Singapore

Souto G (2020) Assignment of financial data as a new business model through open banking [Cessão de dados financeiros como um novo modelo de negócios através do open banking]. Rev Procuradoria-Geral Banco Central 14:13–32
Spiecker I (2018) Right to data protection on the internet in case of collision [Direito à proteção de dados na internet em caso de colisão]. Direitos Fundamentais & Justiça 12(38):15–35
Stiftung Datenschutz (2017) Practical implementation of the right to data portability. Stiftung Datenschutz, Leipzig
Swire P, Lagos Y (2013) Why the right to data portability likely reduces consumer welfare: antitrust and privacy critique. Maryland Law Rev 335:335–380
SynchroniCity (2020) SynchroniCity: delivering a harmonised market for IoT-enabled smart city services. Final Project Report, European Commission's Horizon 2020 Programme, Brussels
Trindade MGN (2020) Platform economy (or trend towards the stock-marketization of markets): distinctive conceptual weightings in relation to the shared economy and collaborative economy and an economic analysis of law approach to economic efficiency gains through the severe reduction of transaction costs [Economia de plataforma (ou tendência à bursatilização dos mercados): ponderações conceituais distintivas em relação à economia compartilhada e à economia colaborativa e uma abordagem de análise econômica do direito dos ganhos de eficiência econômica por meio da redução severa dos custos de transação]. Rev Juríd Luso-Brasileira 4:1945–1980
Viola M, Heringer L (2020) Portability in the General Data Protection Law [A portabilidade na Lei Geral de Proteção de Dados]. ITS Rio, Rio de Janeiro
Vrabec H (2018) Unfolding the new-born right to data portability: four gateways to data subject control. https://ssrn.com/abstract=3176820
Vrabec H, Bansal Y, Gupta A (2023) Squeezing out an imperative right? The right to data portability in the Indian context. Leiden Law Blog. https://www.leidenlawblog.nl/articles/squeezing-out-an-imperative-right-the-right-to-data-portability-in-the-indian-context
Wachter S, Mittelstadt B (2019) A right to reasonable inferences: re-thinking data protection law in the age of big data and AI. Columbia Bus Law Rev 2019(1):494–620
Wang Y, Shah A (2017) Supporting data portability in the cloud under the GDPR. AliCloud Report
Wong J, Henderson T (2019) The right to data portability in practice: exploring the implications of the technologically neutral GDPR. Int Data Privacy Law 9(3):143–155

Chapter 9
New Agenda for Digital Markets: Gatekeepers and the Reconfiguration of Data Flows

9.1 The European Model of Proactive Regulation: Portability and Interoperability in the DMA and Data Act

In the contemporary economy, digital services, and especially online platforms, play an increasingly significant role. However, essential platform services[1] exhibit several characteristics that may be exploited in specific ways.

A distinctive feature of core platform services is their extreme economies of scale, which can result in almost zero marginal costs when adding new users. Additionally, these services exhibit strong network effects, the ability to connect numerous users through multilateralism, significant dependence on both suppliers and users, lock-in effects, absence of multi-homing, vertical integration, and data-driven economic advantages.[2]

[1] According to the Digital Markets Regulation 2022/1925 (Digital Markets Act—DMA), the following are considered "core platform services": (a) online intermediation services; (b) online search engines; (c) online social networking services; (d) video-sharing platform services; (e) number-independent interpersonal communication services; (f) operating systems; (g) Web browsers; (h) virtual assistants; (i) cloud computing services; and (j) online advertising services, including any advertising network, advertising exchange, or other advertising intermediation service, provided by an undertaking that offers any of the core platform services listed in points (a)–(i).

[2] As Nicolas Petit explains, the DMA reflects an approach based on network effects, which have been extensively studied in the digital economy. In these models, the addition of a new user to a platform results in significant marginal benefits for other users, a phenomenon known as the "network effect." This process creates a tipping point, where users tend to concentrate on one or more dominant platforms. The demand for these platforms proves to be stable and relatively inelastic, in contrast to the traditional analysis of dominance, which is limited to the horizontal size of companies. The DMA, therefore, considers not only the dimension of corporate expansion but also how network effects influence the competitive dynamics in the digital market (Petit 2021, p. 529).

D. Copetti Cravo, *Law and the Digital Economy*,
https://doi.org/10.1007/978-3-032-36672-6_9

Such characteristics, when accompanied by potential unfair practices by essential platform services, may negatively affect market contestability. As a result, there may be a significant reduction in consumers' right to choose, leading the service provider to assume the position of *gatekeeper*.

Digital gatekeepers act as true bridges between a wide range of commercial users and an even broader audience of end consumers, thanks to their innovative services. This strategic position not only facilitates transactions and communications on an impressive scale but also enables these gatekeepers to leverage their privileged positions. One of the greatest advantages at their disposal is access to a vast ocean of data generated by interactions on their platforms.

This access is not limited to superficial information; it extends to deep insights into consumer behavior, market trends, personal preferences, and much more. With this data, gatekeepers not only refine and personalize their current services but also identify opportunities to diversify their offerings and enter new markets. This ability to transfer knowledge and resources from one sector to another grants them a formidable competitive advantage, enabling not only the expansion of their areas of operation but also the consolidation of their position as central pillars of the digital economy.

In this context, gatekeepers play a critical role not only in connecting different spheres of electronic commerce but also in shaping the future directions of these connections. Their influence goes beyond that of mere intermediaries; they are architects of digital interaction, whose decisions and strategies have the power to set market standards, influence consumer behavior, and even shape the very structure of the global digital economy.

In this context, even if new entrants or established competitors adopt innovative and efficient practices, the structure of the digital market is such that challenging these giants is a Herculean task. The difficulty of contesting the market is exacerbated by significant barriers to entry and exit.

Massive initial investments are required, the returns on which are not guaranteed and may be unrecoverable in the event of market withdrawal. Furthermore, limited access to critical inputs, such as data, creates an additional gap, reinforcing the position of the *gatekeepers* and hindering the rise of new competitors.

This dynamic can result in markets operating suboptimally or, worse, in systematic failures that undermine the overall functionality of the digital sector. The disproportionate bargaining power of gatekeepers can lead to significant imbalances, negatively impacting both business users and end users. Unfair conditions may become entrenched, manifesting in distorted prices, compromised quality, unfair competition, reduced consumer choice, and stagnation of innovation.

The regulatory framework of the European Union, although comprehensive, faces challenges in dealing with the gatekeepers of the digital economy. Articles 101 and 102 of the Treaty on the Functioning of the European Union (TFEU) provide a legal framework, but their scope is limited to cases of dominance in specific markets and anticompetitive practices, applying mainly after the fact (ex post).[3] While this approach is essential, it is not sufficient to address the complexities and systemic challenges posed by gatekeepers.

In light of this gap, the Digital Markets Act (DMA)[4-5] emerges as a proactive response. This Regulation, enacted in 2022, was designed to address the shortcomings identified by public policies, recognizing that there are no less restrictive measures capable of effectively achieving the same objectives. Thus, the DMA is considered essential for safeguarding public order, protecting user privacy, and combating fraudulent and deceptive commercial practices.

According to the Digital Markets Act (DMA), a *gatekeeper* is a term used to describe certain digital platforms or online intermediaries that hold significant market power. *Gatekeepers* are central to the regulatory framework of the DMA and are subject to specific obligations[6] and rules aimed at ensuring fair competition and protecting the interests of consumers and businesses.

It is worth noting that the Digital Markets Act (DMA) entered into force on November 1, 2022, with most of its provisions beginning to apply on May 2, 2023, when the gatekeeper designation procedure commenced.[7] This document marks a significant turning point after 20 years of discussions regarding the underenforcement of competition laws.[8]

On September 6, 2023, the European Commission designated, for the first time, six gatekeepers—Alphabet, Amazon, Apple, ByteDance, Meta, and Microsoft. Subsequently, on April 29, 2024, Apple was designated as a gatekeeper specifically in relation to its iPadOS, the operating system for tablets, in accordance with the DMA. On May 13, 2024, the Commission also designated Booking as a gatekeeper for its online intermediation service Booking.com. In total, 24 core platform services provided by these gatekeepers have been identified.

---

[3] According to Demircan, the DMA aims to regulate digital markets using an ex-ante methodology with a "per se" approach. Demircan (2023).

[4] Vicente Bagnoli points out that the objective of the Digital Markets Act is to enable platforms to unlock their full potential by preventing unfair practices and weak contestability, thereby allowing both end users and business users to fully benefit from the digital economy. Bagnoli (2021), pp. 133–158.

[5] From the perspective of consumer law, Anna Moskal notes that the DMA misses the opportunity to provide the much-anticipated updated definition of "consumer," which could have led to a recalibration of EU consumer protection law. Furthermore, the DMA does not fully explore the potential of consumer protection. Moskal (2022), pp. 1113–1119.

[6] According to Pınar Akman, it remains questionable whether all the stipulated obligations are sufficiently clear to provide legal certainty, as claimed by the DMA, an aspect that is still under discussion. Akman (2022).

[7] Unlike the traditional logic of competition law, the DMA adopts a lighter informational criterion to allow for the early identification of platforms that occupy the position of *gatekeepers*. The intention is to prevent this qualification from depending on a detailed definition of the relevant market or on complex analyses of market power and position vis-à-vis competitors, enabling a swifter designation of companies and reducing the costs associated with structural tests. Petit (2021), p. 529.

[8] Demircan (2023).

The need for compliance is fundamental for gatekeepers designated under the Digital Markets Act (DMA). Following designation, gatekeepers must comply with the obligations set out in Articles 5, 6, and 7 of the DMA within a period of 6 months. Within this same time frame, they are required to provide the European Commission with a detailed and transparent report describing the measures implemented to ensure compliance with these obligations. In addition, they are required to publish a nonconfidential summary of these reports.

These reports, together with the nonconfidential summary, must be updated at least annually. Transparency and regularity in updating the reports are essential to ensure that gatekeepers continue to comply with the established rules and to enable proper oversight by the European Commission. In this way, the compliance process not only promotes fair competition and protects consumer rights but also strengthens the integrity and accountability of digital platforms in the European market.

Among the obligations imposed on *gatekeepers* by the DMA is the guarantee of data portability. The Regulation establishes that these entities must ensure that end users, as well as third parties authorized by them, have the possibility to obtain, upon request and free of charge, the effective portability of data provided or generated from the use of the core platform service. To this end, they must provide tools that facilitate the exercise of this right, including allowing continuous and real-time access to the relevant data (Art. 6, §9).

As established by the aforementioned article, the *gatekeeper* is required to provide end users and authorized third parties, upon request and free of charge, with effective portability of data supplied by the end user or generated through the user's activity in the context of using the relevant core platform service. This includes providing, at no cost, tools to facilitate the effective exercise of such data portability and encompasses the provision of continuous and real-time access to this data.

This obligation complements the right to data portability provided for in Regulation (EU) 2016/679, as stated in Recital 59 of the DMA. Furthermore, the DMA's portability provisions share several elements with the right to data portability under the General Data Protection Regulation (GDPR), such as (a) the right to receive the relevant data and (b) the right to have the data transferred to a third party.[9]

However, according to Barbara Lazzarotto,[10] the DMA introduces an addition to the right to data portability originally established by the GDPR, expanding its scope from personal data to all data provided by the end user and generated through their activity on a gatekeeper platform, including all legal bases listed in Article 6(1) of the GDPR. Furthermore, unlike the GDPR, the DMA covers both personal and non-personal data. Within the category of personal data, the DMA is also understood to include inferred and derived data, as has been interpreted so far.

Although the DMA states that it applies "without prejudice" to the GDPR, certain questions inevitably arise regarding the interaction between these two instruments. Likewise, it remains unclear whether the data portability provided for in the

---

[9] Geradin et al. (2022).

[10] Lazzarotto (2024).

DMA (which is broader than that of the GDPR) would constitute a *lex specialis* that would prevail over the GDPR.[11]

According to Chinmayi Sharma, the current wording of the DMA provides general guidelines but lacks detailed technical specifications or mandatory frameworks that companies must follow. While this approach may foster flexibility and innovation in interoperability and data portability strategies, it can also result in inconsistent application of the guidelines, potentially leading to market fragmentation or practices that reinforce the dominance of gatekeepers.[12]

To navigate these challenges, Chinmayi Sharma proposes a three-step strategy for implementing the DMA. Initially, the European Union should allow companies a certain degree of freedom to develop interoperability and data portability solutions tailored to specific contexts, thereby fostering a dynamic market for innovative solutions.

In a second stage, it would be essential to bring together experts and stakeholders to analyze current practices, assessing their effectiveness and shortcomings, in order to better understand which technological approaches truly fulfill the objectives of the DMA. Finally, the third phase would involve collaboration among a diverse group of stakeholders and experts to determine the most effective practices for different sectors, based on empirical analyses and normative assessments. In this way, the market could guide regulatory decisions, ensuring that the solutions adopted genuinely serve the purposes of the DMA.[13]

After the initial implementation deadline for gatekeepers to comply with the Digital Markets Act (DMA), the organizations MyData Global, Coalition for Online Data Empowerment, and Ethical Commerce Alliance wrote an open letter expressing concern over the inadequate implementation of data portability under the European Union's Digital Markets Act (DMA). The organizations highlight the lack of compliance by designated gatekeepers and the urgency for the European Commission to take action to ensure the effective implementation of tools that enable recurring data transfers and the realization of real-time, continuous data portability.

They emphasize that data portability is crucial not only for competition and innovation but also for empowering consumers and driving economic growth in the digital age, calling for robust and decisive action from the Commission.

Ultimately, the implementation of data portability under the DMA, despite its significance for competition, innovation, and consumer empowerment, faces challenges. The lack of detailed technical specifications and the flexibility in the application of guidelines may lead to market fragmentation and the perpetuation of gatekeepers' dominance.

The three-step implementation strategy proposed by Chinmayi Sharma,[14] focusing on the analysis of practices, stakeholder collaboration, and the definition of

[11] Geradin et al. (2022).

[12] Sharma (2024).

[13] Sharma (2024).

[14] Sharma (2024).

effective practices for different sectors, presents a promising path to overcoming these obstacles. It is essential that the European Commission heed the call of organizations such as MyData Global and ensure the robust and effective implementation of data portability, guaranteeing that the DMA achieves its objectives and contributes to the development of a fairer and more competitive digital market.

In Brazil, Bill 2768/2022,[15] currently under consideration in the National Congress, seeks to regulate the digital market in the country, in an initiative similar to the European Union's Digital Markets Act (DMA). The aim of the bill is to promote fair competition, protect consumers, and ensure a level playing field in the digital market. Inspired by European guidelines, Bill 2768/2022 introduces mechanisms designed to balance market power and foster innovation in the Brazilian digital sector.

One of the main provisions of the bill is the designation of digital platforms as holders of essential access control power, a concept similar to the "gatekeeper" introduced by the DMA. These holders of essential access control power are platforms with significant market power and, as such, would be subject to specific regulatory obligations to prevent anticompetitive practices.

In Brazil, as with the DMA, Bill 2768/2022 prohibits practices that unduly favor the products or services of holders of essential access control power to the detriment of competition and also addresses the importance of data access and information portability. Holders of essential access control power must ensure that users and businesses can access and transfer their data, thereby increasing user control and promoting competition.

Another similarity between the Brazilian Bill and the DMA is the possibility of investigating anticompetitive practices. Authorities will have the power to investigate holders of essential access control suspected of engaging in market-harming behavior and to impose corrective measures to restore competitive balance.

Article 5 of Bill 2768/2022 sets forth the objectives of regulating digital platforms in Brazil. Among these are economic development with fair competition, access to information and culture, the promotion of innovation, interoperability through open technological standards, and data portability. These objectives reinforce the pursuit of a more competitive and accessible digital environment, aligned with the demands of the global digital economy.

These objectives reinforce the pursuit of a more competitive and accessible digital environment, aligned with the demands of the global digital economy. However, regulating the conduct of major market players (gatekeepers) is only one side of the coin. For free competition and innovation to be effective, it is imperative that the legal framework also advances in the governance of the assets that underpin this market: the data itself. It is within this context of regulating access to information that the Data Act is positioned.

---

[15] Bill 2768/22 aims to regulate digital markets, addressing competition issues that, according to the proposal, require specific regulatory intervention in addition to the actions already undertaken by the Administrative Council for Economic Defense (CADE) in the repression of violations and control of market concentrations. Maranhão and Barros (2023).

The Data Act[16] emerges as a cornerstone in the European Union's strategy to maximize the use and value of data, reflecting a deep commitment to digital transformation and innovation. This Regulation aims to create a robust ecosystem in which data can be accessed and reused in a fair and efficient manner, establishing a solid foundation for a data-driven economy.

Integrated with the Data Governance Act,[17] the Data Act is central to the European ambition of positioning itself as a global leader in an increasingly data-driven society. The Regulation comprehensively addresses the legal, economic, and technical challenges that have limited the full use of data, introducing rules that promise to unlock significant potential, with expectations of an additional contribution of €270 billion to GDP by 2028.

One of the most notable innovations of the Data Act is the preservation of incentives for manufacturers to continue investing in the generation of high-quality data. The Regulation ensures that the costs associated with data transfer are covered while also protecting manufacturers from direct competition with products whose data has been shared. Additionally, the Data Act introduces measures to rebalance bargaining power, especially for small and medium-sized enterprises (SMEs), preventing abuses and contractual imbalances in data sharing agreements. To support these companies, the European Commission will develop model contractual terms to facilitate the drafting and negotiation of fairer agreements.

The Data Act also establishes mechanisms allowing public sector bodies to access and use data from the private sector in exceptional circumstances, such as public emergencies or to fulfill legal mandates, when the data is not otherwise available. This aspect of the Regulation is crucial to ensure a rapid and effective response in crisis situations, while minimizing the impact on businesses.

Furthermore, the Data Act promotes portability between different cloud data processing service providers, introducing safeguards against the unlawful transfer of data. This measure aims to foster a more competitive and transparent data market.

On the other hand, the Data Act revisits the Database Directive from the 1990s, clarifying that databases containing data from devices and Internet of Things (IoT) objects should not have separate legal protection. This revision is essential to ensure that such data can be accessed and used efficiently.

Consumers and businesses will benefit from greater access to data from their devices, enabling its use for after-sales services and value-added solutions such as

---

[16] Metzger and Schweitzer analyze the then draft of the Data Act and highlight that the proposal establishes a horizontal right of access for private and business users of data-generating products, in addition to setting mandatory provisions for standard business-to-business (B2B) contracts between data holders, users, and third parties. Metzger and Schweitzer (2022).

[17] The Data Governance Act (DGA) also refers to data portability. According to Article 29 of the regulation, which establishes the European Data Innovation Board, a specific subgroup is created for technical discussions on standardization, portability, and interoperability of data (as set out in Article 30, points f and g). The inclusion of portability as one of the main focuses of this technical subgroup underscores the importance the DGA places on this crucial aspect of modern data governance.

predictive maintenance. With more detailed information, users—from farmers to construction companies—will be better positioned to make informed decisions about products and services, promoting quality and sustainability in alignment with the objectives of the European Green Deal.

Finally, the Data Act will foster a more competitive data market, where companies and industry players will have expanded access to data, enabling the provision of more personalized after-sales services and the combination of data for the development of new digital services. This more dynamic and innovative environment promises to transform the landscape of the European digital economy, strengthening the European Union's position in the global data economy.

Although the Data Act does not expressly establish a right to data portability, the Regulation introduces a scenario in which consumers and businesses are granted access to data, complementing the right to data portability provided by the GDPR.[18] The proposal is that the Data Act will enhance this right for connected products, allowing consumers to access and transfer any data generated by the product, whether personal or nonpersonal.

According to the Data Act, connected products and related services must be designed and manufactured or provided in such a way that product data and data from associated services are accessible by default. This includes the relevant metadata necessary to interpret and use these data, which will be collectively referred to as "Data."[19]

Access to these Data must be facilitated in a manner that is simple, secure, comprehensive, organized, and provided in a widely recognized, machine-readable format. Furthermore, user access to the Data must be free of charge. In situations where it is relevant and technically feasible, the Data should be made directly available to the user, eliminating the need for a formal data access request.[20]

In B2B relationships, contracts governing data access must be based on fair, reasonable, nondiscriminatory, and transparent terms. These contracts may include compensation, provided it is reasonable and calculated transparently. The Data Act also prohibits unfair contractual terms imposed unilaterally, thereby protecting the interests of all parties involved.[21]

Despite the emphasis on data access, the Data Act acknowledges the need for restrictions under certain circumstances. Access to and use of data may be limited for security reasons or to protect trade secrets. In the case of trade secrets, specific measures must be agreed upon between the data holder and the user to preserve confidentiality. In exceptional situations, where the risk of severe economic harm is high, the data holder may refuse or suspend the sharing of trade secrets. However, such decisions must be justified and notified to the competent authorities, thereby

[18] Lazarottto (2024).

[19] Wilmerhale (2023).

[20] Wilmerhale (2023).

[21] Wilmerhale (2023).

ensuring a balance between the protection of sensitive information and transparency.[22]

The Data Act also establishes specific limitations on data sharing with third parties. The right to share does not apply to data concerning products, substances, or processes that have not yet been launched on the market, unless contractually permitted. This provision aims to protect companies' innovation and competitive advantage. Furthermore, third parties may not make available to gatekeepers the data they receive from data holders. This exclusion is intended to prevent excessive concentration of data in the hands of companies that are already dominant in the digital market.[23]

According to Graef and Husovec,[24] the proposal to exclude gatekeepers from access to data is a controversial issue. Such exclusion could represent a significant limitation for data subjects, who would no longer be able to exercise their right to data portability, guaranteed by the GDPR, to transfer their personal information to a gatekeeper.

In this context of constant evolution and regulatory adjustments, the European Commission introduced the *Digital Omnibus* initiative, which proposes specific amendments to the *Data Act* with the aim of harmonizing the legal text and ensuring its operational efficiency. These changes seek to provide immediate relief for businesses, public administrations, and citizens by reducing interpretative ambiguities and simplifying administrative requirements that might otherwise hinder innovation. By focusing on debureaucratization and procedural clarity, the *Digital Omnibus* aims to serve as a fine-tuning mechanism, essential for fostering competitiveness within the digital single market. In this way, it ensures that the transition to a data-driven economy occurs in a balanced, swift, and, above all, accessible manner for all economic actors, thereby consolidating the practical effectiveness of Europe's ambitions for the sector.

Although European and Brazilian ambitions seek to establish general rules for the data economy, it is within regulated markets that the challenges of implementation and the benefits for consumers become most evident. The transition to a data-driven economy finds fertile ground in sectors that already manage connectivity infrastructure and financial flows. Therefore, a detailed analysis of the lessons learned from the telecommunications and Open Finance sectors is essential to illustrate how portability and data sharing mechanisms operate within complex ecosystems.

---

[22] Wilmerhale (2023).

[23] Wilmerhale (2023).

[24] Graef and Husovec (2022).

9.2 From the Cross-Sectional to the Sectoral Plan: Sharing Ecosystems in Regulated Markets

As the backbone of digital connectivity and more than a traditional public utility, telecommunications services play a crucial role in our modern society, encompassing a wide range of activities and products that facilitate communication and connectivity—pillars upon which the data economy is built.

To understand the regulatory impact on this ecosystem, it is necessary to recognize that there are three distinct categories within this dynamic sector: the provision of telecommunications services themselves, the auxiliary products and services that provide direct support to telecommunications, and the so-called value-added services, which offer complementary functionalities to telecommunications, along with their respective products. The legal definition of "telecommunications services" encompasses the first two categories of activity, while providers of value-added services[25] are considered users of these telecommunications services.[26] Under Law No. 9472 of 1997, the National Telecommunications Agency (ANATEL) is responsible for regulating the telecommunications sector in Brazil.

In recent years, there has been a significant shift in the communications landscape, driven by the rise of over-the-top (OTT[27]) services. These services, such as Voice over IP, instant messaging, and Web-based email, are increasingly favored by consumers and businesses, replacing traditional communication services. However, it is important to note that these OTT services are often not covered by traditional regulatory frameworks, as is the case, for example, with the European Union Directive on privacy and electronic communications (Directive 2002/58/EC).

Furthermore, the advent of the Internet of Things (IoT) has ushered in a new era of interconnection between machines and devices. This intercommunication through electronic communication networks presents new challenges in terms of data protection, privacy, and the confidentiality of communications. In this context, the question arises as to whether regulations should also encompass the transmission of machine-to-machine communications.

---

[25] Unlike telecommunications services, value-added services are not subject, in many places such as Brazil, to state regulation. Therefore, no type of concession or authorization is required for their operation.

[26] Scorsim (2015), pp. 201–220.

[27] Over-the-top (OTT) services, as they are known, are communication and transmission services provided over the Internet. Recently, these services have become ubiquitous thanks to broadband services offered by telecommunications operators and Internet service providers. However, OTT services sometimes complement and at other times replace traditional telecommunications and broadcasting services offered by incumbent licensed operators. These services pose challenges for regulators due to the rapid evolution of the underlying technology. While telecommunications operators advocate for the regulation of OTT services to ensure a level playing field, OTT service providers resist, arguing that their services are innovative and promote the spirit of Internet freedom. Sridhar (2019).

Therefore, as we continue to move toward an increasingly connected society, it is essential that regulation keeps pace with these changes and safeguards the rights to privacy, data protection, confidentiality of communications in all its forms, and the right of choice, from traditional telecommunications services to the latest innovations in digital communications.[28]

The telecommunications sector, according to a study by the United Kingdom government,[29] is a critical and valuable industry, connecting residents and businesses and enabling essential services such as fixed and mobile telephony, broadband, and mobile Internet. These services are increasingly regarded as necessities for most households, fundamental for access to education, participation in the labor market, and communication with friends and family. They are, therefore, widely considered essential goods, with no close substitutes and consumed by all income groups.[30]

The COVID-19 pandemic significantly impacted the market, increasing reliance on Internet access and exacerbating financial pressures on households, with consumption patterns shifting in response to lockdowns and economic uncertainties.[31] The Organisation for Economic Co-operation and Development (OECD) has noted that the complexity of telecommunications markets can lead to lower consumer satisfaction, reluctance to switch to better offers, and difficulty in comparing products. While there may be benefits to changing services or providers, this often requires forecasting and understanding the new service in relation to the current one, as well as concerns about the potential risks associated with switching.[32]

In light of the increasing essentiality of connectivity services, there has also been an expansion in the ways of accessing the Internet, particularly through wireless technologies. In this context, thanks to the development of fast and efficient wireless technologies, public access to the Internet via Wi-Fi networks has become increasingly common. These networks are widely available in public and semiprivate spaces. However, with this growing availability, it has become ever more imperative to ensure the adequate protection of communications transmitted over these networks and to safeguard their confidentiality.

It is important to note that the use of public Wi-Fi networks exposes users to a range of potential risks, such as the interception of personal data and invasion of

---

[28] Electronic communications data have proven to be a valuable source for the development of artificial intelligence (AI), powering solutions such as search engines and automated responses. These data provide extensive knowledge about human behavioral patterns and correlations, although it is currently the syntactic content that enables accurate inferences about users. AI's ability to understand meaning is limited, but through pattern analysis, detailed psychological and behavioral profiles can be created. This information is used to personalize advertisements and influence behaviors, forming a cornerstone of the business model of digital platforms. Czarnocki (2020).

[29] Gov.UK (2023).

[30] Gov.UK (2023).

[31] Gov.UK (2023).

[32] OECD (2009).

privacy. Even when Wi-Fi service is provided as a complement to another service, such as in a store, the privacy of communications must be strictly protected. The lack of adequate security measures can turn these networks into easy targets for cybercriminals, compromising users' sensitive information.

In light of this scenario, it is necessary for electronic communications data to be defined in a manner that is sufficiently broad and technologically neutral to encompass any information related to the content transmitted or exchanged (content of electronic communications), as well as information about the end user of electronic communications services, processed for the purposes of transmission, distribution, or enabling the exchange of electronic communications content. This may include, for example, data used to track and identify the origin and destination of a communication, geographic location, date, time, duration, and type of communication, regardless of the medium or service used.

Furthermore, it is essential that this data be protected regardless of the transmission method—whether by wire, radio, optical, or electromagnetic means, including satellite networks, cable networks, fixed networks (circuit and packet switching, including the Internet), and terrestrial mobile networks. All such data should be considered electronic communication metadata[33] and, therefore, be subject to regulatory provisions that ensure their protection and confidentiality.

Let us now examine the proposed regulatory policies aimed at addressing the situations mentioned above. These policies must not only ensure the protection[34] and confidentiality of user data but also promote competitiveness in the telecommunications market. It is essential that regulations keep pace with technological innovations, ensuring that consumer rights are protected and that the market evolves in a fair and efficient manner. In this way, it will be possible to foster both innovation and security, ensuring that all users of telecommunications services can enjoy the benefits of connectivity in a safe and protected manner.

In January 2017, the European Commission[35] presented a draft Regulation aimed at privacy and electronic communications, with the goal of replacing the current e-Privacy Directive established in 2002. This initiative arises from the need to

[33] According to Batista, metadata also deserve judicial protection, especially because they consist of micro digital fragments that, when cross-referenced, can reidentify an individual. Batista (2023), pp. 11321–11337.

[34] For information on the protection of personal data in the telecommunications sector in Brazil, see Conexis Brasil Digital (2022).

[35] In the current context, it is worth highlighting that the European Commission has played a prominent role in advancing the digital agenda, as reflected in a series of recent initiatives. In February 2024, it introduced a set of measures to promote innovation, security, and resilience of digital infrastructures in Europe. These initiatives aim to sustain the future competitiveness of the European economy by providing fast, secure, and widely accessible connectivity to support emerging technologies such as telemedicine, automated driving, and precision agriculture. The package includes a White Paper on Europe's digital infrastructure needs, a recommendation on the security and resilience of submarine cable infrastructures, and proposals to create a Connected Collaborative Computing Network ("3C Network") to drive the development of innovative technologies and AI applications.

strengthen the security of communications and the confidentiality of data, covering not only traditional telecommunications providers but also other actors, such as information society service providers offering Internet-based services, including VoIP, instant messaging applications, and Web-based email (OTTs).[36]

The main objective of the proposal is to ensure fair conditions for all companies. Unlike the previous directive, the proposed Regulation aims to protect both the content and the metadata of communications. With advances in electronic communication technologies, metadata can reveal more specific details about individuals, such as preferences and habits, compared to the simple traffic data mentioned in the former e-Privacy Directive. This includes, for example, location data, which can now provide more detailed insights into people's lives than before.[37]

In addition to strengthening the security and confidentiality of communications, the proposed Regulation also establishes clearer guidelines regarding tracking technologies, such as cookies, and seeks to achieve greater harmonization among the Member States of the European Union. This harmonization is crucial to ensure that citizens' rights are consistently protected throughout the EU, regardless of where they reside or which services they use.[38]

This initiative represents a response to growing concerns regarding the protection of personal data and individual privacy in the digital context. By replacing the previous directive, which had become outdated in light of rapid technological changes, the newly proposed Regulation, if approved, aims to update the standards to strengthen the security of European citizens' information.[39]

It is important to emphasize that, despite the criticisms and the difficulty in approving a final text after more than 7 years,[40] there are robust justifications and evidence supporting the need for the safeguards sought by the proposed European Union e-Privacy Regulation. The telecommunications sector collects, processes, and stores large amounts of personal data, including call records, messages, and location data. This information can be used to identify individuals, track their movements, and monitor their communications activities.

The vast amount of personal data available makes the telecommunications sector a prime target for cybercriminals seeking to steal information for malicious purposes. Through mobile devices, in addition to obtaining data such as device model, browser type, and geolocation, it is possible to identify which locations are frequented by the owner and how long they remain connected. Internet browsing data can also be obtained, including the websites accessed and the duration of use for each application.[41]

---

[36] European Parliamentary Research Service (2017).

[37] European Parliamentary Research Service (2017).

[38] European Parliamentary Research Service (2017).

[39] European Parliamentary Research Service (2017).

[40] Marimom (2024).

[41] Futurecom (2022).

To protect this data, it is essential that electronic communications data be defined in a broad and technologically neutral manner. This should encompass any information related to the content transmitted or exchanged, as well as information about the end user, processed for the purposes of transmission, distribution, or enabling the exchange of content. Examples include data used to track and identify the origin and destination of a communication, geographic location, date, time, duration, and type of communication, regardless of the medium or service used.

In this way, the European Union's draft Regulation exemplifies the attempt to address the current risks and challenges of communications in the digital age. However, this initiative raises the question of whether it is necessary to create specific laws to address this issue, in addition to the general regulations already in place, such as the General Data Protection Regulation (GDPR).[42]

In addition to concerns regarding protection and confidentiality, the debate over mechanisms capable of enabling the efficient circulation of data among economic agents, particularly through portability, has gained prominence in this context. Although data portability is already provided for in general data protection laws, this right remains largely underutilized, mainly due to the lack of interoperability standards[43] that would allow for its implementation.

It is precisely in this gap that the regulation of specific markets becomes relevant, as it enables the creation of more effective mechanisms to make portability a reality. From this perspective, data sharing in regulated sectors ceases to be a mere bureaucratic requirement and becomes a strategy for openness, enhancing access to and reuse of information. In this sense, data access and sharing should not be viewed merely as isolated obligations but rather as pillars of an integrated and competitive digital infrastructure.

These data-sharing proposals in regulated markets are among the possible approaches that can be employed to enhance access, sharing, and reuse of data throughout the ongoing process of data openness. Just like data openness itself, data access and sharing should not be viewed as a binary concept of "closed versus open." Instead, it is a spectrum with varying degrees of openness. This ranges from internal access and reuse (limited to the data holder), through restricted external access and sharing (unilateral and multilateral), and ultimately culminates in open data—the most extreme form of data openness.[44]

---

[42] According to Cristiana Marimon, adding sector-specific regulations in a kind of "regulatory lasagna" is not the ideal way to address specific challenges. By analyzing certain legislative instruments, one can infer that the legislator thought: "double regulation offers better protection," as if they wanted to translate the German proverb "*Doppel genäht hält es besser*" (better safe than sorry). Marimon (2024).

[43] Data portability differs from other forms of portability, such as number portability in telecommunications. This is because data portability, as a right of the data subject provided for in the GDPR or the LGPD, does not necessarily entail the termination of the original legal relationship but rather ensures access to a copy of the data for domestic reuse or by another controller.

[44] OECD (2019).

Such a trend of data sharing has been anticipated in regulated markets, such as telecommunications, since its characteristics indicate a significant potential to promote consumer welfare, especially in light of the current rise in the cost of living.

It is important to note that telecommunications markets are complex, and navigating a wide range of options can be both technical and time-consuming. Despite the significant variation in consumer characteristics, needs, and usage patterns, there is strong evidence that consumers often do not engage with the market, choosing to remain with their current providers even when this entails a high cost.[45]

It is precisely in this context of low consumer mobility and informational frictions that regulatory initiatives aimed at enabling data portability have emerged. In the United Kingdom, the Open Communications initiative stands out as a specific data mobility measure. This initiative is part of the Smart Data project, which refers to the secure and consent-based sharing of consumer and product data with third-party providers (TPPs). These providers can use such data to offer innovative services to consumers and small and medium-sized enterprises (SMEs). Smart Data goes beyond the data access rights established by the GDPR, providing a platform for the development of more advanced and personalized services.[46]

The implementation of Open Communications in the telecommunications sector aims to expand consumer access to their data and establish common standards for data sharing. The primary focus is to empower end users, from individual consumers to small businesses, enabling them to navigate the communications market more knowledgeably. This will allow them to make better-informed decisions regarding connectivity services, helping them obtain the necessary connectivity at the best possible price.

Open Communications is expected to bring significant benefits to both consumers and SMEs. Among these benefits are the increased adoption of next-generation connectivity services and the empowerment of consumers and SMEs to switch to the best available offers, meeting their connectivity needs and household budgets.[47]

In summary, Open Communications, by operating based on the powers of Smart Data, represents a significant step forward in the way data is utilized in the telecommunications sector, promoting greater transparency and efficiency in the market and empowering users to make more informed and advantageous choices.[48]

Open Communications has already undergone a phase of public feedback analysis through a public consultation in 2023. The purpose of this consultation was to gather opinions on the possible introduction of the Smart Data scheme, called "Open Communications," in the UK telecommunications market.

The consultation aimed to gain a better understanding of the potential benefits and challenges of implementing Open Communications in the UK telecommunications sector. If adopted, this scheme would require broadband and mobile phone

[45] Gov.UK (2023).

[46] Gov.UK (2023).

[47] Gov.UK (2023).

[48] Gov.UK (2023).

companies to provide their customers, upon request, with data about their telecommunications services, such as the price paid, download speed, and data usage.

Furthermore, it should be emphasized that the application of Smart Data logic to connectivity infrastructures is not an isolated phenomenon but rather reflects a broader movement toward openness, whose most advanced paradigm is found in the financial sector. While telecommunications represent the technical "backbone" of the digital economy, the financial ecosystem[49] has served as the true pioneering laboratory for the implementation of large-scale interoperability protocols. From this perspective of regulatory maturity and disruptive innovation, it is also pertinent to analyze the context of Open Finance (financial sector), whose lessons on governance and technical standardization now serve as a compass for other regulated markets.

In the Brazilian context, the financial system has established itself as the most advanced paradigm of sectoral data openness. As noted by Alessandra Pela Sabbag and Lucas de Oliveira Noleto,[50] the Central Bank of Brazil has been making efforts since 2018 to implement Open Banking, an ecosystem aimed at the seamless sharing of information between financial institutions and third parties. In this arrangement, fintechs[51] play a leading role as intermediary agents operating through interoperable technological interfaces, with the goal of streamlining the provision of services. However, the major challenge of this transition lies in the development of robust safeguards to ensure the protection and confidentiality of sensitive banking data circulating in this new environment.

Joint Resolution No. 1, dated May 4, 2020, marked the beginning of the implementation of the open financial system (Open Banking[52-53]) in Brazil. This initiative

[49] In an article written in 2001, Wierzel already reported that clients desired financial aggregation services, provided that security, fraud, and privacy were properly addressed. Furthermore, if financial institutions resisted the trend of aggregation, other companies would fill this gap and win over clients. Such aggregation could generate additional revenue by incorporating services such as investment advisory, portfolio management, and cross-selling. Although the text dates from 2001, many of the concepts discussed remain relevant in the current context of digital financial platforms, highlighting the importance of adequately addressing concerns related to security, privacy, and regulatory compliance to meet client demands and drive the growth of the digital financial sector. Wierzel (2001), p. 457.

[50] Sabbag and Noleto (2019), pp. 1–16.

[51] Fintechs emerged as digitally native companies, offering an innovative alternative to traditional banks. With a focus on accessibility, convenience, and technology, they have grown rapidly and driven the digitalization of financial services worldwide, especially with the popularization of internet banking. Zetta (2024).

[52] Within a context of mismatch between user demands and the services offered by financial institutions, the trend known as *Open Banking* has emerged. This trend is characterized by the opening of banking systems through the creation of interfaces that connect banks' databases to external networks, enabling third-party companies to act as intermediaries in the relationship between financial institutions and their clients. Goettenauer (2018), pp. 109–128.

[53] The concepts of *Open Banking* and *Open Finance* are closely related but not identical. Originally, *Open Banking* referred to an open API standard focused on banking services. Subsequently, the term was replaced by *Open Finance* to reflect the broader regulatory scope, encompassing other

aimed to promote the standardized sharing of data and services among participating institutions, with the objective of fostering innovation, increasing competition, improving efficiency, and strengthening citizenship in the financial sector.

Open Banking has evolved into Open Finance, expanding its scope beyond traditional financial products and services such as accounts and credit operations.[54] It now also includes data on products and services related to foreign exchange, acquiring, investments, insurance, and pension plans. This expansion enables clients to access better terms and a wider range of options across various financial sectors.

With Open Finance, clients are expected to have greater control over their data, being able to decide whether or not to share it with other participating institutions. All security requirements must remain in place to ensure the protection of users' information.

Currently, consumers and users can already request the sharing of their registration data, information on account transactions, credit card transactions, and contracted credit products. This sharing occurs only among institutions participating in Open Finance, always for specific purposes and for a defined period, subject to the prior authorization of the consumer/user.

In addition, it is now possible to make payments within the Open Finance environment, with Pix being the first available method. Payment initiation enables faster and more convenient transactions while maintaining the security of the process.

The governance of Open Finance is established by the Central Bank, which defines the principles, objectives, and rules. A governance structure, composed of representative trade associations, submits proposals to the Central Bank for review and potential regulation.

Security is a fundamental aspect of Open Finance. Multiple layers of security are implemented, including authentication of both consumers and participating institutions. Only authorized institutions may participate, and cybersecurity regulations are enforced. The Central Bank oversees the entire process, and institutions and their executives may be held liable.

Data sharing may only occur after the stages of consent, authentication, and confirmation have been completed through secure electronic channels. The consumer/user's consent must be freely given, informed, prior, and unequivocal, using clear and objective language that specifies the purposes, duration, and data to be shared.

Thus, Open Finance represents a revolution in the Brazilian financial system, fostering greater transparency, competitiveness, and benefits for consumers. With

---

financial services such as investments and insurance, in addition to conventional banking operations. It is important to note that the sharing of financial data is expanding globally, with notable developments in countries such as Australia, India, Brazil, Mexico, Colombia, and Chile, as well as in the traditional markets of the United States, the European Union, and the United Kingdom. Zetta (2024).

[54] The success of financial regulation over the past decade demonstrates that removing regulatory barriers and establishing appropriate conditions for competition, through suitable processes and structures, are effective strategies. With collaboration between regulatory agencies and input from the market, regulation can continue to foster Brazil's economic growth. Cunha e Melo and Abreu (2023).

data control in the hands of clients and the possibility of accessing better products and services, this initiative has the potential to transform the way we interact with financial and insurance institutions.[55]

The analysis of the new regulatory agenda reveals that the digital economy is undergoing a profound transitional phase, in which regulation is no longer merely reactive but becomes proactive and structural. The emergence of entities such as *gatekeepers*—architects of digital interaction who concentrate massive volumes of data and wield control over market access—has demanded a normative response that goes beyond the traditional boundaries of Antitrust Law.

As discussed throughout this chapter, instruments such as the *Digital Markets Act* (DMA) and the *Data Act* in the European Union, as well as Bill No. 2768/2022 in Brazil, represent legislative efforts to transform data portability from an individual privacy right into a systemic tool for promoting competition and innovation.

Addressing the proposed research problem—how to design legal frameworks that reduce fragmentation and regulatory frictions—necessarily involves overcoming the dichotomy between data protection and free enterprise. The European experience demonstrates that legal certainty for the legitimate reuse of data depends not only on prohibitions but also on the creation of technical interoperability obligations and the establishment of clear standards for data sharing. Market fragmentation is mitigated when general data protection regulations, such as the GDPR or the LGPD, interact harmoniously with sector-specific regulations, preventing compliance from becoming an excessive burden for new entrants or a disguised barrier to entry under the guise of privacy protection.

In this regard, sectoral data-sharing initiatives such as Open Communications in the United Kingdom and Open Finance in Brazil offer valuable lessons on reducing regulatory friction. These models demonstrate that secure data sharing is enhanced when there is centralized governance, open technological standards, and specific purposes that directly benefit the end consumer. By delegating the definition of technical standards to specialized regulatory bodies and encouraging collaboration among stakeholders, the system reduces legal uncertainty and fosters an environment in which data reuse is viewed as a driver of economic efficiency rather than as an inherent risk.

Finally, the consolidation of a data-driven economy requires that the institutional framework be flexible enough to keep pace with technological evolution yet firm in the protection of fundamental rights. The path to reducing informational asymmetries and ensuring contestability in digital markets lies in the effective implementation of real-time portability and continuous access to data. Only through coordinated legal frameworks that combat the formation of informational silos by gatekeepers and ensure transparency in data flows will it be possible to build a digital ecosystem that is both secure for citizens and conducive to global innovation. The success of

[55] It is noted that the regulatory measures currently in force for payment institutions and traditional banks, especially with regard to competition and the economic development of companies operating in the financial sector, may have significant impacts. Gonçalves Queiroz Machado et al. (2023), pp. 200–227.

this new regulatory agenda will therefore depend on the ability of states to transform data into circulating assets that drive social welfare and economic justice in the information age.

References

Akman P (2022) Regulating competition in digital platform markets: a critical assessment of the framework and approach of the EU Digital Markets Act. European Law Review, Leeds

Bagnoli V (2021) Designing competition policy in digital markets for developing economies: how the EU can contribute with the Digital Markets Act and Digital Services Act. Rev Defesa Concorrência 9(2):133–158

Batista A (2023) Metadados e o dilema de Collingridge: como compatibilizar novas tecnologias e direitos fundamentais na sociedade da informação [Metadata and the Collingridge dilemma: how to compatibilize new technologies and fundamental rights in the information society]. Contribuciones a las Ciencias Sociales 16(8):11321–11337

Conexis Brasil Digital (2022) Protection of personal data in the telecommunications sector in Brazil. Conexis, Brasília

Cunha e Melo M, Abreu J (2023) Regulation and competition: the case of the Brazilian fintech ecosystem. https://doi.org/10.59262/fgyy58

Czarnocki J (2020) Electronic communication confidentiality in ePrivacy Regulation: how to protect privacy and personal autonomy without hampering AI solutions development. Studia Iuridica LXXXVI

Demircan M (2023) The DMA and the GDPR: making sense of data accumulation, cross-use and data sharing provisions. In: Bieker F, Meyer J, Pape S et al (eds) Privacy and identity management. privacy and identity. IFIP Advances in Information and Communication Technology, vol 671. Springer, Cham, 2022

European Parliamentary Research Service (2017) Reform of the e-Privacy Directive. EPRS, Brussels

Futurecom (2022) Os desafios do uso de dados no setor de telecomunicações [The challenges of data use in the telecommunications sector]. https://digital.futurecom.com.br/tecnologia/os-desafios-do-uso-de-dados-no-setor-de-telecomunicacoes

Geradin D, Bania K, Karanikioti T (2022) The interplay between the Digital Markets Act and the General Data Protection Regulation. https://ssrn.com/abstract=4203907

Goettenauer M (2018) Open banking and the financial sector. Rev Adm Fin 12:109–128

Gonçalves Queiroz Machado C, Ferreira MA, Vitória Ferreira L et al (2023) Assimetria regulatória entre instituições financeiras e instituições de pagamento [Regulatory asymmetry between financial institutions and payment institutions]. Revista Ciências Sociais em Perspectiva 21(41):200–227. https://doi.org/10.48075/revistacsp.v21i41.30621

Gov.UK (2023) Open communications: a smart data scheme for the UK telecoms market. Department for Science, Innovation and Technology, London. https://www.gov.uk/government/consultations/open-communications-a-smart-data-scheme-for-the-uk-telecoms-market

Graef I, Husovec M (2022) Seven things to improve in the Data Act. https://ssrn.com/abstract=4051793

Lazzarotto, B. (2024). The right to data portability: A holistic analysis of GDPR, DMA and the Data Act. European Journal of Law and Technology, 15(1).

Maranhão J, Barros A (2023) Bill 2768/22 and the regulation of digital markets in Brazil. J Digital Law 4(2):45–67

Marimon, C. (2024). Future privacy rules for a digital EU. Telefónica. Retrieved June 12, 2024, from.

Metzger A, Schweitzer H (2022) Shaping markets: a critical evaluation of the draft Data Act. https://ssrn.com/abstract=4222376

Moskal A (2022) Digital Markets Act (DMA): a consumer protection perspective. Eur Papers 7(3):1113–1119

OECD (2009) Policy guidance on radio frequency identification. OECD Publishing, Paris

OECD (2019) Enhancing access to and sharing of data: reconciling risks and benefits for data re-use across societies. OECD Publishing, Paris

Petit N (2021) The proposed Digital Markets Act (DMA): a legal and policy review. J Eur Compet Law Pract 12(7):529–541

Sabbag AP, Noleto LO (2019) Open banking: impasse entre a privacidade de dados e a revolução tecnológica? [Open banking: impasse between data privacy and the technological revolution?]. Revista de Direito e as Novas Tecnologias 3:1–16

Scorsim E (2015) Competência da Anatel para outorgar e fiscalizar os serviços de acesso à internet: limites e possibilidades [Anatel's competence to grant and inspect internet access services: limits and possibilities]. Revista de Direito Administrativo Contemporâneo 21:201–220

Sharma A (2024) Data governance and sharing protocols on digital platforms. J Tech Policy 18:89–104

Sridhar V (2019) Over-the-Top (OTT) services: should they be regulated much like telecom services? In: Emerging ICT policies and regulations. Springer, Singapore

Wierzel KL (2001) If you can't beat them, join them: data aggregators and financial institutions. N C Banking Inst 5:457. https://scholarship.law.unc.edu/ncbi/vol5/iss1/17

WilmerHale (2023) Details of the EU Data Act (1): data access rights and obligations. WilmerHale Privacy and Cybersecurity Law Blog. https://www.wilmerhale.com/en/insights/blogs/wilmerhale-privacy-and-cybersecurity-law/20231204-details-of-the-eu-data-act-1-data-access-rights-and-obligations

Zetta (2024) Open Finance: lessons for the future of Open Finance - the view from Brazil. Zetta, São Paulo. https://somoszetta.org.br/wp-content/uploads/2024/09/Zetta_OpenFinance__ENG_DIGITAL_V1.pdf

Chapter 10
Conclusion

Throughout this work, an analytical path was followed that began with the recognition of the centrality of data as a strategic infrastructure of the digital economy and, progressively, investigated the complex interactions between rights protection, market power, and technological innovation. The central question guiding this journey—*how is it possible to design legal and institutional arrangements capable of reducing fragmentation, mitigating regulatory frictions, and providing legal certainty for the safe and legitimate reuse of data in the digital ecosystems of Brazil and the European Union?*—emerged not as a matter of simple regulatory adjustment but as a challenge that demands a profound reconfiguration of the very logic of governance.

The answer, as has been demonstrated, does not lie in a single law or a single authority but rather in a coordinated governance framework that brings together different areas of law and various institutional competencies in pursuit of a common goal: enabling the safe and beneficial flow of data while simultaneously protecting the dignity and autonomy of individuals.

The argumentative trajectory of this book has demonstrated, first and foremost, the intrinsically dual nature of data. On the one hand, personal data has been consolidated as an extension of one's own personality, the electronic body of the individual in the digital age, whose protection is embodied in the fundamental right to informational self-determination. This perspective, grounded in the frameworks of the GDPR and the LGPD, places the data subject at the center of the ecosystem, endowing them with a bundle of rights designed to ensure control over their information.

On the other hand, data functions as an economic asset of unparalleled value—the input that fuels artificial intelligence (AI) algorithms, structures business models, and sustains enduring positions of market power. This duality—data as a right and data as power—is the primary source of the tensions that characterize the digital economy.

D. Copetti Cravo, *Law and the Digital Economy*,
https://doi.org/10.1007/978-3-032-36672-6_10

Ignoring it, or treating one of its poles as subordinate to the other, leads to incomplete solutions: excessively restrictive data protection may stifle innovation, while an unbridled pursuit of economic exploitation may undermine fundamental rights and consolidate unfair and unbalanced market structures.

The second major finding that emerged from the comparative analysis between Brazil and the European Union was the insufficiency of isolated regulatory approaches. The investigation into digital markets revealed that the traditional mechanisms of each branch of law, when applied in isolation, prove inadequate to address the complexity of the phenomenon. Competition law, with its predominantly *ex post* (after-the-fact) logic, often intervenes too late to correct imbalances in network markets, where *lock-in* effects and the "winner-takes-all" dynamic quickly become entrenched.

Consumer law, although essential for addressing informational asymmetries, faces challenges in confronting the structural power of gatekeepers and the technical barriers that hinder effective choice. In turn, Data Protection Law, if interpreted in isolation, may inadvertently create obstacles to the legitimate sharing of information, increasing fragmentation and compliance costs.

It is at this point that the dialogue of sources has proven to be not only an elegant theoretical construct but also an indispensable methodology for data governance. The articulation among regulatory norms, consumer law, competition law, and personal data protection is not optional but rather a necessity imposed by the inherently cross-cutting nature of data flows.

The effectiveness of protecting both the individual and the market depends on the synergy among the responsible authorities, who must operate in a coordinated manner, sharing information and aligning their oversight and enforcement strategies to create a coherent and predictable regulatory environment.

Within this coordinated framework, the right to data portability has emerged as the legal institution with the greatest transformative potential. Its analysis throughout the chapters has revealed a remarkable conceptual and functional evolution. Portability is no longer seen merely as an individual right, a simple complement to the right of access, but has become established as a powerful instrument of structural governance.

In the context of data protection, it embodies informational self-determination, returning active control over one's electronic persona to the data subject. In the field of consumer protection, it functions as a mechanism to reduce switching costs and the lock-in effect, enabling the genuine exercise of the right to choose.

In the realm of competition, it functions as a pro-competitive remedy, capable of reducing barriers to entry, increasing market contestability, and disciplining the market power of large platforms. In the regulatory context, however, portability assumes an even broader and more structuring role, being incorporated as a central element of normative frameworks designed to organize data flows in a coordinated and predictable manner. Instruments such as the Digital Markets Act (DMA) and the Data Act and sectoral initiatives like Open Finance highlight this transformation: portability ceases to be merely a reactive right of the data subject and becomes a proactive governance mechanism, aimed at creating interoperable ecosystems and enabling markets based on regulated data sharing.

However, the promise of portability is only fully realized when accompanied by interoperability. As demonstrated by the technical and legal analysis, the mere provision of a data file in a "machine-readable format" is insufficient if the destination systems are unable to interpret and meaningfully utilize this information.

True portability requires open technical standards, standardized application programming interfaces (APIs), and a regulatory commitment to removing artificial technical barriers. The experience of sectors such as Open Finance in Brazil and the discussions on Open Communications in the United Kingdom illustrate that data sharing becomes a driver of innovation precisely when there is robust governance that defines the technical rules of the game, ensuring security and fluidity.

The new regulatory agenda for digital markets, embodied in the Digital Markets Act and the Data Act, marks a shift from a predominantly reactive model to a structurally oriented regulatory framework. This approach is based on the diagnosis that, in digital ecosystems characterized by strong network effects, data-driven economies of scale, and concentrated intermediation power—particularly in the hands of gatekeepers—traditional ex post enforcement tools have proven insufficient to preserve contestability and fairness.

In this context, while the DMA operates through asymmetric obligations directed at core platforms, the Data Act seeks to rebalance data access and use across the economy, addressing informational asymmetries and economic dependencies beyond the narrow core of platforms.

Therefore, a necessary step is the implementation of an *ex ante* (preventive) intervention, which imposes direct obligations of real-time portability and interoperability, not as an option but as a condition for operating in the market. This paradigm shift transfers the burden of proof: it is no longer up to the regulator to prove abuse but rather to the *gatekeeper* to demonstrate compliance with its openness obligations.

Bill No. 2768/2022 in Brazil signals alignment with this global trend, seeking to adapt the Brazilian framework to this new reality of proactive regulation. This transition, however, is not without challenges. The rise of generative artificial intelligence and agentic AI systems intensifies the demand for data access while simultaneously increasing the risks of entrapment within closed ecosystems, the so-called walled gardens.

The portability of an AI agent's "memory," encompassing all its context and learning, becomes the new frontier of informational self-determination and competition. Similarly, harmonizing the right to portability with the protection of trade secrets requires a delicate balancing exercise, ensuring that the invocation of secrecy does not become a veto on transparency and data mobility.

Returning to the fundamental question, the answer offered by this work is that the design of an effective legal-institutional framework for data governance in the digital age rests on four essential pillars:

Institutional Synergy The establishment of formal and informal mechanisms for cooperation among data protection authorities, consumer protection agencies, competition authorities, and regulatory bodies, ensuring coordinated action and avoiding conflicting decisions that generate legal uncertainty.
Regulatory and Technical Harmonization The advancement of regulation that not only establishes rights but also defines the technical standards necessary for their implementation. This includes the active promotion of interoperable data formats and open APIs, reducing compliance costs and friction for the legitimate flow of data.
Balance Between *Ex Ante* and *Ex Post* Regulation The combination of robust competition oversight, capable of curbing abuses of market power, with proactive sectoral and cross-sectoral regulation that imposes obligations of openness and interoperability on agents with structural power, such as *gatekeepers*.
Centrality of the Data Subject as a Digital Citizen The understanding that all these regulatory and institutional mechanisms ultimately aim not only at market efficiency but also at empowering the individual. Portability and interoperability are tools for building active digital citizenship, in which the individual is not merely an object of datafication but a rights-bearing subject capable of managing their identity and participating meaningfully in the digital economy.

It is within this context, already outlined in its normative and institutional contours, that a new axis of tension and transformation emerges, situated beyond state borders and directly linked to the geopolitical dynamics of technological innovation. At the same time, the global race for AI intensifies the importance of data flow regulations: the European Union relies on its notion of digital sovereignty, China seeks to project its regulatory influence through multilateral initiatives (including within the BRICS - Brazil, Russia, India, China and South Africa framework), and the United States reinforces selective barriers based on national security. The result is a fragmented landscape, in which the regulation of international data transfers becomes directly tied to the future of artificial intelligence.

The future, therefore, appears to point toward a dual requirement: on the one hand, regulatory frameworks capable of ensuring security, transparency, and fundamental rights in international data flows; on the other, international cooperation mechanisms that prevent excessive fragmentation and allow AI to flourish as a global technology. Instruments such as contractual clauses tailored to AI use, adequacy criteria that consider not only privacy but also algorithmic ethics, and multilateral frameworks for data sharing in sensitive sectors (such as health and the environment) may represent promising pathways.

Ultimately, the journey from the information society to the data-driven economy compels us to shift from a logic of data protection as restriction to a logic of data governance as enablement. The goal is not to dam the flow of information but to build secure, legitimate, and efficient channels through which data can circulate, fostering innovation, knowledge, and social well-being, without ever sacrificing the fundamental rights that form the foundation of a democratic society.

Governing the digital economy is, at its core, governing its most vital resource. The development of a legal and institutional framework that accomplishes this task in a fair, transparent, and coordinated manner is perhaps the most defining challenge of our time.

FSC
www.fsc.org
MIX
Papier | Fördert
gute Waldnutzung
FSC® C083411

Kolibri 360 GmbH
Ferdinand-Jühlke-Straße 7
99095 Erfurt, Deutschland
produktsicherheit@kolibri360.de